Features and Challenges of the EU Budget

Features and Challenges of the EU Budget

A Multidisciplinary Analysis

Edited by

Luca Zamparini and Ubaldo Villani-Lubelli

University of Salento, Italy

EE Edward Elgar
PUBLISHING

Cheltenham, UK • Northampton, MA, USA

Published by
Edward Elgar Publishing Limited
The Lypiatts
15 Lansdown Road
Cheltenham
Glos GL50 2JA
UK

Edward Elgar Publishing, Inc.
William Pratt House
9 Dewey Court
Northampton
Massachusetts 01060
USA

A catalogue record for this book
is available from the British Library

Library of Congress Control Number: 2019930627

This book is available electronically in the **Elgar**online
Social and Political Science subject collection
DOI 10.4337/9781788971928

ISBN 978 1 78897 191 1 (cased)
ISBN 978 1 78897 192 8 (eBook)

Printed by CPI Group (UK) Ltd, Croydon CR0 4YY

Contents

Contributors

Peter Becker, Stiftung Wissenschaft und Politik (SWP), Berlin, Germany

Alessandro Isoni, University of Salento, Lecce, Italy

Robert Kaiser, University of Siegen, Siegen, Germany

Mario Kölling, Spanish National Distance University, Madrid, Spain

Karsten Mause, University of Münster, Münster, Germany

Elsa Perreau, Blomeyer y Sanz, Guadalajara, Spain

Maurizia Pierri, University of Salento, Lecce, Italy

Margit Schratzenstaller, Austrian Institute of Economic Research, Vienna, Austria

Matteo Scotto, Villa Vigoni Research Centre, Menaggio, Italy

Ubaldo Villani-Lubelli, University of Salento, Lecce, Italy

Luca Zamparini, University of Salento, Lecce, Italy

1. Introduction

Luca Zamparini and Ubaldo Villani-Lubelli

The budget has constituted one of the most debated and important issues at the political and at the academic level since the inception of the European Economic Community and in the ensuing evolution to the European Community and to the European Union (EU). The changes in its structure and composition are then crucial elements to understanding of the historical and political developments of the European Union and of its legal and economic perspectives. Given that the EU budget is mainly composed of transfers from Member States to the Union, the political negotiation always begins in the Council, where the heads of state and government define the strategic directions of the Union and set the overall amounts of the programming period. Subsequently, the European Commission presents a proposal that is first approved by the European Parliament and then by the Council of the EU. The Lisbon Treaty aimed at reinforcing the role of the EU Parliament to make the discussion more democratic. In this way, the budget would become a fruitful dialogue between European institutions, which are stakeholders of different interest groups. The financial planning would then become a fundamental open space of political confrontation, despite the expected tensions between institutions.

The current European budget amounts to less than €150 billion. It may appear a very large sum in absolute terms, but it corresponds to only 1 per cent of the yearly gross domestic product generated by the EU countries. With respect to revenues, the budget is funded by the national contributions of the Member States (70%), by the EU's own resources, as customs duties (13%), by national transfers of a share of the VAT (12%), and finally, by taxes charged to European staff and fines paid by companies in the case of violation of the right to competition since 2007 (5%).[1] The latter line of financing has allowed a partial reduction in the contributions/transfers from Member States. With respect to expenditures, their largest share is directed to capital account items. The resources of the budget mainly finance common investment programs that have an added value in their European dimension. The budget thus has

---

[1]   The most relevant cases are represented by Telefonica in 2007, Microsoft in 2008, and most recently, Apple in 2016, Facebook in 2017 and Google in 2018.

a different nature from the national ones which are characterized by largest shares of current account items. Its purpose is to carry out joint actions that would be difficult, or at least more expensive, to finance at Member State level. This mechanism has produced many positive effects in strategic sectors such as energy, transport, information and communication technologies, climate change and research. However, the nature of a budget closely linked to long-term investments has severely limited the Union's ability to react to con-tingencies and emergency situations, as was particularly evident in the migra-tion crisis. Another limit is represented by the imposed balance of the budget that does not allow deficits in peculiar situations. On the other hand, this principle has been deemed necessary in order to have a unanimous agreement of countries characterized by heterogeneous economic structures and cycles. According to Article 312 of the Treaty on the functioning of the European Union, the yearly EU budgets are determined on the basis of the Multiannual Financial Framework (MFF). Its most important aims are the development of expenditures in an orderly manner, the respect for the limits imposed by the EU's own resources and the identification of items of expenditure. The MFF represents the long-term perspective for EU finances and must be related to a period of no less than 5 years.

The MFF for the period 2014–2020 devoted about 80 per cent of its resources to agricultural subsidies (Common Agricultural Policy) and to regional development policies (structural funds and cohesion funds), while just over 6 per cent was allocated to the role of the European Union in the world and only 2 per cent to security and citizenship issues. This financial rigidity has been a huge problem for the solution of complex crises such as those which the EU has had to confront, thus weakening the European institutions themselves. Furthermore, the traditional immobility of the Member States, reluctant to surrender significant shares of their sovereignty, has curbed the EU action.

The negotiation on the MFF for 2021–2027 has taken place in one of the most difficult and controversial phases of the European Union on several fronts. A series of crises, which have occurred almost simultaneously, have called into question the whole European project. After the economic and the single currency crises, the political crisis leading to the rise of nationalism and of sovereignist parties has seen its climax in the referendum on the exit of the UK from the European Union. Its result was followed by the complicated negotiations between the UK and the EU which will lead to the first exit of one of the Member States. Moreover, the continuing migration crisis contributed to making the EU political framework unstable and highlighted the limits of the EU budget for the management of this phenomenon. It is precisely in this context, and on the eve of EU general elections in May 2019, that the Member States and the European institutions were called to plan the MFF 2021–2027, where the political and economic targets to pursue will be settled. As already mentioned, the definition of budget issues and of expenditure items is not just a financial accounting exercise as it represents the clearest and most important political indicator of the path that the European Union will follow in this period.

The present collective book is based on the awareness that a sectorial discussion on the EU budget can only provide a partial understanding. It thus proposes a multidisciplinary approach that considers not only the economic dimension but also the historical, political and juridical ones. This multifaceted analysis of the EU budget allows a much more detailed and profound knowledge not only of the political and economic dynamics within the EU but also of the real level of European integration. The book provides the latest academic research both on a retrospective view of the EU budget development and on the current and future issues and trends. In this framework, some of the following chapters aim at shedding light on the debate and proposals about the MFF 2021–2027, in order to fully understand the various and contrasting stances of national governments and of European Institutions with respect to the EU budget dimension and relevant subjects.

1.1 THE STRUCTURE OF THE BOOK AND ITS CONTENT

The present book is divided into two parts. The first one will review the historical and political profiles of the EU budget. It will first provide a historical analysis of the EU budget and the European integration process. It will then discuss the role of the EU budget between bargaining tool and policy instrument. This will be followed by the study of the democratic deficit in the European Union and of the citizens' attitudes towards the EU budget. Lastly, the political implications of the MFF 2021–2027 will be considered. The second section will analyze the legal and economic perspectives. It will examine the flexibility and unit principles of the EU budget and of the MFF. It will then consider the European framework for monitoring and control of the EU budget. Moreover, it will review its role for growth and competitiveness. It will then provide a discussion of its relevance for the structural balances of Member States. Lastly, it will analyze the effects of Brexit on the EU budget. The main findings emerging from the various contributions will be discussed in the last chapter that concludes the book.

In detail, Part 1 opens with Chapter 2, 'The EU budget and the European integration process: a historical analysis', by Ubaldo Villani-Lubelli. The chapter first states that the EU budget is of fundamental importance for the consolidation and reinforcement of the European political project and for the defense of the values on which the European Union was originally and is still founded.

Throughout the European integration process, the function of the EU budget has been understood as a system of supranational development of all Member States. However, its evolution, especially since the introduction of the own resources system, has gone in a direction not exactly corresponding to the initial intentions. The Member States have both limited and conditioned the autonomy of the budget of the Union and have made the control much more complex and fragmented. The EU budget finances many economic and social initiatives and determines the direction and level of political integration between Member States. Despite this, it is very modest, just around 1 per cent of Community GDP. This chapter also analyzes the historical development of the EU budget from its origins to the political debate on the 2021–2027 MFF, in order to outline the successes, failures and status of the European integration process. Finally, the contribution aims to highlight the anomalous institutional nature of the European Union and the consequent need to provide it with a more substantial and values-oriented budget.

Chapter 3, 'The EU budget between bargaining tool and policy instrument' by Mario Kölling, starts from the assumption that, in the academic and political debate, the EU budget is largely considered a relic of the past that needs a deep reform. The spending structure of the EU budget has evolved according to the EU integration process and subsequent treaty reforms, and according to specific challenges. However, despite numerous proposals for improvements, the reforms of the past did not meet the expectations. The chapter then discusses some theoretical assumptions about the concepts of bargaining tool vs. policy instrument related to the EU budget. The shift between these two possible definitions is first analyzed by considering the evolution of the EU budget headings among the programming periods. The chapter then takes into account the impact of conditionality in budgetary spending and the role of the European Parliament in the negotiation of the MFF. Lastly, the revenue side is studied according to the question of how a reform of the own resources system could support the evolution of the EU budget towards a policy instrument. The chapter argues that the specific characteristics of the EU budget and the negotiation process may not lead to a revolutionary new budget in the next programming period. Nevertheless, the 2021–2027 MFF will reinforce the ongoing paradigm change in the perception of the EU budget, from a budget aimed at compensating Member States for their political compromises to a budget aimed at solving EU-wide problems.

Chapter 4, 'No representation without taxation'. For a history of the budgetary control in the European Union' by Alessandro Isoni, aims to highlight how the complex set of procedures concerning the EU budget mirrors the existence of a democratic deficit in the European Union. Starting from the development of the English constitutional experience, this paper analyses how the procedures in force at European Union level for the budget approval are very far from the Western constitutional patterns, where a clear system of checks and balances is usually established in order to ensure the control of the executive power. In this line, the adopted reforms seem to have only contributed to complicating democratic control over EU budget, eventually leading to a stronger power of Member States. Moreover, the chapter focuses on three important features. The first is the choice adopted by the European "Founding Fathers" to opt for a new funding system, abandoning the *juste retour* principle and creating new complex institutional procedures. The second is a review of bitter struggles among European Member States concerning their financial contribution to the European budget and how this long and exhausting conflict deeply influenced the development of the European integration. Lastly, the chapter tries to propose a new constitutional framework able to ensure a real democratic control on budget issues, through a complete and full involvement of the European Parliament.

Chapter 5, 'Citizens' attitudes towards the EU budget: An overview', by Karsten Mause, states that there is an ongoing debate over the appropriate level of financial redistribution and international solidarity generated via the EU budget. While the opinions of political decision-makers and other experts are relevant, it is also important to take into account what EU citizens – in their role as taxpayers funding the EU budget – think about this budget. National citizens are often considered as the 'principals' of those actors or 'agents' at the EU level being responsible for the EU budget. It can be expected that many principals have an incentive that their taxpayers' money is spent well by the EU. Hence, the chapter gives an overview of the topic of citizens' attitudes towards the EU budget. Using cross-national data from the Eurobarometer public opinion polls, the chapter addresses three research questions. First, it examines how public attitudes toward the EU budget have developed over time. It emerges that in a number of countries public support for an increase in the EU budget increased between 2005 and 2018 despite the fact that one of the EU's biggest crises happened during this investigation period: namely, the financial, sovereign-debt, and economic crisis after 2007/2008. Second, the chapter analyzes whether EU citizens are satisfied with the status quo of the EU budget system. It appears that the legitimation basis for an increase in the EU budget currently remains rather low throughout the EU. Third, it investigates the cross-national differences in citizens' attitudes toward the EU budget. As expected, it turns out that approval rates tend to be higher in EU countries that are net beneficiaries. Moreover, the five EU countries that were bailed out through 'rescue packages' since 2010 are among the 'top-10 countries' with respect to public support for an increase of the EU budget. Lastly, no clear East–West divide with respect to this issue emerges.

Chapter 6, 'The multi-annual financial framework: reforms and path-dependent development of the EU budget' by Robert Kaiser, argues that reforms at the structural level for the 2021–2027 MFF are quite unlikely. This is because the structure of the MFF has proven and still proves to have a certain degree of flexibility, which means that it is capable of incorporating quite substantial changes while at the same time providing all involved actors (mainly at the national levels) with the amount of security needed to commit themselves to a longer-term definition of their burdens and benefits. Changes will probably occur at the instrumental level where it is still possible to agree on new policy objectives or to change certain rules for the distribution of funds. In order to substantiate this assumption, the chapter first presents the conceptual framework that guides the analysis of stability and change of the MFF. It then turns to the structural level of the MFF by examining the overall amount of investments, the duration of the financial framework, the direct linkage between the main expenditure lines and the three most important Union programmes (i.e. for agricultural policies, for structural and cohesion policies, and for research and innovation policies), and the structure of the revenue side. It emerges that the EU budget structure has indeed developed during the last three decades along a solid institutional path. Moreover, the chapter looks at the procedural level elaborating on the main features, such as actors' preferences and coalitions, of the negotiation process. Finally, it evaluates the potential for change at the policy level, especially in funding of research and innovation, in new rules for the distribution of funds to the Member States and in a more comprehensive use of new financial instruments.

Part 1 of the book closes with Chapter 7, 'Towards a closer Intergovernmental Union? The political implications of the MFF 2021–2027 negotiations', by Matteo Scotto. It first considers that the EU budget negotiations have always been characterized by political disputes, mirroring the Union's economic, social and political evolution. The chapter argues that the political debate around the EU budget composition in the 2021–2027 period reflected the state of the European project, namely an unsteady intergovernmental Union, both at the institutional and at the procedural level. This situation is the outcome of the behavior of Member States acting beyond the EU Treaties by means of intergovernmental treaties (such as the Treaty on Stability, Coordination and Governance in the Economic and Monetary Union or *Fiscal Compact*), or intergovernmental organizations (such as the European Stability Mechanism). The chapter also discusses the EU budget from procedural perspectives, identifying the intergovernmental features of budgetary policy up to the 2021–2027 period, in particular by examining how the EU's own resources are organized. Moreover, it states that the Lisbon Treaty consolidated numerous intergovernmental procedures in new policy areas and the EU budget is no exception. The chapter also analyses the political debate in the negotiation process both on the revenue and on the expenditure side, with potential negative consequences on European integration as a whole. Lastly, it considers that, given the turbulent times the EU was facing and the unsteady intergovernmental architecture, the MFF 2021–2027 did not constitute an important factor in the economic, social and political development of the EU. The conservative attitudes of the Member States hampered the capacity of the MFF 2021–2027 to represent, even symbolically, a concrete advance in the European integration process envisaged by the EU Commission.

Part 2 of the book opens with Chapter 8, 'The EU budget and the MFF between flexibility and unity', by Peter Becker. The chapter discusses the conflict and dilemma between the political necessity of budgetary flexibility and the wish for budgetary stability and predictability, hence the tension between these two fundamental principles of budgetary policy. The chapter first discusses the need for budgetary flexibility, by also presenting the current flexibility instruments in the European Union's budgetary policy (among them, the emergency aid reserve, the solidarity fund and the European globalization adjustment fund). It then considers the principle of unity of the budget and introduces the relevant exceptions in European policy. These exceptions either stem from the origins of European budgetary policy, like the European Development Fund, or are based on the legal personality of an institution, like the European Central Bank (ECB) or the European Investment Bank, or they are determined by the division of competencies between the EU and the Member States. Finally, the chapter tries to draw conclusions for European budgetary policy in general and the negotiations on the 2021–2027 MFF in particular. Beyond the controversy over the volume and distribution of funds, the search for a reliable balance between budgetary predictability on the one hand and the need for political adaptability of the budget on the other were an issue of these negotiations. The chapter states that the EU will have to improve its capacity for accurate and proper responses on political challenges through flexibility instruments, inside and outside the MFF, that will have to be brought into line with the budgetary principles of unity and completeness. The most fundamental exception to the budget principle of unity could be a special budget for the Eurozone. The European Parliament's budgetary participation and control rights and thus the democratic legitimacy of the EU budget as a whole must also be taken into account.

Chapter 9, 'The European framework for monitoring and control of the EU budget' by Elsa Perreau, provides an overview of the budget monitoring and control system of the European Union. It states that the Article 310 of the Treaty on the Functioning of the European Union lists the six principles governing the EU budget: unity, universality, equilibrium, annuality, specification, and sound management. Moreover, the Financial Regulation stipulates three main principles on sound financial management: the principle of economy, the principle of efficiency and the principle of effectiveness. On the other hand, the chapter considers four risks to good financial management of EU funds: (a) the funds are not spent according to the rules or for their intended purpose (legality and regularity); (b) expenditures are not accounted for properly (reliability of the accounts); (c) the funds are not spent following sound financial management principles (economy, efficiency and effectiveness); and (d) benefits from the use of the funds do not materialize and the EU budget does not produce EU added-value. The chapter then states that financial accountability takes place internally and externally and involves various EU institutions: the European Commission, the European Court of Auditors, the European Parliament and the Council. The external control by the European Court of Auditors mainly takes place after the implementation of the EU budget. This chapter also reviews the challenges for monitoring and control of the EU budget. While fragmentation and complexity are to some extent inherent to the EU budget because of the structure of the European Union, they have accelerated in the Lisbon era, creating new challenges for budget monitoring and control. The chapter considers four tendencies that have increased fragmentation and complexity: the financial troubles of 2007, the more recent migration crisis of 2015, the increased use of instruments financed only by participating Member States, and the internal fragmentation and complexity within the budget owing to the shift from a policy-driven budget to a demand-driven budget.

Chapter 10, 'Growth, competitiveness and the EU budget', by Luca Zamparini, analyzes two of the most important issues related to all economic systems. The linkages between growth and competitiveness are very important in order to understand the long-term development and also the convergence among different regions pertaining to larger economic areas, such as the EU. The chapter considers the evolution of the EU GDP and of the EU GDP per capita since the inception of the first financial perspective, by displaying the average growth rates in the five periods that have been marked by financial perspectives (Multiannual Financial Frameworks). Moreover, it discusses the competitiveness of the EU and compares it with other world regions (i.e. US and Japan) by taking into account the indicators related to the innovation environment and the reasons for the weak performance of the EU. The chapter also considers the degree of competitiveness in the various NUTS2 regions of the EU. The discussion is based on the results emerging from the Regional Competitiveness Index aimed at providing a measure of economic and social development and at fostering medium- and long-term plans. Lastly, the role of the EU budget for growth and competitiveness, between the first financial perspective that covered the period between 1988 and 1992 and the MFF for the period between 2014 and 2020, is considered. Such analysis is carried out by displaying the historical development of the expenditure commitments of the EU Commission from 1991 to 2018.

Chapter 11, 'The relevance of the EU budget for the structural balances of Member States', by Maurizia Pierri, outlines the key principles governing the European system and focuses on the golden rule of the balanced budget (principle of equilibrium), from the point of view of the European budget and of individual Member States. The regulatory framework of the budgets in Eurozone countries is extremely complicated, for the simultaneous presence of standards deriving from treaties both external and stipulated within the Union law, regulations and directives on monetary policy. The balanced budget rule is due to an international treaty (Fiscal Compact) that requires the balanced budget to be embodied in the countries' rules of law (preferably at constitutional level). The possibility of including the rule of balanced budget even at sub-constitutional level, the difference between nominal and structural balances and the ambiguous identification of justification causes for the violation of the stability standards determine considerable differences in the Countries' behaviors and so a partial ineffectiveness of the so-called *golden rule*. The issues arising from its application are discussed in the last part of the chapter as it considers its implementation (or attempts of implementation) in five EU countries, namely France, Germany, Italy, Slovenia and Spain. These countries were selected given their adoption, or intention to adopt, the balanced budget rule at the constitutional level.

Part 2 of the book closes with Chapter 12, 'Brexit and the EU budget', by Margit Schratzenstaller. Departing from the hypothesis that the Brexit may act as a catalyst for fundamental reforms within the EU budget aiming at strengthening the added value of EU expenditures and revenues, the chapter sketches the pillars of such far-reaching reforms. It states that EU expenditures should only target policy areas in which Member States' un-coordinated actions would be insufficient owing to free riding, coordination problems and cross-border issues and those areas in which common European interests are at stake. Consequently, the EU action is justified either if it results in a higher value compared with separate national actions or if expenditure has a cross-border element. On the revenue side, the introduction of sustainability-oriented tax-based own resources, partially substituting for Member States' national contributions, can strengthen the role of the EU system of its own resources for central EU policies. The chapter then provides an overview of the expected financial implications of the Brexit. The current status of the UK–EU Brexit negotiations implies a twofold financial impact of the Brexit, comprising the one-off "Brexit bill" or "divorce bill" and the permanent "Brexit gap". The chapter states that the exact size of the Brexit gap will depend on various factors, which are highly uncertain, particularly the modalities of Brexit ("hard" or "soft" Brexit) and the future UK–EU financial arrangements. Against this background, the chapter closes with a brief first assessment of the European Commission's proposals for the 2021–2027 MFF. To cover the Brexit gap and to finance the new priorities, the proposals foresee an increase in national contributions as well as new own resources.

The Conclusions, written by the editors on the basis of the issues emerging in the two main parts of the book, are explicitly comparative in orientation. First, they analytically draw the similarities and the heterogeneities of the themes and frameworks discussed in the previous chapters. Secondly, they aim at representing a well-founded contribution to the political and institutional debates on the reforms of the EU budget and their influence on the development of the European Union.

PART I

Historical and political profiles

2. The EU budget and the European integration process: a historical analysis

Ubaldo Villani-Lubelli

2.1 INTRODUCTION

The connection between the EU budget and the history of the European integration process is a relatively new topic in research on political institutions. The structure and composition of the EU budget, however, are crucial elements in understanding political integration in the European Union. Every organization carefully plans its budget to achieve financial and political success (Laffan, 2000; Laffan and Shackleton, 2000; Lindner and Rittberger, 2003; Ackrill and Kay, 2006). In fact, a budget represents the political plan that quantifies future expectations and decides the ways and means of achieving certain goals and values. This is particularly true for the European Union, as will see in the following chapter.

Despite having a modest budget of around 1 per cent of Community GDP, the EU budget finances many economic and social initiatives and determines the direction and level of political integration between Member States. In other words, 'its political significance is [...] much greater than its size' (Ackrill, 2000, 2). Throughout the European integration process, the function of the EU budget has been understood as a system of supranational development of all Member States. However, its evolution, especially since the introduction of own resources, has gone in a direction not exactly corresponding to the initial intentions. This is mainly because the Member States have both limited and conditioned the autonomy of the budget of the Union and have made the control much more complex, parcelized and fragmented (Crowe, 2017). This process was well illustrated in detail in the Monti Report as 'the galaxy around the Eu-Budget'.[1] This galaxy represents both the complex participation of the

---

[1]   See Annex IV of the Monti Report.

Member States and the diversified system of procedures that has emerged around the EU budget, in order to support European policy and values (Monti Report, 2016).

Given that budget resources are defined in the so-called Multiannual Financial Framework, in 2018 negotiations were started for the redefinition of the European budget for the period 2021–2027, during which the Commission proposed a substantial increase in contributions in view of the exit of the UK from the European Union, which will cause an annual deficit of about €14 billion (see Chapter 12).

After a short introduction about the connection between the budget and European values, the following chapter traces the development of the European budget from a historical-political point of view, identifying four macro-phases in order to outline the successes and failures of the European integration process. The first of these is 'From the Treaty of Rome to the first enlargement of the EU', the second is 'From Fontainebleau to the Treaty of Maastricht', the third is 'The Nineties and the Lisbon Treaty' and the fourth is 'The Challenges of the present: The Multiannual Financial Framework 2021–2017'. In the final part of the chapter some concluding remarks on the current development of the EU budget and on the necessity of its substantial increase in order to advance the European integration process will be proposed.

2.2   THE EU BUDGET AND EUROPEAN VALUES

The European budget is unique in its nature and definition. It is mainly an investment budget and its economic stabilization function depends on national Member States. Unlike national budgets, the EU budget must always be in balance and aims to designate financial resources in order to achieve fundamental objectives and political and societal priorities of the European Union following art. 3 of the European Treaty, according to which, social and economic cohesion are an indispensable prerequisite to achieving political aims:

1. The Union's aim is to promote peace, its values and the well-being of its peoples.

2. [...]

The Union shall establish an internal market. It shall work for the sustainable development of Europe based on balanced economic growth and price stability, a highly competitive social market economy, aiming at full employment and social progress, and a high level of protection and improvement of the quality of the environment. [...] It shall combat social exclusion and discrimination, and shall promote social justice and protection, equality between women and men, solidarity between generations and protection of the rights of the child. It shall promote economic, social and territorial cohesion, and solidarity among Member States. [...]

The idea of social cohesion and economic convergence is at the heart of the European model with the aim of avoiding imbalances and ensuring proper functioning of the single market. The guiding principle of the EU is that European economies can converge and that imbalances can be adjusted for greater cohesion. The quantitative and qualitative development of the EU budget was always intertwined with the European political integration process, so that it was a significative and crucial indicator of the status of the latter. Not by chance it was also an important political negotiation point between the EU Member States and European political institutions, regarding the determination of the total volume of resources that should be allocated to the supranational level and their subdivision by areas of intervention. Negotiation on these issues has to deal with the recognition of a fair financial distribution between the EU Member States, in order to safeguard the benefits of EU membership (Ackrill, 2000).

It is also necessary to remember that art. 311 of the Treaty on the Functioning of the European Union named *The Union's Own Resources* explains the connection between budget and Union objectives:

> The Union shall provide itself with the means necessary to attain its objectives and carry through its policies. Without prejudice to other revenue, the budget shall be financed wholly from own resources.

The EU budget represents, in the 2014–2020 program, just 1.05% of the GDP of the EU Member States. The limited budget depends on the fact that public spending in sectors of social interest, such as policy defense, health or pensions, has remained the responsibility of the EU Member States, *de facto* impeding further progress towards European integration.

Despite its current dimension, the EU budget is a fundamental political aspect in the understanding of the present status of the European integration process. Over the years, the composition of the European budget has had a slow but substantial evolution (see Figure 2.1).

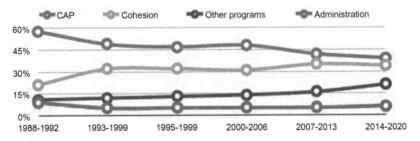

Figure 2.1   *The evolution of the EU budget*

2.3 FROM THE TREATY OF ROME TO THE FIRST ENLARGEMENT OF THE EU

The Rome Treaty (1957), which founded the European Economic Community (EEC), aimed to unite six different national economic areas in order to begin a process to an ever-closer union. Economic integration and political goals were the two intertwined aims.

The six founding countries of the EEC (Belgium, France, Germany, Italy, Luxembourg and the Netherlands) were relatively homogeneous from an economic and societal point of view, so that the Treaty of Rome, except for a vague reference in art. 2, relied on the positive effects that the free market would have in smoothing out economic inequalities. The question of the backward areas remained the responsibility of the individual states except for the south of Italy (*Mezzogiorno*), to which the treaty dedicated a specific protocol. Since the 1957 Treaty of Rome, the normative evolution of the European Economic Community and of the EU has been oriented to the principles of free movement, solidarity, cohesion and socio-economic harmonization.

The Rome Treaty established that the European Council was responsible for post-clearance approval of the budget by unanimous vote. The role of the European Parliamentary Assembly and of the European Commission was limited to an advisory function in the preparation of the budget. Although art. 201 of the Treaty of Rome envisaged the possibility of financing the budget using its own resources and giving the Commission the task of drawing up proposals, the European budget was financed exclusively by national contributions from Member States until 1970. The project of the first president of the European Commission, the German Walter Hallstein, was to realize a more independent budget, in order to create a central Community authority which would be independent of the separate Member States. However, this project was rejected by France. Thus, the European Economic Community was no different from the other international organizations that were founded after the Second World War.

A fundamental and crucial turning point in the history of the development of the EU budget was the establishment in 1962 of the European Agricultural Guarantee Fund. The Fund was a very important tool for financing the Common Agricultural Policy (CAP), which was introduced in the same year to better respond to the aims of the Treaty of Rome: the Council of the European Union liberalized the common market organizations for six agricultural products (cereals, pig meat, eggs, poultry meat, fruit and vegetables, and wine). In addition, rules regarding competition were introduced. These included a schedule to assist intra-community trade for dairy products. Beef and veal were added to the agricultural products, and the European Agricultural

Guidance and Guarantee Fund was also established. Even today the CAP represents the largest component of expenditure on the EU budget.

On 22 April 1970, with the Treaty of Luxembourg a system of own resources in partial replacement of national contributions was introduced for the first time. The EEC self-financed in the following way: (a) with customs duties and other charges levied on imports from outside the Community; (b) with the levies on agricultural products; and (c) with a share of VAT up to a maximum of 1 percent. Otherwise, the possibility of financing the community budget with direct contributions from the Member States remained intact, but with transitory and decreasing importance. Moreover, from an institutional perspective, it was established that the European Assembly would become one of the two decision-making branches with regard to the European budget, even if its powers were still very limited to shared responsibility (art. 1 of the Treaty of Luxembourg).

Starting in the 1970s, firstly by the entry into the EU of the UK, Denmark and Ireland in 1973 and then, later, with the new memberships in the European Economic Community of Greece (1983), Spain and Portugal (1986), it was clear that economic and social distortions owing to enlargement could have taken the project away from its original scope and possibly undermine the political legitimacy of the EEC. Moreover, a document presented by Pierre Werner, the Prime Minister and Finance Minister of Luxembourg, known as the Werner Report, drawn up in 1970, had already underlined the problem of potential economic and social asymmetries within the community and proposed an economic and monetary union:

> Economic and monetary union will make it possible to realize an area within which goods and services, people and capital will circulate freely and without competitive distortions, without thereby giving rise to structural or regional disequilibrium [...] The implementation of such a union will effect a lasting improvement in welfare in the Community and will reinforce the contribution of the Community to economic and monetary equilibrium in the world. [...] To ensure the cohesion of economic and monetary union transfers of responsibility from the national to the Community plane will be essential. (Werner Report, 1970)

According to the Werner report, a modification of the European budget had become fundamental. In fact, the report stated:

> For influencing the general development of the economy budget policy assumes great importance. The Community budget will undoubtedly be more important at the beginning of the final stage than it is today, but its economic significance will still be weak compared with that of the national budgets, the harmonized management to which will be an essential feature of cohesion in the union. (Werner Report, 1970)

The aim was therefore to continue to orient the European budget toward cohesion and to avoid socio-economic imbalances, which would have left behind the weaker regions or countries. Furthermore, according to the next Thompson report, which paved the way for the European Regional Development Fund, the combination of growth and cohesion was a human and moral imperative, without which the very purpose of the European Community was called into question (Thompson Report, 1973).

In 1975 the European Council further strengthened the Parliament's powers, radically changing the division of responsibility introduced by the Treaty of Luxembourg (1970). While the Council retained the right to finally approve compulsory expenditure, Parliament obtained the last word on the adoption of non-compulsory expenditure. It was also established that the Parliament should be given control over the Commission. Finally, it was decided to set up the Court of Auditors, an institution responsible for monitoring the implementation of the Community budget (see Chapter 9).

On the expenditure side, the European Regional Development Fund was introduced and marked the beginning of the European economic cohesion policy – already prepared by the Thompson report – with the aim of allocating resources to the poorest regions of the Community. In 1977, the MacDougall report focused on a 'pre-federal integration' structure in connection with the first direct election of the European Parliament in 1979. The report advanced proposals in some ways truly revolutionary. Among the main ones were: (a) federal expenditure of the order of 5–7% of total GDP and (b) creating a Community Unemployment Fund in order to reduce intra-regional differences in capital endowment and productivity:

> it would have significant redistributive effects and help to cushion temporary setbacks in particular member countries, thereby going a small part of the way towards creating a situation in which monetary union could be sustained. (MacDougall Report, 1977: 13)

The MacDougall report (together with the Marjolin Report, 1975) was the theoretical and substantial basis for the reform of the European budget, which was developed in the 1980s.

2.4 FROM FONTAINEBLEAU TO THE TREATY OF MAASTRICHT

Over the years, it became clear that the initially allocated resources were not sufficient to meet the Community's financial commitments. Hence the need to increase national contributions to the budget to cover expenditure, but this requirement proved to be rather difficult. In June 1984, an agreement was reached at the Fontainebleau European Council to end the 10 year dispute over the size of the UK contribution to the Community budget, given the disproportion between what it paid and the amount it received back in the form of Community funding. With the so-called *Abatement* the UK was granted a reduction of two-thirds of its net contribution.

In order to cope with the need for spending it was also decided that the share of the VAT contribution would increase from 1 to 1.4 per cent. A reflection on a radical reduction of the financing of the European budget was also initiated. Thus, in 1988, during the European Council in Brussels, a small revolution of the European budget came about because the so-called *fourth resource* was created, a national contribution to budget revenues calculated on the basis of gross domestic product (IABDIBP, 1988; Fauri, 2017). Since then, each Member State has contributed to the European budget based on its ability to pay.

In the meantime, the Frenchman Jacques Delors became President of the European Commission and held the office from 1985 to 1995. President Delors, in the context of a necessary and indispensable reform of the community budget, tried to implement the proposals that were elaborated by the above-mentioned reports, with the aim of combining the single market with a strong social dimension by smoothing out regional economic disparities.

The first Delors Package aimed to guarantee the financing of the Community budget. It translated into the 1988–1992 financial perspectives which were approved by the Brussels European Council, on the basis of a proposal prepared the previous year by the Commission chaired by Jacques Delors and aimed at operationalizing the Single European Act of 1987. The package marked an important reorientation of the EU's main spending guidelines, in particular with the transfer of resources from the CAP to cohesion policies. It also introduced a fourth financing resource based on the GDP of the member countries, and set a total ceiling on the total resources to be allocated annually to the Community budget. The first inter-institutional agreement between the Council and the European Parliament was also signed, and after lengthy negotiations, the EEC moved from a five- to a seven-year financial perspective. The reform ratified the transition to the system of Multiannual Financial perspectives; the European Commission made the proposals and both the Council and the European Parliament (budgetary authority) negotiated the agreement.

The second Delors package of 1992, which took shape in the 1993–1999 financial perspectives, established the increase of the ceiling for the resources marked out for the EU budget and strengthened the redistributive component from the expenditure side giving more funds to allocative policies, such as research and transeuropean networks. On the revenue side, the second Delors package essentially confirmed the previous system of own resources, strengthening the weight of the gross national product resource out of the total and maintaining the correction mechanism for the UK. The second Delors package confirms the reduction of contributions to the European budget by the UK.

Thus, in the 1980s, the European cohesion policy was born, introduced with the aim of helping the economic development of the most disadvantaged European regions, so that their per capita income could converge to the average EU income through the adoption of structural funds. At this point it is important to reflect on cohesion policy well beyond the historical phase examined here. The objective of European cohesion policy became even more significant, following the enlargement process that affected the European Union to the countries of the former Soviet-bloc and, starting from 2008 to 2010, with the economic and financial crisis that inevitably increased social inequalities.

Investment in cohesion policy has grown consistently. In the 2014–2020 programming period, about a third of the budget (€352 billion) is earmarked for funding projects that aim to reduce still existing social and economic disparities in European territories. At the same time, this policy is a further catalyst for public and private funding as it often obliges Member States to co-finance by drawing on national budgets.

2.5   THE 1990S AND THE LISBON TREATY

In 1999 the 2000–2006 financial perspectives were adopted by the Berlin European Council after two years of negotiations. Two years before, on 16 July 1997, the Commission of Jacques Santer presented to the European Parliament the 'Agenda 2000' on the future of the policies of the European Union, at the end of the Intergovernmental Conference in Amsterdam. Agenda 2000 was born as a response to the requests made by the Madrid European Council of December 1995, in relation both to the need for a deepening of the pre-accession strategy elaborated following the applications for entry into the EU of the countries of central-Eastern Europe, and the evolution to be given to the Community policies in the face of the challenges posed by the prospect of enlargement of the European Union. However, with Agenda 2000 the European Commission went far beyond this mandate and proposed a more general reflection with two primary objectives: (a) to achieve an initial assessment of the phase of strengthening the process of economic and political integration of the EU; and (b) to propose an institutional reform of the Treaties (already launched under the Single European Act) and outline the future prospects of Community policies in an enlarged Union.

Agenda 2000 was, therefore, a document of broad strategic scope, which outlined the evolutionary scenario of the EU for the beginning of the new millennium. It identified the lines of development of Community policies in a single context, in relation to their compatibility with the new objectives and the new Union fund principles and with the budget constraint imposed by the financial framework defined for the years after 2000. With regard to the strengthening of the EU, recognizing the insufficiency of the amendments made by the Amsterdam Treaty, 'Agenda 2000' established that the development of institutional reforms and the review of the organization and working methods of the Commission, the development of Internal policies and the continuation of the reform of the CAP were indispensable for tackling enlargement, ensuring sustainable growth and increasing employment and improving the living conditions of European citizens.

The package was characterized by a conservative approach. It was elaborated in a context of significant criticality from the political point of view, with the Santer Commission resigning on the eve of the summit, with the need to allocate resources to the candidate countries of the upcoming enlargement and with the pressing requests from four Member States (Germany, Austria, Sweden and the Netherlands) to achieve a reduction in their net contribution to the Community budget. The own resources ceiling was kept unchanged, and the CAP reform was significantly reduced compared with the Commission's proposal for a national co-financing. The changes to the regulation of the structural funds would have limited effects, both in the budget and in the redistribution among the Member States, and it was not possible to abolish the British correction, as initially proposed by the Commission, because of the UK's tenacious opposition. The main innovative aspect was represented by the creation of a new category of expenditure (of 'pre-accession') aimed at supporting the candidate countries in the phase of preparation for entry into the EU and the provision of a margin available to cover the cost of any enlargement during that period (see Pre-accession strategy, Accession criteria).

In December 2005 the 2007–2013 financial perspectives were adopted by the Brussels European Council. They were characterized by the stability of resources and an internal reorganization of the expense categories, with a gradual reduction of agricultural expenditure and a partial exploitation of allocative expenses functional to the pursuit of the objectives of the Lisbon Strategy (research and innovation, employment and sustainable development) and external actions. Neither the financing system nor the UK correction mechanism was reformed, even though a partial change was planned to take place by 2009. With the coming into force of the Lisbon Treaty certain modifications were made to the EU's budget powers, some of which were substantial while others were purely formal. The two most relevant changes were the decreased flexibility to the budget and the partial reduction in spending, the so-called financial perspectives became known as the Multiannual Financial Framework and furthermore the long-term budget planning was constitutionalized through art. 312 of the Treaty on the Functioning of the European Union. Finally, the power of the European Parliament was reduced, despite the apparently greater

Table 2.1   *Multiannual Financial Framework adjusted for 2019*

Commitment appropriations	2014	2017	2018	2019	2020	Total 2014–2020
1. Smart and inclusive growth	52.756	73.512	76.420	79.924	83.661	513.563
1.A. Competitiveness for growth and jobs	16.560	19.925	21.239	23.082	25.191	142.130
1.B. Economic, social and territorial cohesion	36.196	53.587	55.181	56.842	58.470	371.433
2. Sustainable growth: natural resources	49.857	60.191	60.267	60.344	60.421	420.034
of which: market-related expenditure and direct payments	43.779	44.146	44.163	44.241	44.264	308.734
3. Security and citizenship	1.737	2.578	2.656	2.801	2.951	17.725
4. Global Europe	8.335	9.432	9.825	10.268	10.510	66.262
5. Administration	8.721	9.918	10.346	10.786	11.254	69.584
of which: administrative expenditure of the institutions	7.056	8.007	8.360	8.700	9.071	56.224
6. Compensations	29	0	0	0	0	29
Total commitment appropriations	121.435	155.631	159.514	164.123	168.797	1.087.197
as a percentage of GNI	0.9%	1.04%	1.02%	1.01%	1.01%	1.03%
Total payment appropriations	135.762	142.906	154.565	159.235	162.406	1.026.287
as a percentage of GNI	1.01%	0.95%	0.98%	0.98%	0.97%	0.98%
Margin available	0.22%	0.28%	0.22%	0.22%	0.23%	0.24%
Own resources ceiling as a percentage of GNI	1.23%	1.23%	1.2%	1.2%	1.2%	1.22%

Note: GNI, Gross National Income.
Source: European Commission, http://ec.europa.eu/budget/mff/figures/index_en.cfm.

influence afforded by the process of co-decision (in the co-decision process) with the European Council (Benedetto, 2013; Crowe 2017, 437–444).

The total expenditures of the EU budget for the period 2014–2020 amount to € 959.99 billion. They will be funded in the following way: 70% from the national contributions of each Member State on the basis of a mechanism linked to the level of national income, 12% from the national transfers of a portion of VAT, 13% from own resources and 5% from taxes charged to EU staff or fines paid by companies in the event of infringement of the right to competition. In particular, the 2014–2020 EU budget is divided according to Table 2.1.

The most important item remains that of economic and social cohesion. The main objective here is to financially assist the convergence of the poorest regions (i.e. with a GDP of less than 75% of the EU average) and the least developed countries with better-off regions and countries of the European Union. It should be noted that more than half of the planned resources are allocated to countries whose development is lagging behind.

2.6   THE CHALLENGES OF THE PRESENT: THE MFF 2021–2027

Since the 1990s, the Community budget has seen a slow but evident reduction. As can be seen from Figure 2.2, the size of the European Union budget as a percentage of Gross National Income has been reduced from 1.25% in 1993–1999 to 1.03% in 2014–2020.

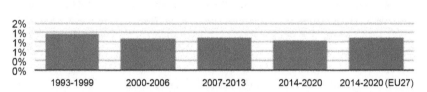

Figure 2.2   EU budget and gross national income

As discussed above, the European Union's funding, since its foundation, has been the subject of controversies and negotiations among the Member States. With the recent economic-financial crisis the conflicts on the European Unions' funding have been at the center of the European political-institutional debate, during which, the forms and limits of the financing of the European budget have emerged. The migration and humanitarian crisis is a clear example of this.

On the one hand it intersects with a differentiated integration of an enlarged Europe, and on the other hand, with the reduced economic capacity of the Member States in times of crisis. The current debate and negotiation process about the Multiannual Financial Framework reflects this crisis.

Starting from the conviction that the European budget in general and the definition of the Multiannual Financial Framework in particular is at a crucial point for achieving the political aspiration and ambition of creating an 'ever closer Union', negotiations on the next Multiannual Financial Framework are coming at a very troubled historical and political phase. If the economic crisis seems to have been overcome, the European Union has a series of wider problems. The next Multiannual Financial Framework has to take into account the withdrawal of the UK which means the loss of an important contributor to the European budget (see Chapter 12). It is impossible to foresee the development of the next Multiannual Financial Framework 2021–2027; the negotiations will go on for the whole of 2019, probably over the European political election on May 2019. However, it is possible to throw light on the political framework in which the negotiations will take place and the European budget will develop. An 'In-depth Analysis' from the Policy Department for Budgetary Affairs of the Union and the European Parliament also takes into consideration the hypothesis of a change in the duration of the Multiannual Financial Framework from seven to five years (or rather 10, a 5 + 5-year cycle). Since art. 312 of Treaty on the Functioning of the European Union establishes that the Multiannual Financial Framework cannot be less than 5 years, the division into two shorter cycles would bring two advantages. In the first place, it would guarantee greater democratic legitimacy because it would be better aligned with the European Parliament and European Commission political mandates. In the second place, a shorter duration would make it more flexible in case of unforeseen events from a political and economic point of view. In other words, at a time of hasty decisions and sudden developments it would be much more politically responsible to choose a shorter term which would allow modifications taking into account current political and social phenomena (DG IPOL, 2017).

The institutional debate on the EU budget is actually a permanent topic. In view of the discussion on it, an important moment of analysis of future prospects of the budget was the work of the group chaired by Mario Monti. The report pointed out, firstly, the necessities of a reform of the EU budget on both the revenue and expenditure sides to address EU priorities and to help solve the challenges of our time, whether they are economic, security-related and geopolitical, social or cultural. Secondly, it stressed the importance for the EU budget 'to focus on areas bringing the highest European added value, for which European action is not only relevant but indispensable' (Monti Report, 2016: 11), as underlined in the first part of this chapter. Moreover, the report emphasized the importance of EU budget, as one of the main tools to achieve the EU goals (Monti Report, 2016).

Through discussion on the new Multiannual Financial Framework, the European Parliament has approved two resolutions on the Multiannual Financial Framework 2021–2027, which involve increasing the budget from less than 1 to 1.3% of GDP (a rise of over 30%), despite Brexit. The main proposed changes are: (a) increasing European public spending (research, innovation, youth mobility); (b) relying more on own resources rather than on national contributions; (c) approval in the European Council by qualified majority instead of unanimity; and (d) aligning the duration of the budget with that of the European legislature.

The European Commission, on the other hand, proposed in May 2018 a new long-term budget (2021–2027) that can fix new political priorities. According to the Monti Report, the socio-political challenges of the last years imposed a strong change in the European budget, thus the European Commission proposed a budget at 1.13% of GDP, €1135 billion for the period between 2021 and 2027 (but including cooperation funds, previously excluded). The European Commission has proposed a small reduction of Common Agricultural Policy and of Cohesion Policy, both by around 5%, in oder to to make it modern, simple and flexible. In fact, in consideration of the fact that the UK is leaving it, the European Union will need either to cut red tape for beneficiaries and managing authorities by making rules more coherent on the basis of a single rulebook, or alternatively set clearer objectives focusing more on performance. The idea is to make the structure of the budget more closely aligned with the Union's priorities. In particular, the recent political challenges (economic, Euro and humanitarian crises) have shown the limits of flexibility in the current EU budget to react quickly and effectively enough. Following the necessity, The EU Commission proposed to create a new 'Union Reserve' to tackle unforeseen events.

An important innovation in the EU Commission's proposal is to strengthen the link between EU funding and the respect of the rule of law, which is a prerequisite for financial management and the effectiveness of EU funding. The Commission proposes a new mechanism to protect the EU budget against financial risks related to generalized deficiencies regarding the rule of law in the Member States. The proposed new instruments would allow the Union to suspend, reduce or restrict access to EU funding in the case of violation of the rule of law. Such a ruling would be proposed by the Commission and adopted by the Council by reverse qualified majority voting.

According to the roadmap for deepening Europe's Economic and Monetary Union presented in December 2017, the Commission set out how new budgetary instruments could be developed within the framework of the EU's public finances, in order to support a stable Euro area and convergence towards the Euro area: (a) a new program to support reforms which, with a total budget allocation of €25 billion, will provide financial and technical support to all Member States for the implementation of priority reforms, particularly in the context of the European semester; and (b) a European investment stabilization function that will help maintain levels of investment in severe asymmetric shocks. Initially, it will operate through 'back-to-back' loans guaranteed by the EU budget with a ceiling of €30 billion, combined with assistance to the Member States to cover the interest burden.

During the first Speech on the State of the Union in September 2015, the President of the European Commission Jean Claude Juncker said that 'No wind favours he who has no destined port – we need to know where we are headed'. He was referring to the imminent future of the European Union (Juncker, 2015). After an entire legislature characterized by deep crisis and political instability, the European Union still does not know where it is headed. The negotiations on the European Budget and the next Multiannual Financial Framework reflect this fundamental ambiguity and uncertainty of the European Union. Not by chance has the European Commission put forward five different scenarios for the European Union by 2025 (White Paper on the Future of European Union 2017). They are as follows:

1. Carrying on – the EU27 continues to focus on jobs, growth and investment by strengthening the single market and by stepping up investment in digital, transport and energy infrastructure.
2. Nothing but the single market – the functioning of the single market becomes the main *raison d'être* of the EU27. Further progress depends on the capacity to agree related policies and standards. This proves easier for the free movement of capital and of goods, which continues tariff-free, than it does in other areas.
3. Those who want more do more – a group of Member States decides to cooperate much more closely on defense matters, making use of the existing legal possibilities. This includes a strong common research and industrial base, joint procurement, more integrated capabilities and enhanced military readiness for joint missions abroad.
4. Doing less more efficiently – the EU27 steps up its work in fields such as innovation, trade, security, migration, the management of borders and defense. It develops new rules and enforcement tools to deepen the single market in key new areas. It focuses on excellence in R&D and invests in new EU-wide projects to support decarbonization and digitization.
5. Doing much more together – on the international scene, Europe speaks and acts as one in trade and is represented by one seat in most international fora. The European Parliament has the final say on international trade agreements. Defense and security are prioritised. In full complementarity with NATO, a European Defense Union is created.

The five scenarios are strictly tied to the EU budget negotiations because they will be determined to a great extent by the level of political and economic integration between the Member States in the immediate future. Table 2.2 shows the possible effects of the five well-known scenarios on some of the most important financial areas.

Table 2.2   *Impact of the five scenarios for EU27 by 2025 on the EU budget*

Scenarios	Carrying on	Nothing but the single market	Those who want more do more	Doing less more efficiently	Doing much more together
Budget size/ volume	Broadly stable	Significantly lower	Somewhat higher	Lower	Significantly higher
Economic, social and territorial cohesion	Lower share	Lower amount	Lower share	Lower share	Higher amount
CAP	Lower share	Lower amount	Lower share	Lower share	Higher amount
New priorities: security/ defense/ migration	High share	No funding	Partly covered by willing Member State	Significantly higher share	Significantly higher share
Revenue	Current system without rebates	Current system without rebates	Current system without rebates; plus new policies financed only by participating Member State	Current system without rebates further simplified; new own resources	In-depth reform beyond scenario 4; new own resources finance significant share of the EU budget

Source: Adapted from Reflection Paper on the Future of EU Finance, European Commission 2017. See also Begg, 2017.

Given the historical difficulty of the European Union to make progress in the integration process, by making the different national interests coincide, it is very difficult to estimate which scenario is the most likely. However, it seems that the first one (carrying on) is the most plausible (Begg, 2017).

After all, the development of the European budget and the present discussion on the Multiannual Financial Framework 2021–2027 cannot take place outside of the political context of individual Member States and the more general European political context. The current political phase of the European Union, with the long period of progressive withdrawal from the European integration process after the referendums in Holland and France firstly blocked the Constitutional Treaty and then culminated with Brexit in June 2016. The emergence of nationalist, sovereignist and sometimes explicitly anti-European movements and parties has meant that the integration process is no longer taken for granted and has called into question the values on which the European Union was founded (art. 3 of Treaty on the European Union). It is in this sticky historical-political framework that the European Union finds itself discussing the next Multiannual Financial Framework. Moreover, the European general election of 2019 and the Brexit process inevitably influenced the budget negotiation. Furthermore, several global challenges (terrorism, climate change, migration phenomena, humanitarian crisis, social inequality) require the European Union not only to progress in its integration process but also to propose a more consistent and efficient budget.

2.7   CONCLUDING REMARKS

During the EU budget discussions the problems of the current institutional structure have come up. The limits of European governance have become evident, in terms of democratic legitimacy and political representation. Furthermore, the disproportion created by the existence of a common monetary policy and the absence of a common fiscal policy and macroeconomic coordination means that a more complex institutional reform is essential (Policy Insight no. 91, 2018; Scenario 5 of the European Commission).

Lastly, it cannot be forgotten that the relationship between political representation and taxation has always been there and is extremely relevant in the constitutional framework. The right to have control of the budget has been of fundamental importance as regards the defining of relations between government and parliament (decision and representation). The reason for this is that the right to control the budget is related to the political-institutional system because the management of public financial resources has direct relevance to the distribution of real power in any given political system (see Chapter 4). The paradox of the European Union is that, while it is not a State but has shared sovereignty at a different level, it has a European single institution framework. In this sense the European Union is the only institutional model of its kind in the world. The European Union is a *Staatenverbund*, a union of States without European sovereignty. It has an exclusive autonomy of decision derived from the will expressed by Member States, in fact its competence is granted by the Member States themselves, but it does not enjoy the so-called *kompetenz-kompetenz*.[2] The Union suffers from this anomalous institutional nature (unprecedented in history) which, especially in the context of the historical evolution of its budget and its difficulty in reforming itself, shows itself still to be an unfinished and incomplete political project.

---

[2]   *Kompetenz-kompetenz* is a German jurisprudential doctrine whose origin dates back to 1871. According to this doctrine a legal body or a State may have jurisdiction to decide on the extent of its own competence on any issue.

The first part of this chapter underlined the close connection between the values on which the European Union is based and the budget. In view of a necessary and indispensable evolution of the European project towards greater integration between the Member States, the reference to values is once again fundamental. In addition to the aforementioned five scenarios presented by the European Commission, Jean-Claude Juncker, in his 2017 State of the Union speech, declared himself in favor of a sixth scenario rooted in decades of his first-hand experience in European politics. This 'sixth scenario' is strictly linked to the defense and re-enforcement of European values:

> Our values are our compass. For me, Europe is more than just a single market. More than money, more than a currency, more than the euro. It was always about values. That is why, in my sixth scenario, there are three fundamentals, three unshakeable principles: freedom, equality and the rule of law. (Juncker, 2017)

The necessity to provide the European Union with a more substantial and values-oriented budget will be the real historical challenge in the next decade, in order to put freedom, equality and rule of law at the political core of the European project.

REFERENCES

Ackrill, R. (2000), 'The European Union Budget, the Balanced Budget Rule and the development of common European Policies', *Journal of European Public Policy*, 20 (1), 1–19.

Ackrill, R. and Kay, A. (2006), 'Historical-institutionalist perspectives on the development of the EU budget system', *Journal of European Public Policy*, 13 (1), 113–133.

Begg, I. (2017), The EU Budget after 2020, Sieps European Policy Analysis, September.

Benedetto, G. (2013), 'The EU budget after Lisbon: rigidity and reduced spending?', *Journal of Public Policy*, 33 (3), 345–369.

Crowe, R. (2017), 'The European Budgetary galaxy', *European Constitutional Law Review*, 13, 428–452.

DG IPOL (2017), The next Multiannual Financial Framework (MFF) and its Duration, Budgetary Affairs, European Parliament, October.

Fauri, F. (2017), *L'Unione Europea. Una storia economica.* il Mulino, Bologna.

IABDIBP (1988), 'Interinstitutional Agreement on Budgetary Discipline and Improvement of the Budgetary Procedure', *Official Journal of the European Communities, L*, 185/33, 15 July.

Juncker, J.-C. (2015), 'State of the Union 2015 – time for honesty, unity and solidarity', European Commission, 9 September.

Juncker J.-C. (2017), 'State of the Union 2017 – catching the wind in our sails', European Commission, 20 September.

Laffan, B. (2000), 'The big budgetary bargains: from negotiation to authority', *Journal of European Public Policy*, 7 (5), 725–743.

Laffan, B. and Shackleton, M. (2000), 'The Budget. Who gets what, when, and how', in H. Wallace and W. Wallace (eds), *Policy Making in the European Union*. Oxford, Oxford University Press, pp. 211–240.

Lindner, J. and Rittberger, B. (2003), 'The creation, interpretation and contestation of institutions – revisiting historical institutionalism', *Journal of Common Market Studies*, 41 (3), 445–473.

MacDougall Report (1977), 'Report of the Study Group on the Role of Public Finance in European Integration', Volume I, Brussels, April.

Marjolin Report (1975), 'Report of the Study Group Economic and Monetary Union 1980'.

Monti Report (2016), 'Future financing to the EU. Final report and recommendations of the High Level Group on Own Resources', December 2016.

Reflection Paper on the Future of EU Finance (2017), European Commission.

Thompson Report (1973), 'Report on the regional problems of the enlarged community', Commission of the European Communities, COM(73)550.

Werner Report (1970), 'Report to the Council and the Commission on the realization by stages of economic and monetary union', Supplement to Bulletin of the European Commission, 11.

White Paper on the Future of European Union (2017), 'Reflections and Scenarios for the EU27 by 2025', European Commission, COM(2017)2025, March.

3. The EU budget between bargaining tool and policy instrument

Mario Kölling

3.1 INTRODUCTION

The budget of the European Union (EU) is *sui generis* for several reasons: the relationship between its 'small' size and the EU's 'broad' functions; the relationship between the benefits of its investments for all Member States and the intensity of budgetary negotiations; and its evolutionary character. In fact, the negotiations of the Multiannual Financial Frameworks (MFF) are more than purely financial negotiations about budgetary costs and benefits of different Member States since they determine the means by which the EU can fulfil its objectives and policy priorities. Over successive programming periods, a significant amount of budgetary resources has been mobilized through a growing number of EU financial instruments. These resources have contributed in a determined way to guaranteeing food security and a fair income for farmers and have fostered the social and economic cohesion within the EU by infrastructure building, training of workers and unemployed as well as the modernization of the administration, among others.

Analysing the different programming periods, several authors confirm that the EU budget has been (slowly) moving from a budget based on the rationale that richer EU countries help poorer EU Member States in exchange for their engagement in the process of economic integration and because of positive economic returns for them, to a budget that addresses challenges and risks common to all EU Member States (Núñez Ferrer and Katarivas, 2014; Heinemann, 2015; Rubio, 2017). In this context, the spending structure of the EU budget has evolved according to the EU integration process and subsequent treaty reforms, and according to specific challenges (Cipriani, 2014).

This chapter will take this argument as a starting point and it will explore different indicators that could demonstrate this evolution. It will firstly analyse the concepts of 'bargaining tool' and 'policy instrument'. Secondly, it will consider the evolution of the different budget headings, as well as the flexibility instruments within the budgetary system. In addition, it will examine the impact of conditionality in budgetary spending and the role of the European Parliament (EP) in the negotiation of the MFF. Finally, the revenue side will be studied according to the question of how a reform of the own resources system could support the evolution of the EU budget towards a policy instrument.

It appears that the specific characteristics of the EU budget and the negotiation process may not lead to a revolutionary new budget in the next programming period. Nevertheless, the MFF 2021–2027 will reinforce the ongoing paradigm change in the perception of the EU budget, from a budget aimed at compensating Member States for their political compromises to a budget aimed at solving EU-wide problems.

3.2 SOME THEORETICAL ASSUMPTIONS REGARDING THE CONCEPTS OF BARGAINING TOOL VS. POLICY INSTRUMENT

The concepts of 'bargaining tool' and 'policy instrument' are ambiguous and need to be clarified. If we understand the EU budget as a bargaining tool, we assume that specific features of the expenditure and revenue side were established benefiting specific Member States in exchange for their support in other decision-making processes. Historical accounts suggest that powerful Member States determined EU policy formation and induced the cooperation of weaker Member States with side-payments (Moravcsik, 1998). The 'imaginative' use of the budget (Nuñez Ferrer, 2007) as a bargaining tool to reach compromises among Member States fostered exchange relations between beneficiary countries and the contributors. In this sense the budget satisfied the demands of specific Member States and not common EU-wide objectives.

If the EU budget is considered as a policy instrument, it is possible to assume that it is used as an instrument to be activated in specific circumstances, e.g. when a country is affected by an exogenous risk or a negative event that is not under its own control. The logic of the spending instruments would stem from the insight that Member States might be confronted with the same risks but at a different moment (Fernandes and Rubio, 2012). The EU budget as policy instrument may also be applied for situations in which all Member States seem to be confronted with the same risks. These risks may not be very clearly defined and may not materialize in the short-term perspective, but there is a common understanding of the risk. In order to address the risk all Member States agree to invest not according to geographic criteria but with specific purposes based on the assumption that a coordinated action of the EU could help to prevent the risk and transform the challenge into an opportunity, by a process in which 'a number of separate political organizations [states] enter into arrangements for making joint decisions on joint problems' (Friedrich,

1955: 517). Nevertheless, the question remains: how could we operationalize the concepts of bargaining tool and policy instrument?

Firstly, an analysis of the evolution of the different budget headings may help to answer the question of whether spending programmes contribute to common EU challenges or if they benefit a very specific number of Member States, e.g. a specific geographical location of beneficiaries. Moreover, the temporal analysis of EU spending and EU priorities could determine if spending programmes generate 'European added value' and support common European objectives, e.g. programmes that require actions at the European level because they are too large for a single Member State, programmes that generate synergy effects through the collaboration of several Member States or programmes that have a cross-border dimension. In this sense the 'European added value' refers to spending categories at the EU level which are not only politically meaningful, but also economically viable (Heinemann, 2011). Similar to spending programmes in federal countries, the EU budgets – as a policy instrument – would finance those public goods that are common to all Member States, such as large-scale research, environment protection, cross-border infrastructure, or defence (Musgrave, 1959). Nevertheless, according to the principle of subsidiarity, spending programmes would cover a small number of policies which have a clear supranational nature (Begg, 2009). The subsidiarity and proportionality principles are paramount in the EU and laid down in the Treaty of the European Union (TEU). Based on these principles, the EU would only perform those tasks that cannot be performed effectively at a more immediate or local level and only acts to the extent that is needed to achieve its objectives. The principle of additionality underlines this practice, meaning that the EU spending programmes would not replace but rather complement national policy programmes.

Secondly, the chapter will give evidence from the negotiation procedure arguing that interlinked intergovernmental negotiations may lead to bargaining situations in which one Member State will be compensated in one negotiation for supporting demands of other Member States in a parallel negotiation. On the contrary, if there are no secondary negotiations or bargaining chips to exchange, there will only be weak incentives to establish linkages and for using the budget as a bargaining tool. If budgetary negotiations are conducted with no temporal and thematic link to other negotiations, the focus may be more on common challenges. Related to this, if budgetary negotiations were conducted primarily by Member State governments, the logic of *juste retour* may prevail. If there are other actors involved in the negotiations, which may defend a European wide interest, this logic may lose intensity. In this sense, the role of the EP in the negotiation process will be carefully assessed.

Furthermore, the chapter will consider the flexibility of the MFF as an indicator which allows a re-assignation of resources not based on intergovernmental bargaining but on decisions which involve the EU institutions. The degree of flexibility depends on at least four parameters: the duration of the MFF and the number of headings; the margins available within each expenditure ceiling and the capacity to make use of them; the existence of special instruments to react to unforeseen circumstances; and the degree of inbuilt flexibility in EU spending programmes (Rubio, 2017).

As an indication of change in the logic of the budget, we will also add the possibility of using it as a sanctioning and/or incentive instrument, in the sense that resources are conditioned to the fulfilment of political and/or economic objectives. Using the EU budget as a policy instrument may require budget support to be tied to general political conditions and its impact increased by being attached to conditions that support overall policy objectives. Conditionality as a policy tool used by the EU to attain specific governance goals could contain positive incentives and negative incentives (e.g. optional or mandatory suspension of funding).

Finally, in order to consider the EU budget as policy instrument, it will be argued that the EU should have independent control of its financial resources sufficient to perform its own functions. Although this principle is enshrined in article 311 of the Treaty on the Functioning of the European Union (TFEU), the lack of the ability to raise revenues from its own sources may be the main reason why we still cannot define the budget as a policy instrument.

3.3   ANALYSIS

3.3.1   The Evolution of the EU Budget Headings

Owing to the reform resistance of the EU budget, the Sapir report in 2003 labelled the EU budget as a historical relic. It stated that expenditures, revenues and procedures were not always consistent with the present and future state of EU integration (Sapir, et al. 2003). According to the report, the fact that around 80% of the annual budget was in 2003 allocated to the Common Agricultural Policy (CAP) and to the Cohesion Policy could only be explained from a historical perspective. Both policies have been frequently criticized for not being oriented towards European public goods.

Analysing the different budget headings, it is possible to confirm that policy strategies increasingly determined the EU spending priorities and budget implementation and the consequent shift from traditional spending headings towards spending on other policies. The Lisbon Agenda added a new role to the MFF 2007–2013, prioritizing investments in R&D and competitiveness. Rather than an instrument to reduce regional disparities, EU Cohesion Policy started to be portrayed as a delivery vehicle to achieve the Lisbon goals of competitiveness, growth and jobs all over the EU territory (Chambon and

Rubio, 2011). Moreover, the traditional spending policies were designed towards the goal of achieving economic and social cohesion but also for the delivery of public goods that are common to all Member States. The Lisbon Treaty increased the role of the Cohesion Policy and introduced a third dimension: territorial cohesion (Article 158 TFEU). The Cohesion Policy also played an important role beyond its traditional objectives within the framework of the European Economic Recovery Plan (European Commission, 2008). This trend has been reinforced since 2010 with the adoption of the Europe 2020 Strategy, in which the EU set out its aims to 'promote a more resource efficient, greener and more competitive economy' and to become the most competitive region in the world (European Commission, 2010). Finally, the MFF 2014–2020 established a clear link between the budgetary headings and the Europe 2020 Strategy (European Commission, 2011). Indeed, besides semantic enhancements, spending programmes under sub-heading 1a ('Competitiveness for growth and jobs') started to contribute to the fulfilment of the Strategy. In particular, the promotion of research, innovation and technological development, as well as specific actions in favour of the competitiveness of enterprises and small and medium-sized enterprises were set out. The MFF 2014–2020 increased resources for these spending programmes by 37% compared with the MFF 2007–2013. On the other hand, spending programmes on traditional headings, e.g. sub-heading 1b ('Economic, social and territorial cohesion'), were reduced.

Moreover, significant changes in the heading 'Security and Citizenship' were introduced with respect to the 2007–2013 period. Starting from a low level, the budget allocation for this heading has grown by around 27%, including a diversified range of programmes related to asylum and migration and initiatives in the areas of external borders and internal security. Heinemann (2011) underlined the potential for significant European added value of this heading, since many aspects of asylum and migration policy, including external borders and internal security, are based on long-term common risk perceptions, which affect all EU Member States. The same trend can be confirmed for the heading 'Global Europe', which supports programmes in the interests of all Member States, e.g. the neighbourhood policy and the pre-accession assistance, as well as solidarity actions beyond EU borders.

Considering the annual budget, it is possible to confirm this development. By 2017, resources in Cohesion Policy were reduced by 24% compared with 2016. Resources under the heading 'Security and Citizenship' increased by 24% and funds to support refugee integration, security, border control and migration management were almost doubled. For 2018, the EC added for the first time a budget line of €40 million for defence research cooperation, in addition to increasing the Horizon 2020 budget for defence-related research by 7.3%.

Regarding the MFF 2021–2027, the EC already stressed before the negotiation started, that future programmes need to address policy objectives related to emerging economic and social challenges (European Commission, 2017a, b). The MFF 2021–2027 proposals, finally launched by the EC in May 2018, underline investments with clear European added value. Although the proposal was a clear disappointment both in terms of the resources envisaged and of its structure and funding, compared to previous MFFs. It can be confirmed that it contained modifications in line with the trajectory started with the MFF 2007–2013 and that gradually turn the budget into a political instrument. In this sense, the traditional spending headings, CAP (from 2021: Natural resources and environment) and Cohesion Policy (Cohesion and values), will be reduced by 5% and 7% in relation to the current MFF. Moreover, most of the investments in both policies will be re-directed towards programmes that generate jobs and growth, especially for small and medium-sized enterprises that are committed to digital technologies, innovation and industrial modernization. On the other hand, the EC proposed to increase funding for urgent policy priorities, including research, innovation and the digital economy (European Commission, 2018a).

3.3.2 Linkage of Budgetary Negotiation with Institutional Negotiations

The EU is a negotiated democracy with several parallel and vertical negotiations. Negotiation agreements of the MFFs have always passed as package deals which affected both EU budget expenditure and other policy commitments such as EU enlargements. In this sense the EU budget historically played an important role in the EU integration process, making it acceptable for Member States through specific financial compensations for anticipated losses. These 'compensations' were on the one hand institutionalized into the EU budgetary structure and on the other hand allocated to spending programmes following quantitative arbitration among policies (Cipriani, 2014). This development emerges when considering the outcomes of the successive MFF negotiations.

The first MFF was agreed for the period 1988–1992 (Delors I package) and was negotiated in parallel with the Single European Act, where some Member States linked their support for the internal market to an increase in structural funds. Spain, Greece and Portugal insisted on a doubling of these funds as a strict *quid pro quo* for agreeing to the Delors I package (Brennan, 2006). The final agreement included a significant increase in budgetary resources and the Cohesion Policy funds were doubled from 1988 to 1992 (Wagner, 2001; Laffan, 2000).

The MFF 1993–1999 (Delors II package) also contained a significant increase in structural and cohesion funds as a basis for the preparation of Member States for the single currency. In this sense, several Member States related their approval of the economic and monetary union to increasing funds for structural actions. Moreover, the negotiations on the Delors II package took place in the aftermath of the Danish 'No' vote on the TEU, when most Member States had a strong interest in demonstrating both unity and the capacity of the EU to reach agreements (Kölling, 2014).

In 1999, the MFF for the period 2000–2006 secured the necessary resources to finance the eastern enlargement process of the EU. Again, several Member States conditioned their support for the enlargement to specific transition periods and increasing spending in Cohesion Policy.

The negotiation of the MFF 2007–2013 could be considered as a turning point. Even though some Member States tried to link the negotiation of the MFF to the debate on the ongoing treaty reform, both negotiations were not carried out in parallel, and for the first time redistributive and financial negotiations were not linked to normative or constitutional debates. The negotiation outcome included a modest increase in resources, although the MFF 2007–2013 contained more resources and a new link between spending programmes and a policy strategy oriented towards sustainable growth and competitiveness was also established.

The MFF 2014–2020, negotiated during the financial and economic crisis and not in parallel with institutional negotiations resulted in a reduction in the overall budget for the first time. Moreover, a clear link between spending programmes and policy strategy as well as between spending programmes and conditionality was established. Although the negotiations on the MFF 2021–2027 were not directly related to the institutional reform of the EU, specific concerns of Member States, e.g. the migration crisis, influenced the spending priorities of the EU budget. Nevertheless, the EU budget was not used as a side payment in order to get the approval of institutional reforms but as an instrument to address a common challenge.

3.3.3   Negotiation Procedure

The EU's budget has been traditionally negotiated between Member States which considered the specific budgetary headings as acquired 'budgetary rights'. These were 'institutionalized' by the unanimity rule, which fostered the reform resistance of the budget. However, the growing number of national interests made it increasingly difficult to reach consensus on budgetary decisions. Over the years, the European Parliament has assumed a new role in the negotiation of the MFFs, primarily without treaty reforms (Heritier, 2017). On the one hand, using the first mover strategy, the EP increased its negotiation power. On the other hand, the EP engaged in cross-area linkage, demanding more resources in turn for supporting other policy reforms. During the MFF 2014–2020 negotiations, after the Lisbon Treaty gave the EP a new formal role in the adoption of the MFF regulation, the EP could approve or reject the agreement reached by the European Council. Having a veto power in the adoption of the MFF, the EP was able to demand more flexibility and specific spending programmes. However, the EP has not only a new formal role in the final phase of the negotiation, it has become one of the major players from the very beginning of the negotiation process by a 'politicization' of the discussion on the MFF and the introduction of budgetary goals which aim to represent the common interest of the EU.

3.3.4 Major Flexibility

Debates to enhance the flexibility of the MFF have become increasingly important since the 2000s. Over the past few years, the limitations of the EU budget and in particular the MFF model, in terms of both its financial capacity and its institutional framework, have become apparent. Being framed by the MFF, the annual budget cannot re-prioritize spending to meet collective needs or to respond rapidly to changing or unforeseen eventualities. Nevertheless, during the past financing periods the flexibility of the budget has been increased, both related to the temporal dimension but also among budgetary headings. This has led to less budgetary control by the Member States and to an increase in the discretionality of EU institutions.

Within MFF 2007–2013 the budgetary authority could depart by up to 5% from the financial agreement. Moreover, the financial instruments, e.g. the Emergency Aid Reserve, the European Union Solidarity Fund, the Flexibility Instrument and the European Globalization Adjustment Fund, could provide extra resources above the annual financial framework ceiling. Within the MFF 2014–2020, the main novelties were the provisions to maximize the use of margins between headings and years, up to 10% (rather than 5%) with respect to the overall financial envelope set out in the MFF, and to strengthen the Flexibility Instrument, which has been extensively used, e.g. to react to the refugee crisis (Rubio, 2017). A large flexible financing instrument outside the budget (the European Fund for Strategic Investment) was also created. Important limitations still exist, since these instruments were not designed for prolonged or multiple crises but to respond to specific and time-limited events (Nuñez Ferrer, 2017). In addition, these instruments are not based on additional financial resources and are financed with future payments or commitment appropriations which limit the margin for the following annual budgets. In this sense and despite these changes, EU spending programmes are still very rigid and the bulk of resources are pre-allocated for the whole seven-year period.

Overall, the EC proposed a more flexible budget for the 2021–2027 period by: (a) improving the existing mechanisms; (b) increasing flexibility within and between programmes; and (c) creating a new 'Union Reserve' to tackle unforeseen events and to respond to emergencies in areas such as security and migration (European Commission 2018a).

3.3.5   Increased Conditionality

There have always been certain levels of conditionality (positive and negative) within EU re-distributive policies (e.g. the underlying principles, procedures and agreed objectives of spending programmes). However, this conditionality was self-imposed and compliance was based on soft mechanisms as well as related to national characteristics and not always to the EU objectives (Kölling, 2017). Based on this experience, the Sapir report concluded already in 2003 that the key principle of conditionality should be strengthened. Later, the Barca report demanded a stronger conceptual foundation of Cohesion Policy allowing a better link between conditionality and solidarity as well as conditionality and subsidiarity (Barca, 2009). In this context, conditionality requires budget support to be tied more strictly to political conditions, which may lead to changes in (national) policymaking according to EU objectives. This policy conditionality follows a different logic than the infringement procedure or the fulfilment of regulatory requirements but may also, in case of violation, lead to the suspension of EU funding.

Until the MFF 2007–2013, only the Cohesion Fund was subject to macroeconomic conditionality[1] and allocation related to the compliance of the Maastricht criteria. The conditions were adopted by the Council and not legally binding for beneficiary countries,[2] and enforcement mechanisms had a voluntary character – such as peer pressure. For example, in 2012, the Commission proposed to suspend €500 million of Cohesion Fund commitments for Hungary owing to the country's failure to address their excessive government deficit – but no further action was taken.

Since the MFF 2007–2013, conditionality has been expanded and deepened but it is still applied very carefully. The MFF 2007–2013 also included positive incentives developing specific programmes focusing on key European priorities, such as employment, social inclusion, skills research and innovation, energy and resource efficiency. The Cohesion Policy was reoriented from

---

[1]   Article 4 of Regulation (EC) 1084/2006.
[2]   Article 121 of the Treaty on the Functioning of the European Union.

focusing only on the goal of achieving economic and social cohesion in order to also promote the objectives of the Lisbon agenda.

Unlike the previous programming period, in the MFF 2014–2020 all five European Structural and Investment Funds[3] became conditional on the respect of economic governance objectives and procedures. The Common Strategic Framework implemented conditionality through three instruments: ex-ante conditionality; macroeconomic conditionality; and ex-post conditionality (European Commission, 2017c). Concentrating the resources on the national objectives, the Commission established for the first time a performance framework based on measurable indicators in line with the country recommendations for structural reforms and the Europe 2020 objectives. Furthermore, the budget support for development policy has evolved from the traditional treaty-based development policy approach to a configuration interlinking development aid with migration policies.

Although conditionality tools were far more sophisticated in the 2014–2020 programming period than in the previous 2007–2013 term, the Commission considered the use of the negative conditionality as a last resort tool in case of persistent misbehaviour of a country. On the basis of the Europe-wide debate on conditionality, the Commission included a specific proposal on this topic in its proposals for the MFF 2021–2027. It recommended, on the one hand, including respect for fundamental values and for the rule of law as preconditions for EU funding. On the other hand, it proposed reinforcing the link between the annual recommendations within the European semester with concrete indications for investments from the EU budget (European Commission 2018b). In this context, it may be entirely possible that the non-fulfilment of a country-specific recommendation (i.e. regarding the assistance for refugees) could be the basis of a sanction in the near future. This would create an additional incentive for Member States to comply with the recommendations and it would also result in a better linkage between EU re-distributive policies and the fulfilment of EU policy objectives.

3.3.6 Own Resources

While the spending structure of the EU budget has undergone an important evolution during the past decades, the present situation concerning own resources is still closely linked to the nature of the budget at the time it was established. This is the main reason for the growing gap between ambitions

---

[3] The European Regional Development Fund, the European Social Fund, the Cohesion Fund, the European Agricultural Fund for Rural Development and the European Maritime and Fisheries Fund.

and genuine fiscal autonomy for the EU. Revenue coming from the 'GNI resource' (gross national income) and the weight of this resource among the total revenues of the EU budget has increased over the last few years, while the traditional own resources have lost importance. In 2015, more than 85% of EU financing was based on statistical aggregates derived from GNI and VAT.

The focus on juste retour or on net balances by national governments is mainly due to this structure of the revenue side of the EU budget. The concentration of national contributions to the EU budget led to the creation of the British rebate in 1984, and to a complex system of smaller rebates for other countries. Similar to the protections of Member States that benefit from specific redistribution, such as the agricultural sector, the rebates allow wealthier Member States to limit their contributions to the EU budget (Benedetto, 2017).

Several reform proposals have been presented during the past decades to ensure the financial autonomy of the EU and to provide it with its own resources that are necessary to attain its objectives and to carry through its policies (Blanchard et al., 2015; Calmfors, 2015). Although there is still no consensus on what kind of tax bases would be the best EU revenue source, there is a common understanding that an increased financial autonomy and less dependence on the GNI-based resources would foster the development of the EU budget towards a policy instrument. According to the High-Level Group on Own Resources, the Union must mobilize common resources to find common solutions to common problems (Monti et al., 2016).

3.4   CONCLUSIONS

An Eurobarometer survey in 2017 ascertained that for 43% of respondents the EU should have more financial resources at its disposal because of its political objectives. This represented an increase of 6% with respect to 2015.[4] Nevertheless, the EU budget seems still to be a budget for specific sectorial demands and not a European budget to address the actual concerns of the EU citizens. Faced with new policy objectives, the EU budget is still in a situation of a disconnection between spending and EU priorities. Although the EU has assumed new objectives, the 2021–2027 MFF still underlines the path dependency of the EU budget. However, the Brexit may represent an important moment leading to a new path including a reform of existing budgetary institutions in the future MFFs.

---

[4]   Special Eurobarometer 461, Designing Europe's Future – Trust in Institutions, Globalization Support for the Euro, Opinions about Free Trade and Solidarity, 28 June 2017.

This chapter aimed to analyse different indicators which support the argument that the EU budget is evolving from a negotiation tool to a policy instrument. It considered the development of the different budget headings. Despite the similarity in the names of budget headings, there have been many advances towards refocusing spending on areas of EU added value. Even the Cohesion Policy has become a tool to finance the adoption of EU standards and to achieve EU objectives. In this sense, while the EU budget has during the past decades aggregated numerous but uncoordinated spending programmes, the budget has become since 2007 more coordinated and focused on the delivery of public goods. The chapter also analysed the linkage of budgetary negotiation with institutional negotiations. Since the MFF 2007–2013, the MFFs were not negotiated in parallel with other negotiations which reduced the possibility of side payments and policy solutions for specific Member States. The unanimity rule in adopting the MFF still favours package deals but, considering the increasing heterogeneity of preferences among Member States, it also allows the concentration on programmes which generate added value at the EU level.

The evolution of the EU budget towards a policy instrument is marked by: (a) the increasing role of the EP in the MFF negotiations; (b) the greater use of flexibility (also for unforeseen challenges); and (c) the increased conditionality in the re-distributing policies of the MFFs.

The chapter also considered that the current own resources system presents several obstacles. Many tax instruments could potentially be mobilized to either replace or complement the current EU budget resources. However, a reform of the revenue side of the budget seems to be still far away. Although the MFF 2021–2027 may not lead to a revolutionary new budget, the negotiation outcome may reinforce the ongoing paradigm change in the perception of the EU budget, from a budget aimed at compensating Member States for their political compromises to a budget aimed at solving EU-wide problems. Accordingly, the EU financial resources should be aimed more at investments rather than at mere expenses.

REFERENCES

Barca, F. (2009), *An Agenda for a Reformed Cohesion Policy – A Place-based Approach to Meeting European Union Challenges and Expectations*. Report prepared at the request of Danuta Hübner, Commissioner for Regional Policy.

Begg, I. (2009), *Fiscal Federalism, Subsidiarity and the EU Budget Review*. Swedish Institute for European Policy Studies, Stockholm.

Benedetto, G. (2017), 'Institutions and the route to reform of the European Union's budget revenue, 1970–2017', *Empirica*, 44 (4), 615–633.

Blanchard, O., Erceg, C. J. and Lindé, J. (2015), 'Jump starting the Euro Area recovery: would a rise in core fiscal spending help the periphery?' NBER working paper, no. 21426.

Brennan, P. (2006), 'Negotiating the Delors 1 Package. Making a success of the single act', unpublished working paper.

Calmfors, L. (2015), 'The role of fiscal rules, fiscal councils and fiscal union in EU integration'. IFN working paper no. 1076.

Chambon, N. and Rubio, E. (2011), 'In search of the "best value for money": analyzing current ideas and proposals to enhance the performance of cap and cohesion spending', working paper, produced in the framework of the workshop 'The Post 2013 Financial Perspectives: Re-thinking EU Finances in Times of Crisis', Turin, 7–8 July 2011.

Cipriani, G. (2014), *Financing the EU Budget: Moving Forward or Backwards?* Economic Policy, CEPS, Brussels.

European Commission (2008), 'European economic recovery plan', COM(2008)800 final.

European Commission (2010), 'Europe 2020 – a strategy for smart, sustainable and inclusive growth', COM(2010)2020.

European Commission (2011), 'A budget for Europe 2020', COM(2011) 500 final.

European Commission (2017a), 'Reflection paper on the future of EU finances', COM(2017)358.

European Commission (2017b), 'White Paper on the future of Europe', COM(2017)2025.

European Commission (2017c), 'The value added of ex ante conditionalities in the European Structural and Investment Funds (ESI funds)', Brussels, SWD(2017)127 final.

European Commission (2018a), 'A modern budget for a union that protects, empowers and defends – the Multiannual Financial Framework for 2021–2027', COM(2018)321 final.

European Commission (2018b), 'Proposal for a regulation of the European Parliament and of the Council on the Protection of the Union's Budget in case of generalised deficiencies as regards the rule of law in the Member States', COM(2018)324 final.

Fernandes, S. and Rubio, E. (2012), 'Solidarity within the Eurozone: how much, what for, for how long?', *Notre Europe*, policy paper 51.

Friedrich, C. J. (1955), 'Federal constitutional theory and emergent proposals', in A. W. Macmahon (ed.), *Federalism: Mature and Emergent*. Doubleday, New York.

Heinemann, F. (2011), 'European added value for the EU Budget', in Daniel Tarschys, *The EU Budget, What Should Go In? What Should Go Out?* Swedish Institute for European Policy Studies, working paper, vol. 2011:3.

Heinemann, F. (2015), 'Strategies for a European EU budget', working paper for the Brussels Symposium, 14 January 2016, *FiFo*, pp. 91–108.

Heritier, A. (2017), 'The increasing institutional power of the European Parliament and EU policy making', EIF working paper, 2017/01, http://hdl .handle.net/1814/45825 (accessed 19 December 2018).

Kölling, M. (2014), *Preferencias e instituciones: un análisis comparativo de las negociaciones del Marco Financiero Plurianual de la UE*. Centro de Estudios Políticos y Constitucionales, Madrid.

Kölling, M. (2017), 'Policy conditionality – a new instrument in the EU budget post-2020?', Swedish Institute for European Policy Studies, European Policy Analysis, 2017:10.

Laffan, B. (2000), 'The big budgetary bargains: from negotiation to authority', *Journal of European Public Policy*, 7 (5), 725–743.

Monti, M., Daianu, D., Fuest, C., Georgieva, K., Kalfin, I., Lamassoure, A., Moscovici, P., Simonyte, I., Timmermans, F., and Verhofstadt, G. (2016), *Future Financing of the EU*. Final report and recommendations of the High Level Group on Own Resources, December 2016.

Moravcsik, A. (1998), *The Choice for Europe: Social Purposes and State Power from Messina to Maastricht*. Cornell University Press, Ithaca, NY.

Musgrave, R. (1959), *The Theory of Public Finance*. McGraw–Hill, New York.

Nuñez Ferrer, J. (2007), *The EU Budget: The UK Rebate and the CAP – Phasing them both out?* Report, Centre for European Policy Studies.

Núñez Ferrer, J. and Katarivas, M. (2014), 'What are the effects of the EU Budget? – Driving force or drop in the ocean?' CEPS Special Report, no. 86, CEPS, Brussels.

Rubio, E. (2017), 'The next Multiannual Financial Framework (MFF) and its flexibility'. European Parliament, Policy Department for Budgetary Affairs, http://www.europarl.europa.eu/RegData/etudes/IDAN/2017/603799/IPOL _IDA(2017)603799_EN.pdf (accessed 19 December 2018).

Sapir, A., Aghion, P., Bertola, G., Hellwig, M., Pisani-Ferry, J., Rosati, D., Viñals, J. and Wallace, H. (2003), *An Agenda for a Growing Europe: Making the EU Economic System Deliver*. Report, Independent High-Level Study Group established on the initiative of the President of the European Commission.

Wagner, W. (2001), 'German foreign policy since unification. Theories meet reality', in R. Volker (ed.), *German Foreign Policy Since Unification. Theories and Case Studies*. Manchester University Press, Manchester, pp. 296–322.

4. 'No representation without taxation'. For a history of budgetary control in the European Union

Alessandro Isoni

4.1   INTRODUCTION

Since the establishment of feudalism, one of the main features of European Medieval kingdoms had been the political bargaining between the king and the representatives of different estates, usually concerning who had to pay taxes and what was the 'right' level of taxation (Van Caenegem, 1995). Usually, monarchs justified their requests with the need to support wars and crusades, while barons and commons were reluctant to give money to the kings, because in their opinion the strenghtening both of the royal prerogatives and of the royal budget threatened the country's liberties (Maitland, 1908). As a matter of fact, every time kings needed money, a hard and exhausting negotiation took place, eventually leading to a sum granted by representatives to the king, with this latter obliged to come back to them every time the treasure chest was empty.

It is not by chance that the largest part of the Western constitutional experience developed around the budget and the power to levy taxes and that it was characterized by the bitter confrontation between the sovereign presumptions of monarchs and the struggle for liberties of Diets, Cortes, Parliaments and so on. As a matter of fact, before a medieval king that could exercise only two functions – *jurisdictio* (administration of justice) and *gubernaculum* (the power to make peace and war) – the right to deny money to the monarchs was the strongest weapon that barons and commons could use (McIlwain, 1947). On the other side, the famous sentence 'No taxation without representation' fixed once and for all the seminal character of budget issues in the birth of constitutional law. It was interpreted as the means adopted by peoples of limiting power and safeguarding personal prerogatives and proprieties, through the adoption of recurring meetings to discuss how to collect money and, overall, control how it was going to be spent (Strayer, 1970). Military affairs and budgetary issues are closely related to the birth and development of states in modern Europe, and they represent some of the features that contributed to identify a state rather than a previous kind of socio-institutional organization (Hoffman and Norberg, 1994; Victor, 1997; Glete, 2002).

From the Magna Carta to the French Revolution, passing through the fall of the Stuarts in England and the American Revolution, fiscal questions have always represented the spark that started the fire of revolutions, so witnessing the importance of budget in the constitutional framework and strongly contributing to understanding whether we face a constitutional state or an absolute state or, worse, a dictatorship (Holt, 1985; Harris and Taylor, 2013; Palmer, 1964). Before analyzing the European Union (EU) budget issues, it is worthwhile to underline that budget questions represent constitutional issues concerning the way people have chosen to live together and the degree of democracy and social justice within a certain society.

Taking into consideration this important premise, the chapter will focus on three important features: first, the choice adopted by the European 'Founding Fathers' to opt for a new funding system, abandoning the *juste retour* principle and creating new complex institutional procedures; and second, a review of bitter struggles among European Member States concerning their financial contribution to the European budget and how this long and exhausting conflict deeply influenced the development of the European integration. Lastly, the chapter will try to contribute to imagine a new constitutional framework able to ensure a real democratic control on budget issues, through a complete and full involvement of the European Parliament.

4.2   A BAROQUE ARCHITECTURE

The bargaining on the budget is one of the main evidences that help law scholars and political scientists to recognise a constitutional state, i.e. a political organization established on a checks and balances system and where the power is not in the hands of a single person or political body. If the executive power has the right to levy taxes without prior approval by representatives of the people who have to pay them or, rather, if it is impossible to control how money is spent, there is something wrong in the 'constitutional' framework of that political organization (Loewenstein, 1957).

As we have seen, the whole Western constitutional history could be summarized as the attempt to create tools of control on the executive power, while this latter has always demonstrated its preference to act avoiding controls, justifying this with the need to adopt swift decisions to give an answer to questions arising from society (Downing, 1992).

Both at the state level and at the international level, a political organization needs money to fulfill its purposes and, for this reason, the executive body has to provide a draft of budget. Historically, the budgets of the first international organizations created after the end of the First World War were based on the adoption of the *juste retour*. This principle stated that every Member State had to contribute to the common budget, being given the sum they could have in return thanks to the investments made by the international organization itself (Galey, 1988). In this way, states adopted a selfish attitude, aiming to defend national interests, in spite of having a cooperative approach, able to generate long-term advantages deriving from their membership (Waltz, 1979).

Jean Monnet, one of the 'Founding Fathers' of the European integration, was aware of this attitude since he had been Deputy Secretary General of the League of Nations between 1919 and 1923, when he resigned because of difficulties provoked by a laborious decision-making process and by the decision to adopt the *juste retour* principle for the newborn organization (Duchêne, 1994; Brown Wells, 2011). The need for unanimous consent to the budget, together with the delays in the payment of single national contributions led Monnet, when he imagined the first draft of a new organization with the purpose of pooling the French and German coal and steel production, to prefer a system able to ensure low but sure resources, not depending on the unpredictable political will of Member States (Fleury, 1999).

When the European Coal and Steel Community (ECSC) and then the European Economic Community (EEC) were established, the main goal was to avoid the contribution system usually adopted in the international organizations – the United Nations was then experiencing the same difficulties that had led the League of Nations to collapse – in order to create a financial system capable of sustaining the activities of the new organizations (Northedge, 1986; Housden, 2011). The supranational concept itself was created with the aim of shadowing national interests, so as to create a common interest where the Member States could recognize their own advantages within a complex framework (Isoni, 2014).

The so-called 'Empty Chair crisis' provoked by Charles de Gaulle in 1965 amply demonstrated how Monnet was right and what risks the EEC was going to face: who had to pay for the launch of the European Agricultural Guidance and Guarantee Fund? De Gaulle was the strongest supporter of an intergovernmental approach, which in his opinion was the only way to ensure French interest. Paradoxically, the solution adopted for solving the first serious crisis in the European integration history established a system built on two pillars: on the one hand, the French President achieved a unanimous decision-making process when issues concerning resources were discussed but, on the other, he allowed an own resources system to be created for the EEC, especially because he correctly thought that the Common Agricultural Policy (CAP) needed a great deal of resources (Moravcsik, 2000). The perspective of seeing the French agricultural sector heavily financed by communitarian resources pushed De Gaulle to accept this new system, even if the other five Member States were worried that the transfer of budgetary power from national governments to the European Commission could lead to a democratic deficit (Isoni, 2015).

In order to solve this problem, in 1970 a budgetary procedure was imagined that involved the European Parliament – not yet directly elected – controlling the European Commission. As a matter of fact, the whole constitutional framework was envisaged according to a checks and balances system rather than a democratic one, eventually failing to put a closer relationship between the executive and the representative power (Ehlermann and Minch, 1981; Taylor, 1983). On the other hand, the own resources system was established on agricultural and customs levies, that proved very soon unable to ensure the funding of all activities that the EEC was going to implement, so leading to add, in 1978, a Value Added Tax (VAT) contribution, while at the same time direct national contributions were withdrawn. In 1988, a contribution system founded on a percentage share of gross national income (GNI) of each Member State was developed (Shackleton, 1990; Laffan, 1997).

The history of European integration was characterized, especially during the 1970s and 1980s, by disputes on budgetary issues management, which featured two main characters: on the 'domestic' side, the recurring request for involvement of the European Parliament, especially after the 1979 direct elections; and, on the 'external' side, the UK and its will to renegotiate the heavy contribution imposed by European partners in order to accept British membership (Laffan, 2000). The resolution demonstrated by Margaret Thatcher was an important factor in settling the problem of the British contribution in 1985, alongside the role of the European Parliament, which demonstrated its strong-willed attitude in 1980 and 1985, vetoing the entire annual budget of the EU (Isaac, 1984; George, 1990). As a matter of fact, the unanimity requested to reform the EU budget procedures put the question at a standstill from an institutional point of view, obliging a solution to be found on which all Member States would agree (Ackrill and Kay, 2006). All of the reforms adopted in these years originated by a slow decision-making process, which led to progressive reduction of the VAT levy, eventually leading to an own resources system established on three pillars: the long-lasting common external customs tariff on imports from third countries, which counts for about 12% of EU revenue; a levy of 0.3% on national VAT paid in each Member State (11% of EU revenue); and a contribution of 1.23% of GNI that each state has to pay, accounting for 76% of the EU revenue.

After discussing the revenue side of the EU budget, it is important to consider the expenditure one. Regarding the latter, it is useful to analyze a set of financial tools before examining the role of the European Parliament and the main complications in attaining its ever more active role in the EU budget decision-making process (Rittberger, 2005).

In 1988, an Inter-Institutional Agreement was signed with the goal of involving the European Commission, the Council and the European Parliament in the elaboration of a seven-year multiannual budget, conceived as a way to help new Member States – Greece (1981), Portugal and Spain (1986) – who were very concerned about CAP funds and European Regional Development Fund (Begg and Grimwade, 1998). The importance of this program in creating a cohesive system led to a greater stability than in the first phase of the integration process, making the budgetary questions very difficult to discuss and eventually reform, especially because each Member State held a veto power on reform proposals (Ackrill, 2000). The Lisbon treaty itself did not change the unanimity system in order to reform the budgetary issues, while there has been a worsening of the context as a consequence of the EU being enlarged to 28 Member States.

As a matter of fact, the Lisbon treaty provided a framework founded on two sides. On the revenue side, the budget of the EU is established on the traditional system of 'own resources', imagined in 1970 and then little modified. Nowadays, the 'own resources' derives from the three above-mentioned pillars.

In 1988, the European Commission, the Council of Ministers and the European Parliament established the financial perspective, the predecessor of the Multiannual Financial Framework (MFF) now in force, that represents the main political tool to plan the budget for seven years (see Chapter 3). Before the Lisbon treaty, the Member States could amend the MFF and the European Parliament could exercise its veto power, while now it is more difficult to amend it.[1] According to article 312 of the Lisbon treaty 'the financial framework shall determine the amounts of annual ceilings on commitment appropriations by category of expenditure and on the annual ceiling on payment appropriation', while before the coming into force of this treaty it was possible to determine a maximum and actual rate of increase in the budget, through an agreement by the European Commission, the Council and the European Parliament (Tsebelis, 2002 and Chapter 2).

The new Article 314 (Treaty on the Functioning of the European Union, TFEU) outlines a Budgetary Procedure similar to the codecision, because it seems that both the Council and the European Parliament are forced to search for a compromise, through the adoption of amendments and, overall, in order to avoid the rejection of the whole budget. If this circumstance should happen,

---

[1]   The only way to amend the MFF is for Council to use a passerelle, as provided for Article 18(7) TFEU.

according to Article 315 (TFEU), only one-twelfth of the budget of the previous financial year could be spent each month. As a matter of fact, the European Commission has the power to present the Draft of Budget by 1 September each year, while the Council is obliged to give a first reading by 1 October and approve it with a qualified majority voting. Within seven weeks, the European Parliament has the power to give a first reading: the budget is adopted unless some remarks are presented. In this case, a new and really complicated procedure begins. With an absolute majority vote, the European Parliament could propose amendments, which are discussed by the Council within a week: if in this second reading the Council accepts with a qualified majority vote the European Parliament amendments, the budget is adopted. Otherwise, a conciliation phase opens. In a three week period, the new budget draft must be discussed and approved both by the European Parliament (with a simple majority) and by the Council (qualified majority vote). In case the agreement is not reached, there is the possibility of temporary, monthly budgets until the new budget is approved.

4.3 TAKE A WALK ON THE TAX SIDE

Both articles 314 and 315 aim to ensure the normal working of the EU, through the budgetary continuity. This determines a reduction of importance of veto power that the European Parliament used in the past in order to attain political goals. The lower influence of the European Parliament concerning the power to propose or impose reforms is only one feature of the will of European Member States to retake control of EU inner dynamics, where the actual driving force for reforms is now the European Council, the most intergovernmental institution (Eggermont, 2012 and Chapter 7). The pivotal role played by Member States is well represented by the provisions concerning the implementation of the budget, that according to the Lisbon treaty has to be managed by the European Commission in cooperation with Member States, while the European Parliament has only a consultative power, so is not influencing the agenda setting (Pollack, 2003 and 2010). One of the most important outcomes of the Lisbon treaty concerning the Budget Procedure lies in the fact that, even if the European Parliament is a partner in the agenda setting of the European Commission during the initial phase, the possibility of making internal reforms through the Parliament itself is now very difficult. The real power to propose and adopt reforms lies in the political bargaining within the European Council, where governments could act without democratic control.

The different reforms adopted since 1988 deeply modified the original pattern concerning budget, characterized by disputes between the UK and other Member States on the amount of the British contribution and, on the internal side, by the hidden struggle between the Council and the European

Parliament in order to establish who should actually control the budget. The crucial issue has always been the expenditure side, without worrying about the revenue one, even if it accounts for only 1% of the EU's GNI.

Margaret Thatcher's famous will to 'to have her money back', on the contrary, highlighted that there was no agreement on how much single Member States had to pay. This represented an example of the conflict between net contributors and net beneficiaries of the EU funds, renewing the long-standing question concerning the *juste retour* principle (Tonelli, 1981; Richter, 2008). Moreover, there was a revenue of a position ensured to the Six founder states, amply demonstrated by the fact that almost 80% of the EU budget was spent for the CAP and for the regional policies (Bouvet and Dall'Erba, 2010).

The introduction of the multiannual budget planning, established both on the financial perspective and on an interinstitutional agreement, did not change the real nature of issues concerning the EU budget (Chapters 2, 3 and 8). The latter has a great importance in the whole political life of the EU, deeply influencing the role of the EU in the world and in the lives of EU citizens (Rant and Mrak, 2010; Schild, 2008 and Chapter 5).

As a matter of fact, the EU budget is very important, since it allows understanding of who is 'winning' and who is 'losing' at the EU level. Nonetheless, the modest size of the EU budget from the financial point of view, and the massive concentration of funds in support of European farmers and less-developed regions, amply demonstrate that these two groups are stronger than others and, overall, that they are well organized to defend their position against pretensions coming from other groups. Therefore, the anti-European discourse will be less radical in those countries who benefit of European funds or, better, among those people who directly have an EU revenue (Chapter 5).

In this complex framework, the European Parliament could play a very important role in reducing the systemic risk, acting in different directions. It may also serve specific electoral interests, contributing both to strengthen its institutional role and to affirm the European interest in those of Member States. Concerning the EU budget, the European Parliament could help to direct European policies towards new fields in order to enlarge competencies and the awareness of citizens about EU policies. In addition, the Council in all these years has amply demonstrated its propensity to ensure the stability of the system, leaving little space for non-compulsory expenditure, favoured by the lack of internal unity in the European Parliament, as a consequence of national and political cleavages and of a high rate of absenteeism.

It is thus very difficult to find an institutional actor that could deploy unifying policies and strategies, because of the presence of national, political, sectorial and party cleavages. These also strongly influence the direction adopted by each institution, reducing the opportunities to reform this complex system. As a matter of fact, the whole budgetary procedure is a path-dependent process, where only small changes seem possible and where the inner orientation is towards an intergovernmental approach rather than a supranational one, even if changes in governments are frequent.

According to this perspective, the Council is at the center of this constitutional framework, avoiding bitter confrontations among states through the Council Committees, which keep the debate at expert level, without featuring political issues and, eventually, using some expenditures as a way to reward pretensions in other fields. In this line, the role of the European Commission is very important, because it has the expertise to solve questions among states, together with the ability to offer solutions when the Council and the European Parliament disagree on some issues.

Paradoxically, the democratization of the European political system greatly contributed to worsening the situation, especially because electoral interests are very important and amply influence the behavior of political actors. For example, the European Parliament before 1979 used to act as a supranational body, as a consequence of the indirect election of the MEPs, which allowed them not to respond to a political constituency. After the first direct elections, the MEPs began to behave as their national colleagues, trying to give an answer to the requests arising from their electorate (Priestley, 2008). This change of attitude marked the management of Structural Funds, where national interest was closely related to electoral interest (Pollack, 1995).

In order to solve the institutional conflicts among different actors and interests, in 1982 a Joint Declaration was signed by the European Parliament, the European Commission and the Council, which aimed to ensure that the budget procedure should be managed in a cooperative manner, so as to avoid an attrition of interinstitutional life. On the other side, the European Parliament during the 1980s could benefit from the struggle among Member States regarding own resources, swinging between states favorable to increased expenditures and states devoted to austerity policies. The institutional framework changed after 1985, under the new President of the Commission, Jacques Delors, who succeeded in reducing expenditures and reattained an autonomous role, less dependent on the policies adopted by the European Parliament, also through a more technocratic approach (Enderlein and Lindner, 2006).

The following years were characterized by an increasing role of the Commission, which was able to shift the negotiation on budget from a political level to an administrative one, coming back to its original role of political broker, since the ECSC High Authority experience. The ever more technical expertise needed in order to manage EU budget also pushed the European Parliament to shift a large part of the decision-making phase to expert committees, so reducing the space for struggles and divisions within the assembly (Mayhew, 2009).

4.4   THE EUROPEAN PARLIAMENT: NO REPRESENTATION WITHOUT TAXATION

In the 2010s, the economic crisis strongly influenced the political debate, characterized by a massive euro-skeptical attitude in large parts of civil society, even in those countries that benefit most from EU investments, given that the European integration is considered as the main threat to national identities and traditional ways of life (FitzGibbon, Leruth, Startin, 2016). To counter this euro-skeptical attitude, a wider debate on the general idea behind the allocation of EU levies and funds could be useful for the whole European integration process. In this line, the discussion of the Multiannual Financial Framework could be the circumstance when policy-makers, MEPs, national MPs, simple citizens, groups or, more simply, the whole European civil society could discuss the evolution of European integration, either as a return to a single market or, preferably, as a political union aiming towards the creation of the United States of Europe (see, among others, Holzhacker, 2002, Chapters 2, 7 and 8).

Until now, the whole budget issue has been characterized by the original sin of the European integration, i.e. the unresolved dispute on the nature of the EU. According to the legal scholars that firstly studied the three European Communities, the treaties signed in Paris in 1951 and in Rome in 1957 did not move away from the traditional patterns designed in the first half of the twentieth century. In other words, the ECSC, the EEC and the European Atomic Energy Community were consistent with the League of Nations and the United Nations, both established through an agreement among states. According to this internationalist explanation, it is quite normal for Member States to discuss issues concerning budget within the Council and the European Council, two institutions where the intergovernmental approach prevails on the supranational principle (Moravcsik, 1993 and 1995).

The adoption of a constitutional point of view allows appreciation that budgetary issues are one of the biggest reasons for the distance of European citizens from the EU (Weiler, 2001 and 2011). As a matter of fact, the historical review presented above demonstrates the internationalist attitude characterizing the European political institutions. It is generally known that the European Communities outlined a *sui generis* legal framework, with a constitutional nature, proved by: (a) the provision of a complex set of institutions; (b) the creation of a European law; and (c) the establishment of the Court of Justice of the European Communities (CJEC) devoted to solving legal questions between states and the European Communities and between European firms and consumers and their national states when the latter did not observe communitarian rules. Some pillars of the entire communitarian law – such as the primacy of the EU law, the direct applicability of EEC regulations, the direct effect (vertical and horizontal) of EEC directives, all established through a famous judgement of the CJEC – amply demonstrated how the new supranational organization was closer to a new state than to a traditional international agreement. Its main aims were to create a new legal framework able to avoid further wars among European states and to ensure stability and prosperity to European peoples (Hitchcock, 2004; Gilbert, 2012). The adoption of this conceptual viewpoint obliges us to reconsider the relationships between the European Parliament and the other institutions. Until now, the European Parliament has always acted as an institutional counterpart to the Council, corroborating the idea that the institutional dynamics concern the struggle between a democratic side and an intergovernmental one (Puetter, 2012). In other words, the European Parliament has always performed the role of the defender of a more democratic European integration, considering the other institutions as adversaries, only concerned with defending the prerogatives of Member States and opposing to every project devoted to promoting further integration and democracy (Greven, 2000).

However, if a real democratization could occur, the European Parliament should be the place where the struggle on the budget would take place, where it is possible or, better, desirable, to discuss the two different features concerning every budget: how to levy taxes and where to spend resources. In this way, within the European Parliament we could assist the formation of real political parties, established on a clear and sharp idea of society, with an agenda submitted to the judgement of electors, independent from national governments and able to transfer at European level issues arising from national debates, through the reversal of the traditional constitutional principle: no representation without taxation. The discussion on taxes could be the only way to proceed to the full Europeanization of political life, so increasing the possibility that the most important questions affecting European citizens could be debated and solved at the most appropriate level of governance, according to the subsidiarity principle. The European Parliament could become the only place where democratic struggle takes place, introducing in the EU constitutional framework the normal dialectic between the representative power and the executive one (Mény, 2009). As a result of this transformation, the first and most important outcome could be the radical reform of the own resources system, which is a nonsense from a constitutional point of view, since it is simply useless to have financial funds in cases in which there is no freedom to decide how to spend them. Currently these decisions are taken with a complex procedure where every EU institution acts in order to obtain more political exposure to the detriment of other actors, forgetting to pursue a communitarian interest able to surpass national interests.

In 1979, some months after the first direct election of the European Parliament, the rapporteur for the 1979 budget, Mr Bangemann, highlighted how, besides the absence of personal relationships between MEPs and civil servants working in the European Commission and in the Council, the main threat that could lead budget procedures to fail was the absence of a prearranged agreement on the main political goals and on the financial framework of the European budget (Bangemann, 1979). Unfortunately, the subsequent experience amply confirmed his assumption, given the continuing discussion on the struggle among EU actors and between EU institutions and Member States, and on the goals of the European integration after the conclusion of the single market program and the establishment of the Economic and Monetary Union (Fabbrini, 2015).

Once the kind of integration has been chosen, the EU budget itself could be the mirror of a supranational attitude, avoiding decisions concerning tax levies being adopted at intergovernmental level. On the contrary, they would be discussed and adopted in a complex framework involving a democratic side – the European Parliament – and a technocratic body – the European Commission – both engaged in an effort to better distribute weights and benefits among EU citizens.[2] In this way, there could be a bearable level of conflict, where the struggle for resources is the premise that allows discussion of how to develop the European integration and who should benefit from the spending of the EU resources (Lindner, 2006). Since the budget bargainings have often a zero-sum character, it would be useful to increase the cooperation among different actors, through compromise, in order to ensure advantages for all or, at least, that in the next round benefits could shift to the advantage of current losers (Benedetto and Milio, 2012). The risks implied in the budget bargaining could be a consequence of conflicts arising in other fields or, vice versa, could reflect other issues, in both cases contributing to weaken a fragile constitutional framework. The EU needs a cooperative attitude, because it lacks all of the other symbolic values usually evoked in order to maintain unity, as nation,

---

[2]   What Jenks (1943) wrote is very interesting, when, after analyzing the experience of the League of Nations, he reflected how 'the first question requiring consideration in any general survey of future possibilities is whether the system of government contributions should be replaced or supplemented by any other method of financing. Would it, for instance, be practicable to single out distinctive sources of revenue which could be made independent of national control and assigned to world bodies for the financing of their work? (…). It may be thought that such international taxation is conceivable only within a highly integrated supra-national federation, and that for general international purposes we must continue to rely upon financing by contributions. If that view would prevail it would still be worth consideration whether such contributions should necessarily continue to be exclusively contributions from Governments'.

language or a common culture (Della Sala, 2010; Magnusson-Hansen and Wiener, 2010).

REFERENCES

Ackrill, R. (2000) 'The European Union Budget, the Balanced Budget Rule and the development of common European Policies', *Journal of Public Policy*, 20(1), 1–19.

Ackrill, R. and Kay, A. (2006) 'Historical-institutionalist perspectives on the development of the EU budget system', *Journal of European Public Policy*, 13(1), 113–133.

Bangemann, M. (1979) 'La procédure budgétaire de 1979: l'équilibre néces-saire de la répartition des pouvoirs entre le Conseil et le Parlement', *Revue du Marché commun*, 226(2), 169–184.

Begg, I. and Grimwade, N. (1998) *Paying for Europe*. Sheffield Academic Press, Sheffield.

Benedetto, G. and Milio, S. (eds) (2012) *European Union Budget Reform. Institutions, Policy and Economic Crisis*. Macmillan, Basingstoke.

Bouvet, F. and Dall'Erba, S. (2010) 'European Regional Structural Funds: how large is the influence of politics on the allocation process?', *Journal of Common Market Studies*, 48(3), 501–528.

Brown Wells, S. (2011) *Jean Monnet, Unconventional Statesman*. Lynne Rienner, Boulder, CO.

Della Sala, V. (2010) 'Political myth, mythology and the European Union', *Journal of Common Market Studies*, 48(1), 1–19.

Downing, B. M. (1992) *The Military Revolution and Political Change: Origins of Democracy and Autocracy in Early Modern Europe*. Princeton University Press, Princeton, NJ.

Duchêne, F. (1994) *Jean Monnet. The First Statesman of Interdependence*. W. W. Norton, New York.

Eggermont, F. (2012) *The Changing Role of the European Council in the Institutional Framework of the European Union: Consequences for the European Integration Process*. Intersentia, Cambridge, MA.

Ehlermann, C. D. and Minch, M. (1981) 'Conflicts between community institutions within the budgetary procedure, Article 205 of the Treaty', *Europarecht*, 39(2), 202–215.

Enderlein, H. and Lindner, J. (2006) 'The EU Budgetary procedure in the constitutional debate', in Jeremy Richardon (ed.), *European Union: Power and Policy-Making*. Routledge, Abingdon, pp. 187–205.

Fabbrini, S. (2015) *Which European Union? Europe after the Euro Crisis*. Cambridge University Press, Cambridge.

FitzGibbon, J., Leruth, B. and Startin, N. (2016) *Euroscepticism as a Transnational and Pan-European Phenomenon: The Emergence of a New Sphere of Opposition*. Routledge, Abingdon.

Fleury, A. (1999) 'Jean Monnet au Secrétariat de la Société des Nations', in Georges Bossuat and Andreas Wilkens (eds), *Jean Monnet, l'Europe et les chemins de la Paix*. Publications de la Sorbonne, Paris, pp. 31–42.

Galey, M. E. (1988) 'Reforming the regime for financing the United Nations', *Howard Law Journal*, 31, 543–574.

George, S. (1990) *An Awkward Partner. Britain in the European Community*. Oxford University Press, New York.

Gilbert, M. (2012) *European Integration: A Concise History*. Rowman & Littlefield, Lanham, MD.

Glete, J. (2002) *War and State in Early Modern Europe: Spain, the Dutch Republic and Sweden as Fiscal-military States, 1500–1660*. Routledge, London.

Greven, M. Th. (2000) 'Can the European Union finally become democratic?' in Greven M. Th. and L. W. Pauly (eds), *Democracy Beyond the State? The European Dilemma and the Emerging Global Order*. Rowman & Littlefield, Lanham, MD, pp. 35–61.

Harris, T. and Taylor, S. (eds) (2013) *The Final Crisis of the Stuart Monarchy: the Revolutions of 1688–1691 in their British, Atlantic and European Contexts*. Boydell, Woodbridge.

Hitchcock, W. I. (2004) *The Struggle for Europe: the Turbulent History of a Divided Continent, 1945–2002*. Anchor Books, New York.

Hoffman, P. T. and Norberg, K. (eds) (1994) *Fiscal Crises, Liberty, and Representative Government, 1450–1789*. Stanford University Press and Burke, Stanford, CA.

Holt, J. C. (1985) *Magna Carta and Medieval Government*. Hambledon Press, London.

Holzhacker, R. (2002) 'National Parliamentary scrutiny over EU issues: comparing the goals and methods of governing and opposition parties', *European Union Politics*, 3(4), 459–479.

Housden, M. (2011) *The League of Nations and the Organisations of Peace*. Pearson Longman, New York.

Isaac, G. (1984) 'Le 'problème' de la contribution budgétaire du Royaume-Uni', *Revue Trimestrielle de Droit Européen*, 20(1), 107–122.

Isoni, A. (2014) 'Jean Monnet, the UN administrative system and the creation of the ECSC high authority', in Lorenzo Mechi, Guia Migani and Francesco Petrini (eds), *Networks of Global Governance: International Organisations and European Integration in a Historical Perspective*. Cambridge Scholars, Newcastle upon Tyne, pp. 61–76.

Isoni, A. (2015) 'The Common Agricultural Policy (CAP): achievements and future prospects', in Massimo Monteduro, Pierangelo Buongiorno, Saverio Di Benedetto and Alessandro Isoni (eds), *Law and Agroecology. A Transdisciplinary Dialogue*. Springer, Berlin, pp. 185–206.

Jenks, C. W. (1943) 'Some legal aspects of the financing of international institutions', *Transactions of the Grotius Society*, 28, 92–93.

Laffan, B. (1997) *The Finances of the European Union*. Macmillan, Basingstoke.

Laffan, B. (2000) 'The big budgetary bargains: from negotiation to authority', *Journal of European Public Policy*, 7(5), 53–71.

Lindner, J. (2006) *Conflict and Change in EU Budgetary Politics*. Routledge, Abingdon.

Loewenstein, K. (1957) *Political Power and the Governmental Process*. The University of Chicago Press, Chicago, IL.

Magnusson-Hansen, H. and Wiener, A. (2010) Studying contemporary constitutionalism: memory, myth and horizon', *Journal of Common Market Studies*, 48(1), 21–44.

Maitland, F. W. (1908) *The Constitutional History of England*. Cambridge University Press, Cambridge.

Mayhew, A. (2009) 'The EU budget: not "fit for purpose" but change is afoot, gradually', in Roger Liddle (ed.), *After the Crisis: A New Socio-economic Settlement for the EU*. Policy Network, London, pp. 63–76.

McIlwain, C. H. (1947) *Constitutionalism: Ancient and Modern*. Cornell University Press, New York.

Mény, Y. (ed.) (2009) *Building Parliament: 50 Years of European Parliament History 1958–2008*. Office for Official Publications of the European Communities, Luxembourg.

Moravcsik, A. (1993) 'Preferences and power in the European Community: a liberal intergovernmentalist approach', *Journal of Common Market Studies*, 31(4), 473–524.

Moravscik, A. (1995) 'Liberal intergovernmentalism and integration: a rejoinder', *Journal of Common Market Studies*, 33(4), 611–628.

Moravcsik, A. (2000) 'De Gaulle between grain and *Grandeur*. The political economy of French EC policy, 1958–1970 (Part 2)', *Journal of Cold War Studies*, 2(3), 4–68.

Northedge, F. S. (1986) *The League of Nations: its Life and Times, 1920–1946*. Leicester University Press, Leicester.

Palmer, R. R. (1964) *The Age of the Democratic Revolution*. Princeton University Press, Princeton, NJ.

Pollack, M. A. (1995) 'Regional actors in an intergovernmental play: the making and implementation of EC structural policy', in Carolyn Rhodes and Sonia Mazey (eds), *The State of the European Union, Vol. 3, Building a European Polity?* Longman, Harlow, pp. 361–390.

Pollack, M. A. (2003) *The Engines of European Integration: Delegation, Agency and Agenda Setting in the EU*. Oxford University Press, Oxford.

Pollack, M. A. (2010) 'Theorizing EU policy-making', in Helen Wallace, Mark A. Pollack and Alasdair R. Young (eds), *Policy-making in the European Union*. Oxford University Press, Oxford, pp. 15–43.

Priestley, J. (2008) *Six Battles That Shaped Europe's Parliament.* John Harper, London.

Puetter, U. (2012) 'Europe's deliberative intergovernmentalism: The role of the Council and European Council in EU economic governance', *Journal of European Public Policy*, 19(2), 161–178.

Rant, V. and Mrak, M. (2010) 'The 2007–13 financial perspective: domination of national interests', *Journal of Common Market Studies*, 48(2), 347–372.

Richter, S. (2008) 'Facing the monster "Juste Retour" on the net financial position of Member States vis-à-vis the EU budget and a proposal for reform'. EU-Consent EU-Budget Working Paper no. 7.

Rittberger, B. (2005) *Building Europe's Parliament Democratic Representation beyond the Nation-State*. Oxford University Press, Oxford, pp. 114–142.

Schild, J. (2008) 'How to shift the EU's spending priorities? The Multi-Annual Financial Framework 2007–2013 in perspective', *Journal of European Public Policy*, 15(4), 531–548.

Shackleton, M. (1990) *Financing the European Community.* Pinter, London.

Strayer, J. R. (1970) *On the Medieval Origins of the Modern State*. Princeton University Press, Princeton, NJ.

Taylor, P. (1983) 'The EC crisis over the budget and the agricultural policy: Britain and its partners in the late 1970s and early 1980s', *Government and Opposition*, 17(4), 397–413.

Tonelli, R. M. (1981) 'Le juste retour: une loi communautaire? (IV)', *Revue du Marché commun*, 251, 477–491.

Tsebelis, G. (2002) *Veto Players: How Political Institutions Work*. Princeton University Press and Russell Sage Foundation, Princeton, NJ.

Van Caenegem, R. (1995) *An Historical Introduction to Western Constitutional Law*. Cambridge University Press, Cambridge.

Victor Lee (1997) *The Clash of Civilizations: War-making and State Formation in Europe*. Polity, Cambridge.

Waltz, K. N. (1979) *Theory of International Politics*. Newbery Award Records, New York.

Weiler, J. H. H. (2001) 'Federalism without constituonalism: Europe's *Sonderweg*', Kalypso Nicolaïdis and Robert Howse (eds), *The Federal Vision: Legitimacy and Levels of Governance in the United States and the European Union*. Oxford University Press, Oxford, pp. 54–72.

Weiler, J. H. H. (2011) 'The political and legal culture of european integration: an exploratory essay', *International Journal of Constitutional Law*, 9(3–4), 678–694.

5. Citizens' attitudes toward the EU budget: an overview

Karsten Mause

5.1   INTRODUCTION

According to Article 174 of the Treaty on the Functioning of the European Union (TFEU), '[i]n particular, the Union shall aim at reducing disparities between the levels of development of the various regions and the backwardness of the least favored regions'. A policy instrument used by the European Union (EU) to reduce these disparities is the EU budget and its redistribution system (Doménech et al., 2000; De la Fuente and Doménech, 2001; Jacoby, 2008; Laffan and Lindner, 2014; Crowe, 2017). The EU budget can be interpreted as a form of international financial solidarity between the Member States of the EU. Economically weaker Member States get more money from the EU budget than they have paid into this budget. That is, via the EU budget, taxpayers' money is transferred from economically 'stronger' Member States (i.e. the so-called 'net payers') to economically 'weaker' ones (i.e. the 'net-receiver States').

There is an ongoing debate over the issue of whether the level of financial redistribution and international solidarity generated via the EU budget is sufficient. Basically, three positions can be distinguished. Some argue that the EU budget should be considerably increased (e.g. more money for EU-financed investment programs) in order to help economically weaker countries to solve their societal problems, such as unemployment (see, e.g. Enderlein et al., 2012; Habermas, 2013; Nida-Rümelin et al., 2013; Enderlein and Haas, 2015; Macron, 2017). Other observers find that the *status quo* is sufficient. Still others argue that international solidarity has been overstretched in the sense that the financial burden of the net-payer countries and its citizens/taxpayers is too high (see, e.g. Willeke, 2011; Deutsche Welle, 2018).

While it is important what political decision-makers, journalists, economists, political scientists, legal scholars, and other experts think about the EU budget and its size, structure, and degree of redistribution, it seems to be no less important to take into account what EU citizens – in their role as taxpayers funding the EU budget – think about this budget. From a democratic-theory perspective, the question of what EU citizens/taxpayers think about the EU budget focusses on the legitimacy of this mechanism of international redistribution and solidarity (see also Crowe, 2017). In this perspective, for analytical purposes national citizens are often considered as the 'principals' of those actors or 'agents' at the EU level who are responsible for the EU budget. It can be expected that many principals have an incentive for their taxpayers' money to be appropriately spent by the EU. The sketched principal–agent relationship, which concerns the aspect of the legitimacy of the EU and its various actors and institutions, is analyzed in detail in the politico-economic literature on delegation and accountability in the EU context (see, e.g. Bergman, 2000; Bovens, 2007; Scharpf, 2015).

Against this background, the purpose of this chapter is to contribute to the policy debate and multidisciplinary literature on the EU budget by giving an overview of the topic of citizens' attitudes toward the EU budget. More specifically, using the best available data from the cross-national Eurobarometer public opinion polls (including internationally comparable survey questions/items), this chapter addresses the following research questions. Section 5.2 examines how public attitudes toward the EU budget have developed over time. Section 5.3 analyzes whether EU citizens are satisfied with the status quo of the EU budget system. Section 5.4 investigates the cross-national differences in citizens' attitudes toward the EU budget. Finally, Section 5.5 draws some conclusions.

5.2 THE DEVELOPMENT OF PUBLIC ATTITUDES TOWARD THE EU BUDGET OVER TIME

In several Eurobarometer waves, representative samples of citizens in various European countries were asked at different points in time whether they agree with the following statement: 'The EU should have greater financial means given its political objectives' (see, e.g. European Commission, 2018). The first time this survey question was included in the Eurobarometer was spring 2005 (fieldwork: May/June 2005). At the time of writing this chapter, the most recent data on this survey question was provided by the spring 2018 Eurobarometer wave (fieldwork: March 2018). Looking at the development of public attitudes toward the EU budget between the mid-2000s and spring 2018, it turns out that in several countries public support for an increase in the EU budget surged over time (see Table 5.1, column 4). More precisely, in 18 of the 28 considered countries the approval rates increased between 2005 and 2018. This is good (bad) news for those policymakers, experts, and citizens who currently are in favor of (against) a larger EU budget.

Table 5.1   *Citizens' attitudes toward the EU budget*

		'Pro increase in EU budget' (Eurobarometer March 2018)	'Against increase of EU budget' (Eurobarometer March 2018)	'Don't know' (Eurobarometer March 2018)	Change in 'pro increase' from Eurobarometer May 2005 to Eurobarometer March 2018 (in percentage points)
		(1)	(2)	(3)	(4)
Denmark	DEN	19%	67%	14%	+2
Slovakia*	SVK	23%	61%	16%	+2
Netherlands	NED	25%	66%	9%	+3
Sweden	SWE	25%	63%	12%	+4
United Kingdom	UK	25%	49%	26%	±0
Latvia*	LAT	26%	61%	13%	-4
Austria	AUT	27%	67%	6%	+5
Slovenia*	SLO	27%	64%	9%	-1
Finland	FIN	29%	62%	9%	+6
Lithuania*	LTU	29%	50%	21%	+5
Estonia*	EST	33%	41%	26%	-11
France	FRA	33%	50%	17%	-3
Italy	ITA	34%	46%	20%	-3
Luxembourg	LUX	34%	52%	14%	+4
Czech Republic*	CZE	36%	55%	9%	+7
Germany	GER	39%	42%	19%	+14
Belgium	BEL	42%	57%	1%	+5
Croatia*	CRO	42%	45%	13%	-2
Bulgaria*	BUL	43%	30%	27%	-1
Spain	ESP	45%	35%	20%	+14
Romania*	ROM	48%	37%	15%	-15
Poland*	POL	49%	33%	18%	+6
Malta	MLT	50%	18%	32%	-4
Greece	GRE	51%	31%	18%	+1
Portugal	POR	53%	30%	17%	+9
Ireland	IRL	55%	28%	17%	+24

		'Pro increase in EU budget' (Eurobarometer March 2018)	'Against increase of EU budget' (Eurobarometer March 2018)	'Don't know' (Eurobarometer March 2018)	Change in 'pro increase' from Eurobarometer May 2005 to Eurobarometer March 2018 (in percentage points)
Hungary*	HUN	59%	25%	16%	+10
Cyprus	CYP	66%	18%	16%	+9

Note: * Eastern European EU country.
Source: Author's own illustration based on Eurobarometer (EB) data.

Moreover, this finding is remarkable insofar as one of the EU's biggest crises happened during this investigation period: namely, the financial, sovereign-debt, and economic crisis after 2007/2008 (see, e.g. Mause and Schlipphak, 2016 for more details on this multiple crisis). In this context, another interesting finding is that those EU countries that were bailed out via specific bailout funds since 2010 show increases in approval rates: Greece (+1 percentage point), Ireland (+24), Portugal (+9), Spain (+14), and Cyprus (+9). To avoid a sovereign default, in 2010 Greece was bailed out in a joint effort by the Member States of the EU, the European Central Bank and the International Monetary Fund. This was the first sovereign bailout in the history of the EU as a community of states founded after the Second World War, in the middle of the twentieth century. After the 2010 Greek bailout, Ireland, Portugal, Spain and Cyprus also received bailout packages by the 'Troika' of the EU, the European Central Bank and the International Monetary Fund in order to avoid the sovereign default of these countries (Vaubel, 2012; Sinn, 2014; Mause, 2018). Many observers interpret these bailout operations as another form of international solidarity among the EU Member States (see, e.g. Bechtel et al., 2014, 2017; Stoeckel and Kuhn, 2018).

The sharpest increases in approval rates between 2005 and 2018 occurred in the populations of Hungary (+10 percentage points), Germany (+14), Spain (+14) and Ireland (+24). On the other hand, in nine out of 28 countries the approval rates decreased between 2005 and 2018; most notably in Romania (−15 percentage points) and Estonia (−11 percentage points). Interestingly, according to the Eurobarometer data, in the UK public support with respect to the specific policy issue under analysis remained stable over time: both in 2005 and in 2018, only 25% of the population supported an increase in the EU budget.

Attentive readers might have noticed that, in 2005, the starting year of the analysis, not all 28 countries displayed in Table 5.1 were EU Member States.

As mentioned above, the spring 2005 Eurobarometer wave (fieldwork: May/ June 2005) was the first wave in which the analyzed EU budget item was included. Hence, it should be kept in mind that, in the cases of Bulgaria and Romania (EU accession in 2007), as well as Croatia (EU accession in 2013), the aforementioned EU budget question in the spring of 2005 was a hypothetical or prospective one. However, respondents from Bulgaria, Romania and Croatia most likely were aware that their respective governments had already officially applied for accession to the EU at the time that the Eurobarometer interviews were conducted (i.e. May/June 2005). These countries' accession candidate status was the reason why they were included in the spring 2005 Eurobarometer. In the cases of Bulgaria and Romania, the official EU application process started in 1995; in the case of Croatia in 2003.

Moreover, one may object that the wording of the analyzed Eurobarometer item ('The EU should have greater financial means given its political objectives') is rather vague and does not directly and explicitly ask respondents whether they would like to see an increase of the EU budget. However, this objection is unfounded as respondents actually had two other answer options (i.e. here the Eurobarometer uses a three-scaled item). Instead of supporting the aforementioned *statement I* or simply stating 'don't know', respondents could also agree to the following *statement II*: 'The EU's political objectives do not justify an increase in the Union's budget' (see, e.g. European Commission, 2018). As respondents were asked 'With which of the following two statements do you most agree?', and as *statement II* explicitly mentions 'the Union's budget' and the possibility of 'an increase' of this budget, it is safe to say that respondents were aware that the Eurobarometer interviewer talks about the EU budget.

5.3   EU CITIZENS AND THE EU BUDGET: SATISFIED WITH THE STATUS QUO?

In the previous section, we investigated whether citizens' attitudes toward the EU budget changed over time. Analyzing the development of public opinion on this issue between the pre-crisis year 2005 and 2018, it turned out that in the majority of countries (i.e. 18 out of 28 countries) public support for an increase in the EU budget increased in the considered period of time (see Table 5.1, Column 4). This empirical finding may be interpreted as 'good news' by those policymakers, experts, and citizens who currently are in favor of a larger EU budget within the debate about the EU budget and its size, structure, and degree of redistribution. However, despite the observable upward trend with respect to approval rates in 18 countries, it should be emphasized that the legitimation basis for an increase in the EU budget currently remains rather low throughout the EU.

As mentioned above, at the time of writing (July 2018), the most recent data on the analyzed EU budget item is included in the results of the spring 2018 Eurobarometer wave. In March 2018, representative samples of citizens in 28 EU member states were asked whether they agreed with the following statement: 'The EU should have greater financial means given its political objectives' (European Commission, 2018; total sample: $N = 27{,}988$ citizens). Looking at citizens' current attitudes toward the EU budget, Table 5.1 (Column 1) shows that only in five out of 28 countries (i.e. Greece, Portugal, Ireland, Hungary, Cyprus) were a majority of respondents in March 2018 in favor of an increase in the EU budget. In three of these countries – Greece (51%), Portugal (53%), and Ireland (55%) – we observe only a narrow majority in this respect.

This suggests that public support for a larger EU budget currently is rather low in many nation states belonging to the EU club. According to the analyzed Eurobarometer data, only in one-fifth (18%) of EU Member States would such a policy reform be supported by the majority of people. The greatest opposition against an increase of the EU budget can be observed among the populations of the Netherlands (66%), Denmark (67%), and Austria (67%; see Table 5.1, Column 2). Put differently, if policymakers implemented a reform that increased the EU budget then such reform step would be made on a rather weak legitimation basis (we return to this point in the concluding section).

Unfortunately, the Eurobarometer does not explicitly and directly ask EU citizens (a) whether they are satisfied with the current amount of the EU budget and/or (b) whether they would like to see a reduction of this budget. The lack of these interesting and obvious questions may be interpreted as further empirical evidence for the thesis that the European Commission does not have an incentive to produce 'bad news' that questions the process of (further) European integration (Nissen, 2014; Höpner and Jurczyk, 2015). In this context, it should be mentioned that the Eurobarometer is a 'survey requested and co-ordinated by the European Commission', as one can read on the title page of each Eurobarometer poll (see, e.g. European Commission, 2018). However, the results presented above on the basis of the Eurobarometer survey items (I) 'The EU should have greater financial means given its political objectives' and (II) 'The EU's political objectives do not justify an increase in the Union's budget' at least allow the aforementioned conclusions to be drawn with respect to the issue of how strong or weak the legitimation basis of the *status quo* of the EU budget currently is in the different EU Member States (Chapters 2 and 7).

It is clear that the most recent public opinion data with respect to the EU budget provided by the spring 2018 Eurobarometer poll is just a snapshot, and that public opinion on this policy issue might change in the future. For instance, events might happen at the national or the supra-national EU level (e.g. cases of misappropriation of EU funds) that might lead to a shift toward greater opposition to an increase in the EU budget. It is certainly also possible that events may happen at the national and/or EU level that increase public support for a surge of the EU budget (e.g. successful infrastructure projects funded out of the EU budget). In this context, it can be expected that public opinion toward the EU and its budget to some extent is influenced by media reports, that is, by the way in which journalists report the issue of how policymakers at the national and EU levels spend taxpayers' money via the EU budget system (Chapter 3).

5.4   CROSS-NATIONAL DIFFERENCES IN CITIZENS' ATTITUDES TOWARD THE EU BUDGET

Table 5.1 shows that the approval rates measuring public support for an increase in the EU budget range from 19% in Denmark to 66% in Cyprus (see Column 1). This brings us to the question of what explains the considerable differences between EU Member States with respect to public support for an increase in the EU budget. On closer inspection, it turns out that approval rates tend to be higher in EU countries that are net beneficiaries of the EU budget system. This pattern is illustrated by Figure 5.1 where the net-receiver states, who show a positive budget balance within the EU budget system, can be found above the horizontal zero line (the country codes are explained in Table 5.1). At the same time, with the exception of Cyprus (negative budget balance = €–23.4 million; approval rate = 66%), in none of the net-payer states (displayed below the horizontal zero line) did a majority of respondents support a larger EU budget which – *ceteris paribus* – would result in higher net payments of these countries. The statistical analysis confirms a significant positive correlation between approval rates and the net payments a country receives (Spearman's rho = 0.444, significant at the 5% level; $p = 0.0178$; $N = 28$).

   This result is hardly surprising if one looks at the EU from the narrow perspective of a fiscal cost–benefit analysis: citizens in countries that are net receivers (*net payers*) understandably have nothing against (*something against*) an increase of the EU budget as their country would benefit (*lose*) from this increase. Put differently, those who are the beneficiaries of the EU budget structure apparently have nothing against a reform leading to more international solidarity. An interesting case in this respect is the UK. In this country, not only were many citizens skeptical of a further increase in the EU budget (indicated by the relatively low approval rate of 25% in column 1 of Table 5.1), but in addition, it turned out that the UK's net-payer position in the EU budget – alongside immigration and other policy issues – was an important factor in the considerations of those UK citizens who voted to leave the EU (Fidrmuc et al., 2016; Owen and Walter, 2017).

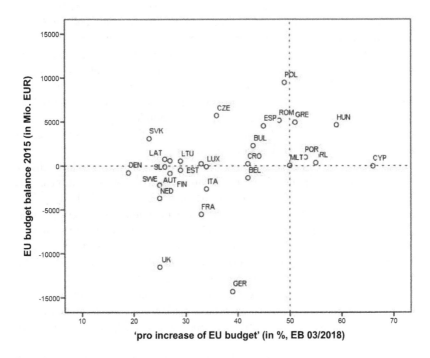

Figure 5.1   *EU budget balance and public support for increase in EU budget*

Source: Author's own illustration based on the EU budget data (European Commission 2015) and data from the March 2018 Eurobarometer (EB). The country codes are explained in Table 5.1.

In this context, another remarkable finding is that the five EU countries that were bailed out through 'rescue packages' since 2010 (see Section 5.2 above) are among the top-10 countries with respect to public support for an increase in the EU budget: Spain (approval rate = 45%), Greece (51%), Portugal (53%), Ireland (55%) and Cyprus (66%). In addition, these countries were also net beneficiaries in the redistribution scheme of the EU budget – during the financial, sovereign-debt and economic crisis (i.e. 2007/2008 and beyond) as well as in the time before the crisis (the reference year used here is 2005).

The net-receiver/net-payer winner/loser logic depicted above can be observed in other redistribution schemes in which jurisdictions of different economic/fiscal strength are involved; see, for example, German citizens' attitudes toward the fiscal equalization scheme that redistributes taxpayers' money across the 16 German *Länder* (Petersen et al., 2008; Jacoby, 2008;

Blesse et al., 2017). It should be mentioned, however, that there are two countries that do not fit into the aforementioned pattern: Slovakia and the Czech
Republic show relatively low approval rates for an increase in the EU budget
(23% and 36%, respectively) although these countries are among the largest
beneficiaries of this redistribution mechanism. In 2015, Slovakia's surplus
amounted to €3.1 billion; the net-receiver position of the Czech Republic
amounted to €5.7 billion. In light of the relatively large net payments both
countries receive, it is somewhat surprising that public support for an increase
in the EU budget is not higher in these countries as they would both – *ceteris
paribus* – benefit from such a policy reform.

In this context, it is also noteworthy that there is no clear East–West divide
with respect to the policy issue under investigation: Eastern European EU
countries, which are marked by an asterisk in Table 5.1, do not show system-
atically and significantly higher approval rates than other EU Member States.
On the contrary, there is a negative correlation between approval rates and the
dummy variable 'East' that takes the value of 1 in the case of the 11 Eastern
European EU countries (point biserial correlation coefficient *pbis* = −0.0248).
However, this correlation is not statistically significant ($p = 0.9004$; $N = 28$).
Note that, to analyze the relationship between a metric-scaled variable (e.g.
the Eurobarometer data) and a dichotomous variable (e.g. the dummy variable
East/West), usually the point biserial correlation coefficient is used (Cleff,
2014).

At this point, one may argue that the cases of Slovakia and the Czech
Republic indicate that the apparently 'irrational' response behavior of respondents in these countries is due to the fact that citizens are poorly informed about
the EU budget and their country's current position (net payer vs. net receiver)
in this redistribution scheme. This may be true and the considerable number of
respondents stating 'don't know' (see Table 5.1, column 3) seems to confirm
this statement. The percentage of 'don't knows' ranges from 1% in Belgium to
32% in Malta. Some observers may generally question whether it makes sense
to ask 'ordinary' EU citizens about 'technical' or 'expert' issues such as the
EU budget (Shepherd and Scully, 2002, p. 176; McCormick, 2015, p. 283),
and it has to be acknowledged that the 'European budgetary galaxy' (Crowe,
2017) is a rather complex system.

The data presented above suggest that the claim that 'ordinary' citizens have
no idea about the EU budget is exaggerated. The aforementioned net-receiver/
net-payer winner/loser pattern that can be observed in the cross-national public
opinion data suggests that citizens seem to be well aware whether their country,
in monetary terms, is a net payer or a net receiver in the EU. This information
is communicated at the national level through political parties and the media,
for example. Nevertheless, given 'the complexity of the Union's budgetary
system [...] future reforms aimed at making the system more comprehensible

for citizens' (Crowe, 2017, p. 430) would not be amiss from the point of view of many observers (Chapters 4 and 8).

5.5 CONCLUSIONS

This chapter has provided some insights into citizens' attitudes toward the EU budget as a mechanism of international redistribution and solidarity. This budget system redistributes taxpayers' money from the 'richer' to the 'poorer' Member States of the EU. At the time of writing (July 2018), there is an ongoing debate over the issue of whether the EU budget should be increased in the future, implying a higher level of international solidarity among EU Member States. It remains to be seen, however, whether and how the size, structure, and degree of redistribution of the EU budget will be changed in the future. As the above analysis has demonstrated, public support for the reform step 'increase in EU budget' is currently rather low. In the spring 2018 Eurobarometer poll, only in five out of 28 countries were there (narrow) majorities in favor of an increase in the EU budget; and with the exception of Cyprus (approval rate = 66%), which constitutes a special case for several reasons (Theodore, 2015), in none of the net-payer states would a majority of people support such a reform step.

Of course, policymakers may increase the EU budget without taking into account what citizens and taxpayers in the EU think about this reform step. To my knowledge, in no EU Member State do citizens have the power to directly act as a veto player in the sense that they would get the opportunity to vote on the issue at hand in an 'EU budget referendum'. Still, citizens' preferences in this particular policy area may play a role in national elections and elections to the European Parliament (Kriesi, 2012; Mause and Schlipphak, 2016; Foster and Frieden, 2017; Dustmann et al., 2017). If, for example, many citizen-voters have the impression that taxpayers' money is wasted at the EU level, then this will most likely have an impact on the election results of 'Anti-EU' parties. The 2016 Brexit referendum illustrates this point. There, an important factor in the decision calculus of those citizens voting for Brexit was the UK's net-payer position within the EU budget's redistribution mechanism (Fidrmuc et al., 2016; Owen and Walter, 2017).

Consequently, those policymakers interested in enhancing the legitimation basis of the EU budget as a form of international solidarity could try to better inform the public about the objectives and functioning of this redistribution mechanism. This includes reporting 'success stories' in the form of successful projects realized through the money received via the EU budget. In other words, it can be expected that taxpayers – even those in net-payer states – will be more supportive of the EU budget when they observe that they receive value for money. At the same time, it can be expected that each additional 'horror story' (i.e. wasteful spending, political corruption, etc.) reported by the European Court of Auditors (see, e.g. Court of Auditors of the EU, 2013), the European Anti-Fraud Office (see, e.g. OLAF, 2016) or another 'waste watcher' is grist to the mills of Euroskeptics.

REFERENCES

Bechtel, M. M., Hainmueller, J. and Margalit, Y. (2014), 'Preferences for international redistribution: the divide over the Eurozone bailouts', *American Journal of Political Science*, 58 (4), 835–856.

Bechtel, M. M., Hainmueller, J. and Margalit, Y. (2017), 'Policy design and domestic support for international bailouts', *European Journal of Political Research*, 56 (4), 864–886.

Bergman, T. (2000), 'The European Union as the next step of delegation and accountability', *European Journal of Political Research*, 37 (3), 415–429.

Blesse, S., Berger, M., Heinemann, F. and Janeba, E. (2017), 'Föderalismuspräferenzen in der deutschen Bevölkerung', *Perspektiven der Wirtschaftspolitik*, 18 (2), 145–158.

Bovens, M. (2007), 'Analysing and assessing accountability: a conceptual framework', *European Law Journal*, 13 (4), 447–468.

Cleff, T. (2014), *Exploratory Data Analysis in Business and Economics: An Introduction Using SPSS, Stata, and Excel*. Springer, Heidelberg.

Court of Auditors of the EU (2013), *Annual Report on the Implementation of the Budget concerning the financial year 2012*. Brussels.

Crowe, R. (2017), 'The European budgetary galaxy', *European Constitutional Law Review*, 13 (3), 428–452.

De la Fuente, A. and Doménech, R. (2001), 'The redistributive effects of the EU budget: an analysis and proposal for reform', *Journal of Common Market Studies*, 39 (2), 307–330.

Deutsche Welle (2018), 'German economists slam Macron's Eurozone reform agenda', *Deutsche Welle News*, 22 May, https://p.dw.com/p/2y8tW (accessed 19 December 2018).

Doménech, R., Maudes, A. and Varela, J. (2000), 'Fiscal flows in Europe: the redistributive effects of the EU budget', *Review of World Economics*, 136 (4), 631–656.

Dustmann, C., Eichengreen, B., Otten, S., Sapir, A. and Tabellini, G. (2017), *Europe's Trust Deficit: Causes and Remedies*. CEPR Press, London.

Enderlein, H. and Haas, J. (2015), 'What would a European Finance Minister do? A proposal', Policy paper 145. Jacques Delors Institute, Berlin/Paris.

Enderlein, H., Bofinger, P., Boone, L., de Grauwe, P., Piris, J.-C., Pisani-Ferry, J., Rodrigues, M. J., Sapir, A. and Vitorino, A. (2012), *Completing the Euro:*

A Road Map Towards Fiscal Union in Europe. Report of the 'Tommaso Padoa–Schioppa Group'. Jacques Delors Institute, Berlin/Paris.

European Commission (2015), *EU Budget 2015. Financial Report*. Luxembourg.

European Commission (2018), *Standard Eurobarometer 89: Public Opinion in the European Union. Fieldwork March 2018. Annex*. Brussels.

Fidrmuc, J., Hulényi, M. and Tunali, C. B. (2016), 'Money can't buy EU love: European funds and the Brexit referendum'. CESifo Working Paper no. 6107.

Foster, C. and and Frieden, J. (2017), 'Crisis of trust: socio-economic determinants of Europeans' confidence in government', *European Union Politics*, 18 (4), 511–535.

Habermas, J. (2013), 'Democracy, solidarity and the European crisis', in A.-M. Grozelier, B. Hacker, W. Kowalsky, J. Machnig, H. Meyer and B. Unger (eds), *Roadmap to a Social Europe*. Social Europe, London, pp. 4–13.

Höpner, M. and Jurczyk, B. (2015), 'How the Eurobarometer blurs the line between research and propaganda'. MPIfG Discussion Paper no. 15/6.

Jacoby, W (2008), 'Side payments over solidarity: financing the poor cousins in Germany and the EU', *German Politics*, 17 (4), 470–487.

Kriesi, H. (2012), 'The political consequences of the financial and economic crisis in Europe: electoral punishment and popular protest', *Swiss Political Science Review*, 18 (4), 518–522.

Laffan, B. and Lindner, J. (2014), 'The budget: who gets what, when, and how?', in H. Wallace, M. A. Pollack and A. R. Young (eds), *Policy-making in the European Union*, 7th edn. Oxford University Press, Oxford, pp. 220–242.

Macron, E. M. (2017), 'Initiative for Europe', speech by M. Emmanuel Macron, President of the French Republic (Sorbonne speech), Paris, 26 September.

Mause, K. (2018), 'Governing the market for sovereign bailouts', in G. Eusepi and R. E. Wagner (eds), *Debt Default and Democracy*. Edward Elgar, Cheltenham, pp. 17–35.

Mause, K. and Schlipphak, B. (2016), 'Increasing winners–losers gap? Increasing euroscepticism? Exploring the economic crisis' conflict potential', in T. Krieger, B. Neumaerker and D. Panke (eds), *Europe's Crisis: The Conflict-theoretical Perspective*. Nomos, Baden-Baden, pp. 111–132.

McCormick, J. (2015), *European Union Politics*, 2nd edn. Palgrave Macmillan, Basingstoke.

Nida-Rümelin, J., Hirschel, D., Meyer, H., Meyer, T., Möller, A., Scheer, N., Schwan, G. and Schwengel, H. (2013), *We Need a Europe That is Truly Social and Democratic*. Social Europe, London.

Nissen, S. (2014), 'The Eurobarometer and the process of European integration. Methodological foundations and weaknesses of the largest European survey', *Quality and Quantity*, 48 (2), 713–727.

OLAF (2016), *European Anti-Fraud Office: 2016 Annual Activity Report*. Brussels.

Owen, E. and Walter, S. (2017), 'Open economy politics and Brexit: insights, puzzles, and ways forward', *Review of International Political Economy*, 24 (2), 179–202.

Petersen, T., Scheller, H. and Wintermann, O. (2008), 'Public attitudes towards German federalism: a point of departure for a reform of German (fiscal) federalism? Differences between public opinion and the political debate', *German Politics*, 17 (4), 559–586.

Scharpf, F. W. (2015), 'Political legitimacy in a non-optimal area', in O. Cramme and S. B. Hobolt (eds), *Democratic Politics in a European Union under Stress*. Oxford University Press, Oxford, pp. 19–47.

Shepherd, M. and Scully, R. (2002), 'The European Parliament: of barriers and removed citizens', in P. Norton (ed.), *Parliaments and Citizens in Western Europe*. Frank Cass, London, pp. 153–177.

Sinn, H.-W. (2014), *The Euro Trap. On Bursting Bubbles, Budgets, and Beliefs*. Oxford University Press, Oxford.

Stoeckel, F. and Kuhn, T. (2018), 'Mobilizing citizens for costly policies: the conditional effect of party cues on support for international bailouts in the European Union', *Journal of Common Market Studies*, 56 (2), 446–461.

Theodore, J. (2015), *Cyprus and the Financial Crisis: The Controversial Bailout and what it Means for the Eurozone*. Palgrave Macmillan, Basingstoke.

Vaubel, R. (2012), 'The political economy of sovereign bailouts in the Eurozone', in J. Brodský (ed.), *Today's World and Václav Klaus. Festschrift in Honour of Václav Klaus, President of the Czech Republic*. Fragment, Prague, pp. 323–328.

Willeke, F.-U. (2011), *Deutschland, Zahlmeister der EU. Abrechnung mit einer ungerechten Lastenverteilung*. Munich: Olzog Verlag.

6. The Multiannual Financial Framework: reforms and path-dependent development of the EU budget

Robert Kaiser

6.1 THE MULTIANNUAL FINANCIAL FRAMEWORK 2021–2027: THE CONTEXT FOR THE POST–2020 BUDGET

The European Union has started the negotiation process for the post-2020 Multiannual Financial Framework (MFF) confronted by various crisis phenomena. On 2 May 2018 the European Commission published its proposal for the budget 2021–2027 whereby it suggests investing €1135 billion or 1.11% of the EU's gross national income (GNI) for the seven year period (European Commission, 2018). This overall amount represents a significant increase from the current MFF (which amounted to 1.03% GNI), but it remains slightly lower than the predecessor (2007–2013), which amounted to 1.12% GNI.

The proposal for such a total investment appears, on the one hand, to be reasonable. It corresponds with a broad agreement among EU institutions and Member States' governments on the need for substantial reforms of EU integration. In September 2016, the European Council initiated the so-called Bratislava process, a period of reflection among Member States on changes that are required to make the European Union more efficient in terms of the current challenges, such as migration, security and defence as well as economic and social development (European Council, 2016). This process led to the Rome Declaration of the leaders of the 27 remaining Member States (after the Brexit), the European Parliament and the European Commission, who committed themselves to making the European Union a place that is 'safe and secure', 'prosperous and sustainable', that provides for 'social progress' and that will have a 'stronger' role on the global scene (European Council, 2017). In parallel, the European Commission prepared a 'White Paper on the Future of Europe' (European Commission, 2017a) in which it presents five scenarios illustrating the paths the European Union could take until 2025. The White Paper also establishes the link between the different reform options and the consequences for the budget, as each of the five scenarios is discussed, *inter alia*, against the impact it would have on the future MFF.

On the other hand, there are also good arguments in favour of a more focussed budget that concentrates financial resources on measures that can be implemented more efficiently at the European level while providing more room for domestic policy initiatives at the national level. Many Member States still have not yet overcome the economic and social downturn after the 2008 financial crisis. With the so-called Brexit only few months away, the EU has to face the departure of its third-largest net contributor, and across Europe, left- and right-wing populist parties are gaining growing support for their anti-EU agendas, while there are serious conflicts among Member States over issues like migration policy. There is, without doubt, a growing concern that the European Union is involved in too many issues in which it seems to fail to provide an undisputed added value. Therefore, negotiations about the future European financial resources will take place again, as has often been the case, in difficult times. Compared with earlier phases, however, the current situation appears to be different not because of the existence of a crisis, but because of the manifold levels of conflicts and crises. In this situation, it is plausible to suggest two different alternative outcomes for the post-2020 MFF.

Firstly, one could argue that over the last three decades the institution of the financial perspective has developed into a path-dependent structure that will further solidify as long as the perception of a crisis situation does not convince the relevant actors of the need to change path. Under such a perspective, the assessment of the given situation would be based less on the level of efficiency of the institutional structure than on the level of security and stability it provides. Since the end of the 1980s, the establishment of a long-term budget perspective has clearly proven its ability to generate a high level of certainty about the interests, preferences and strategies of the actors (mainly the Member States) involved in the negotiations. This holds even for an era of European integration in which 15 new Member States entered the EU and during which the intensity of political integration significantly increased. In this respect, the MFF is not only a budget for investments at the European level, but also a solid mechanism for the redistribution of financial resources among EU Member States. Moreover, the large-scale EU funding programmes cannot easily be changed as they have been evolved as stabilizing factors over a longer period of time. Consequently, actors who benefit from these programmes, either financially or politically, both at the European and the national levels, will not refrain from the benefits if the crisis does not force them to do so.

Secondly, one could also state that the various crisis phenomena have opened a 'window of opportunity' for path-changing reforms of the budget. This would require that the actors involved perceive the current situation as a moment in which change is needed and/or possible. There are, however, certain institutional preconditions for such a reform opportunity. One important precondition would be that the given institutional structure lost (at least some of) its capacity to provide actors with benefits they were used to obtaining from it in the past. Another precondition would be that there are relevant actors on the scene that capitalize on that situation by acting as policy entrepreneurs providing momentum and concepts for change. Proposals for change could be of varying scale and magnitude. They could address the structural dimension of the MFF by putting into question, for example, the main policy objectives and the related expenditure programmes or the means used to provide the EU with financial resources. They could, however, be also of limited scale focusing on the distribution of money across relatively stable budget lines or, on an even lower instrumental level, on the rules that are applied to the transfer of investment to the Member States.

In this chapter, it will be argued that reforms at the structural level for the post-2020 MFF are quite unlikely. This is because the structure of the MFF has proven and still proves to have a certain degree of flexibility, which means that it is capable of incorporating quite substantial changes while at the same time providing actors (mainly at the national levels) with the amount of security needed to commit themselves to a longer-term definition of their burdens and benefits. Changes will probably occur at the instrumental level where it is still possible to agree on new policy objectives or to change certain rules for the distribution of funds. In order to substantiate this assumption, the remaining chapter will proceed in the following way. Section 6.2 will present the conceptual framework that guides the analysis of stability and change of the MFF. In Section 6.3, we turn to the structural level of the multiannual financial framework, showing that it has indeed developed during the last three decades along a solid institutional path. Section 6.4 looks at the procedural level elaborating on the main features, such as actors' preferences, and coalitions, of the negotiation process. In Section 6.5, we will evaluate the potential for change at the policy level while Section 6.6 summarizes the main findings.

6.2 THE MULTIANNUAL FINANCIAL FRAMEWORK AS A COMPLEX INSTITUTIONAL STRUCTURE

The EU's Multiannual Financial Framework is a complex institutional structure. The complexity mainly emerges from three distinct features.

First of all, there is a large variety of actors involved in the negotiation process who coordinate their interests in a consensual mode across different territorial levels. The EU's system of multilevel governance can be characterized best as a non-hierarchical institutional architecture in which decisions are taken as a result of consensus-oriented negotiations 'among nested governments at several territorial tiers' (Marks, 1993: 392). The consensus orientation does, however, not prevent an inter-institutional competition for competencies within the European political system, which is certainly stronger than at the national level. Inter-institutional competition already exists in the early phase of agenda-setting in which actors may build upon convictions that reforms are necessary and may engage in policy entrepreneurship. In public policy research, the concept of policy entrepreneurship aims at providing explanations for the existence and the (sometimes unexpected) outcome of agenda-setting processes in which a political actor (i.e. the policy entrepreneur) succeeds in proposing and pushing through his problem solution strategy even against the anticipated resistance of other political actors whose agreement is needed for the implementation of this solution. Kingdon's (1984) concept of the policy entrepreneur is quite useful in this respect as it clearly allows for the characterization of the European Commission as the 'natural' policy entrepreneur in budget politics. The Commission is not only equipped with the required information and technical resources, but it also has the prime role in formal agenda-setting procedures and has established a comprehensive system of standing and ad-hoc committees as well as expert groups, which allow for the early coordination of legislative proposals with representatives from the Member States and with private actors. Owing to the financial and economic crisis, however, the Commission's entrepreneurial role has been challenged by a gradual transition of the European Council from an informal forum of the Heads of State and Government to the EU's future control center. With the entering into force of the Lisbon Treaty, the European Council gained the status of a formal institution of the European Union, which 'shall provide the Union with the necessary impetus for its development' (Article 15 TEU). Actually, the European Council goes much further. Not only do the Heads of State and Government meet much more often than originally foreseen, but the more important aspect is that the European Council regularly claims responsibility for decisions on issues (by consensus) on which the Council could not find an agreement (based on qualified majority) before (Chapter 7). The multilevel character of the EU also implies that there are many actors involved who may act either as 'institutional' or 'partisan' veto players (Tsebelis, 2002), thus limiting the freedom of action especially for national governments. Institutional veto players play a role primarily in federalized or regionalized EU Member States where central governments often have to act in agreement with regional governments or second chambers. Partisan veto players, such as interest groups, political parties, etc., vary significantly in their importance across different Member States, but we can at least assume a relevant role for them (a) in policy areas in which large EU expenditure programmes exist (especially in agricultural policies) and (b) in countries in which populist parties with anti-EU agendas put a lot of political pressure on national governments.

Secondly, the negotiation process usually takes more than three years and therefore always contains the risk that unexpected events impact on the negotiations in an unforeseeable way. It is important to note that the process starts well before the European Commission presents its proposal. Before this happens, working groups of the Council have been involved in order to make sure that the preferences of the Member States are already considered when the Commission prepares first drafts of the MFF. Because of that, the early phase of preparation is much more driven by an administrative than by a political logic which induces to some extent the planning of the new on the basis of the existing structure. Moreover, certain political phenomena may impact on the negotiation process in a way not anticipated by the political actors. In 2007, for example, the Commission launched a broad public consultation process on the future budget ('the budget review') to ensure full involvement of all stakeholders as well as of Member States' governments at a very early stage of preparation of the MFF 2014–2020. For the Commission, this could have been a basis for legitimizing a reform proposal for the next MFF hinting at the positions Member States had already put forward. However, these assumptions got weaker during 2009/2010, as the publication of the budget review – owing to its postponement from the expected date in the first half of 2009 to October 2010 – finally ran in parallel to the actual start of the preparations for the next MFF. The budget review thus became a victim of the economic and financial crisis, because Member States were not very keen anymore to initiate comprehensive reforms but focused mostly on national crisis prevention measures. Timing and the sequence of events are therefore crucial factors for the outcome of the budget negotiations. As for the post-2020 MFF, it is already apparent that the various reform declarations and reflection papers mentioned in the introduction of this chapter will not significantly influence anymore the upcoming negotiation process. European policy actors are currently much more concerned about whether Brexit will take place in a coordinated or a 'hard' way. The political instability caused by electoral successes of populist parties in some Member States has even promoted the idea of concluding the next MFF before the elections to the European Parliament in May 2019. Although this is not very likely to happen, it would be the first time since the 'invention' of the MFF that a deal on the new budget was made more than 18 months before the current MFF expires.

Thirdly, the final MFF agreement needs unanimous support from all Member States' governments. Owing to this decision rule, the negotiation process is likely to be determined by established conflict lines and actor coalitions that already had a strong impact in the past. Traditionally, budget negotiations at the EU level follow the logic of net-payer countries (organized as 'Friends of Better Spending') vs. net-recipient countries (united in the group of the 'Friends of Cohesion'). These groups are, however, not always equally strong and powerful (see Section 6.4.1 and Chapter 5). Owing to Brexit (which will cause the overall GNI of the European Union to decrease) and the relatively positive economic development in some receiving countries, Member States that were traditionally net-recipients of the EU budget could move into the camp of the net-payers (Chapter 12). Apart from that, some traditional net-payers (especially Germany and France) have already signalled that they are willing to contribute more in order to compensate for the British contribution while other net-payers (for example, Austria and the Netherlands) oppose that. Given that, it is quite likely that the net-payers camp will be less united than it was in the last negotiation round.

Taking the three features together, it can be assumed that the post-2020 MFF will neither be a comprehensive reform nor a document of stagnation. Rather, it will comprise elements of stability as well as elements of change. The assumption of stability originates from the fact that the main role of institutions is 'to reduce uncertainty by establishing a stable (but not necessarily efficient) structure to human interaction' (North, 1990, p. 6). Even in the presence of different crises and challenges for European integration, the overall structure of the MFF has repeatedly proven its capacity to establish a basis for conflict resolution and consensus on the budget. It has ended a period of severe political conflicts among Member States about annual EU budgets that hampered European politics in the 1970s and 1980s. Today, the level of uncertainty is quite high and because of that, political actors involved in the process have little incentive for institutional experiments.

Historical institutionalism (Hall, 1986; March and Olsen, 1989; Campbell et al., 1991; Steinmo et al., 1992) provides for the assumption that complex institutional structures, once they have become established as an institutional compromise between elites, tend to develop along a specific path as long as they produce increasing returns for the actors involved. Increasing returns can be of a very different kind: the established MFF structure provides actors, especially national governments, with a significant amount of security about their future contributions to the budget as well as the financial backflows they can expect. They can profit from experience from the past in order to assess how changes within and across budget heading may impact on their respective balance. Keeping the structure also provides at least some security about actor preferences and actor coalitions.

6.3 CONTINUITY AND CHANGE AT THE STRUCTURAL LEVEL

There are hardly any reasons to assume that the structure of the post-2020 MFF will significantly change. This holds for the four most important components: the overall amount of investments, the duration of the financial framework, the direct linkage between the main expenditure lines and the three most important Union programmes (i.e. for agricultural policies, for structural and cohesion policies, and for research and innovation policies), and the structure of the revenue side.

6.3.1　The Overall Amount of Investments

The political game that is played in terms of the maximum ceiling of a new MFF is quite predictable. It always follows the same rules. The European Parliament's role is to set the highest amount proposed in the debate. With reference to the new European challenges and the deficits of the current MFF, the parliament tends to propose a maximum ceiling far beyond what can be accepted by Member States, at least by the net-payers. In a resolution of 14 March 2018, the EP did exactly that, claiming that an expenditure ceiling of 1.3% GNI is needed in order to achieve 'a stronger and a more ambitious Europe' (European Parliament, 2018). Subsequently, the ball was in the field of the net-payers. They are traditionally focused on the 1% GNI limit. In the current process, that role was taken over by Austria, Denmark, the Netherlands and Sweden. They suggest no increase in contributions, but a smaller budget that produces better results.[1] The European Commission is normally eager to place its proposal in the middle, providing both the Parliament and the net-payers with some arguments that the proposal is closer to what they expected. The Commission's plan to reach a maximum ceiling of 1.11% GNI is already closer to the net-payer's position. Moreover, if it is considered that the European Commission plans to reintegrate the European Development Fund into the MFF, the commitment appropriations for the post-2020 MFF are even lower than for the 2014–2020 budget (€1138 billion vs. 1135 billion). It seems obvious that the Commission was very much interested in presenting a proposal that could finally get support even from net-payers. They would have to accept, however, that the budget will not decrease as a consequence of the Brexit.

In the end, there are good reasons to assume that the post-2020 MFF will not generate the same level of investments as the current MFF does. This

---

[1]　'EU budget hawks under attack', Politico, 23 April 2018.

*Table 6.1   EU Budget payment ceiling in percent of EU GNI (European
                  Parliament 2018: 2; European Commission 2017b: 7)*

1988–1992	1993–1999	2000–2006	2007–2013	2014–2020	2021–2027*
1.15	1.18	1.06	1.07	0.98 (1.03)**	1.11

Notes:
*   as proposed by the European Commission.
** higher value includes the European Development Fund.

assumption does not, however, consider the aspect that the British government
might finally accept significant transfers ('the final bill') to the EU as a condition for the Brexit. Without those transfers, keeping the budget at the current
level would not only put considerable burden on many net-payers, it would
also mean that even net-beneficiaries would have to agree to higher national
contributions. It is, however, also not very likely that the post-2020 MFF will
be cut exactly at the level of the British contribution. There is obviously enor-
mous pressure to provide sufficient financial means for the new challenges.
To a certain extent, funds could be taken from the agricultural budget, which
will most likely further decrease. However, there is very little redistribution
mass in the two other areas of cohesion as well as research and innovation.
Increasing revenues would, of course, be an option, but it's not a plausible one
for the next MFF.

  With a maximum ceiling of 1.11% GNI (or even lower) the post-2020 MFF
would be within the limits of earlier financial frameworks with a seven year
duration. It would be higher than the MFFs from 2000 to 2014, but still lower
than the financial framework of 1993–1999 (see Table 6.1).

6.3.2   The Duration of the Financial Framework

A second important aspect regarding the structure of the forthcoming MFF concerns its duration. According to the treaty (Article 312 TFEU), the MFF shall
be established for a period of at least five years. The European Commission,
during the budget review in 2010, for the first time discussed the option to
prolong the duration to 10 years, with a substantial review after five years ('5
+ 5'). The European Parliament advocates in favour of only five years, but
also considers the five plus five years option acceptable. The main reason for
the parliament is to align the MFF period with the five-years mandate of the
Commission and the Parliament (cf. European Parliament 2006).

  At first sight, the justification for a deviation from the current seven year
period seems reasonable. If the MFF negotiations should be concluded before
the next elections, the European Parliament that decides on the MFF would
not control its implementation afterwards. If the MFF is decided only after the

elections, the new European Parliament has to accept the political positions of its predecessor but would be involved in the management of the MFF for only half of its duration.

Nevertheless, for at least two reasons, a change towards five years (or even 5 + 5 years) is unlikely. Firstly, it would provoke considerable technical adjustments to the most important EU funding programmes without providing a substantial functional advantage. Secondly, and probably more importantly, the change would intervene into the institutional equilibrium between the Parliament and the Council. It would provide the Parliament with the opportunity to politicise budget negotiations even more. Therefore, it seems rather unlikely that EU Member States would support such a proposal. Being aware of that, the European Commission's proposal for the post-2020 budget is based on a seven-year duration and it does not include any discussion of alternatives.

6.3.3 The Strong Linkage Between the Main Budget Headings and the Three Most Important Union Programmes

Ever since the first MFF in 1988, the by far largest share of EU investments were delegated to only two large expenditure programmes: the funds of the Common Agricultural Policy as well as the regional and cohesion policies. Over the decades, their share of the overall budget decreased, but still amounted to roughly 75% even in the MFF 2014–2020. This clearly indicates that the European Union went into a path-dependent expenditure structure not simply because of the importance of the two policy areas, but mainly because of the fact, that the actors involved became acquainted with calculating their burdens and benefits as well as the degree of solidarity among the Member States on the basis of these mega-funds. Taking this into consideration, it comes not as a surprise that changes did not often occur in terms of the ceilings of the MFF, but more within them. This means that the character of both the agricultural and the regional policies have significantly changed over time, but not that much their importance within the EU budget.

It can therefore be assumed that both trends (a moderate decrease of the share of the largest expenditure programmes and the integration of new priorities into established headings) will continue. Looking at the Commission's proposal for the post-2020 budget, it becomes evident that the proposed investments into the new areas of migration, security and defense require cuts in agricultural and regional policies, but at least the regional and cohesion policies are to some extent compensated by the transfer of funding programmes that are currently still delegated to other budget headings. As Table 6.2 shows, the agricultural policy (organized under the new heading 'natural resources and environment') could face a significant cut in overall investments and still a moderate decrease in terms of the share of the budget.

Table 6.2   *Changes in MFF headings 2014–2020 to 2021–2027 (ECA 2018: 10)*

MFF headings	Changes in billion EUR	Changes in percent	Percent of the overall MFF 2021–2027
Natural Resources and Environment	−63	−16	29.7
Cohesion and Values	+4.7	+1	34.5
European Public Administration	+4.8	+7	6.7
Neighbourhood and the World	+12.6	+13	9.6
Single Market, Innovation and Digital	+49.9	+43	14.6
Migration, Security and Defence	+43.1	+359	4.9

Table 6.3   *Proposed Changes of the MFF structure 2014–2020 to 2021–2027 (ECA 2018: 7)*

Programme	Amount of investment in billion EUR	Moves from heading of MFF 2014–2020 …	… to heading of MFF 2021–2027
Erasmus and others	16.6	1a: Competitiveness for Growth and Jobs	2: Cohesion and Values
Nuclear Safety	1.9	1a: Competitiveness for Growth and Jobs	4/5: Migration, Security and Defence
Food and Consumer	2.1	3: Security and Citizenship	1: Single Market, Innovation and Digital
Creative Europe	5.2	3: Security and Citizenship	2: Cohesion and Values
EU Aid initiative	0.3	4: Global Europe	2: Cohesion and Values
Union Civil Protection	0.1	4: Global Europe	4/5: Migration, Security and Defence

At first sight, these changes are quite fundamental. Closer inspection, however, reveals that the increase of investments in areas of new priorities are largely realized by proposing fresh money. As Table 6.3 indicates, the European Commission was much less motivated for reform in terms of the redistribution of funds across budget lines. The respective changes are limited, and sometimes only of symbolic nature. They are significant, however, in terms of one specific pattern. The EU Commission used substantial funds that were now delegated to the new heading of 'cohesion and values' in order to prevent a substantial decrease of investments in regional policy. This shows, on the one hand, that the path-dependent structure of the MFF is quite stable even at the level of established budget headings. On the other hand, it becomes obvious that the post-2020 MFF will mainly lose its innovative approach if Member States should reject to compensate for the British budget contribution.

6.3.4 The Revenue Side

The EU budget is mainly financed (roughly 70%) by national contributions of the Member States based on their respective GNI. The share of national contributions to the budget has steadily increased over the last decades. It is widely accepted that this development provides advantages and disadvantages. The main merits are that it allows for steady, reliable and predictable revenues, it corresponds with the principle of subsidiarity and it establishes a relatively fair system of burden sharing among Member States. The disadvantages are, however, that the dominance of national contributions support the juste retour logic, meaning the attitude of Member States' governments to evaluate their contributions on the basis of their individual financial benefits from the EU budget.

In February 2014, a 'High-level Group on Own Resources' was established to reflect on 'more transparent, simple, fair, and democratically accountable ways to finance the EU' (High Level Group on Own Resources, 2016). It was chaired by former European Commissioner, Mario Monti. The group comprehensively reviewed the structure of the MFF and made proposals that quite substantially deviate from the current situation (especially in terms of abolishment of all rebates and in view of a 'new mix' of own resources). The first reactions in the Council on the Monti-report revealed that many Member States do not show much appetite for a revision of the system of own resources. Sweden, Croatia, Poland, Latvia, Greece, Denmark, Germany and the Netherlands confirmed that the current system works well. Some of the cohesion countries, such as Romania, Hungary, Latvia and Greece, took the opportunity to express early on their interest to keep the so-called traditional policies (e.g. agriculture, cohesion) in place.[2] The German government, in an official report issued by the Federal Ministry of Finance, even argued that claims made by the European Parliament and the Commission to establish new tax-based own resources for the European Union, could be mainly motivated by political considerations, meaning that those taxes could broaden or strengthen competences at the European level.[3]

---

[2] 'Several finance ministers feel that the current system of resources works well', Agence Europe 27.01.2017.
[3] Bundesministerium der Finanzen, 2017: Hochrangige Arbeitsgruppe für Eigenmittel ('Monti-Gruppe'), Berlin, 23.02.2017.

This does not mean, however, that recommendations made by the Monti-Group will not play a role in the upcoming negotiations. One has to consider, that the group was equally comprised of representatives from all three EU institutions involved in the negotiations on the post-2020 MFF. Given that the final report was unanimously supported by all members of the group it is quite difficult to see how Member States' governments could fully ignore recommendations that were supported even by Council representatives. It can be, therefore, concluded that new own resources will play a certain role in the negotiation process. It also seems realistic that there will be a soft entry into that field at a relatively low impact level for the Member States. In this respect, the delegation of resources gained from the European Emission Trading System (ETS) would be a relevant candidate providing own resources stemming from a common European carbon tax. There will be, however, not a paradigmatic change away from the dominance of the national contributions. The simple reason is that all measures proposed by the Monti-Group score lower than the current own resources on the indicator of 'limiting political transaction costs' (High Level Group on Own Resources, 2016: 89).

6.4   CONTINUITY AND CHANGE AT THE PROCESS LEVEL

The negotiation process for the multiannual financial framework is traditionally characterized by two main factors: (a) the net-payer/net-receiver logic as the main basic conflict line, characterized by the stability of the actor's preferences and the creation of coalitions at the side of the Member States' governments; and (b) the importance of a reconciliation of interest between France and Germany as a dynamic factor that often paved the way for compromise. Looking at the upcoming negotiations for the post-2020 budget, there are indications that the stability of all three factors is diminishing which could cause much more intense debates than in the past.

6.4.1   The Net-payer/Net-receiver Logic

The net-payer vs. net-receiver logic, which has its origins mainly in Margaret Thatcher's fight since 1980 to reduce Britain's payments, has gradually intensified since 1998. Ahead of the preparations for the MFF 2006–2006, the first that fully integrated the ten Central and Eastern European countries, four net-contributor countries (Austria, Germany, the Netherlands, and Sweden) informed the European Commission that they consider their negative budgetary position as 'excessive relative to their prosperity' (Commission of the European Communities 1998: 23). Until December 2003 the group of net-contributors had further consolidated. Well before the negotiations on the MFF 2007–2013 six net-contributors (Austria, France, Germany, the Netherlands, Sweden, and the United Kingdom) published a letter in which they aired their common understanding to limit the overall ceiling of the MFF to 1% of the EU's GNI (Brehon and Kaiser 2013: 50). Only with the MFF 2014–2020, the net-contributor vs. net-beneficiary logic materialized in form of two 'camps' in which almost all Member States were organized: the net-contributors as the 'friends of better spending' (Austria, Finland, France, Germany, Italy, the Netherlands, and Sweden; but not the UK anymore) and the net-beneficiaries as the 'friends of cohesion' (Bulgaria, Czech Republic, Estonia, Greece, Hungary, Latvia, Lithuania, Malta, Poland, Romania, Slovakia, Slovenia, and Spain). Considering the outcome of the negotiations it can be said that the camp of the net-contributors 'scored a victory', mainly because they were in a much favourable strategic position vis-à-vis the net-beneficiaries whose camp was weakened by the fact that some of the members were already beneficiaries of stabilization funds offered during the Euro-crisis.

In general, it is quite likely that the net-contributor vs. net-beneficiary logic will prevail also in the upcoming negotiations, but under different premises. As Haas and Rubio (2017: 9) have shown, the net-contributors would be quite differently affected if the post-Brexit MFF would maintain the level of current spending, reduced only by the amount of EU transfers from the UK. Austria, Germany, the Netherlands and Sweden would be confronted with an increase of their national contributions by 14–16% while other members of the 'friends of better spending' would face a significantly lower increase of expenditures of about 7%. Apart from that, the four countries with the highest burden are also the countries that currently profit from a rebate on the British rebate, meaning that they must pay only 25% of their normal financing share needed to correct the British rebate. Therefore, these four countries might establish a coalition aimed at maintaining rebates even beyond 2020 as correction mechanisms for net-contributor countries.

Coalition building could become much more difficult compared to earlier negotiation rounds. This holds for the existing coalitions, but also for new interest formations. The 'friends of better spending' are already weakened by the fact that Britain as one of the strongest ally is not available anymore. Moreover, given that the French and German governments have already agreed to provide more financial resources to the European Union, the camp of the net-payers who clearly opt for a decrease of the budget after the Brexit has significantly lost influence. Similar to 2010–2013, the 'friends of cohesion' are also not very strong and united. This holds because of their divide between Euro-members and Non-Euro-members, but also in light of the fact that more and more EU Member States are on the brink of becoming net-payer countries. They could be more concerned about the change of certain rules for obtaining subsidies from the main expenditure programmes (see Section 6.5) and less about the overall amount of money available from them. And finally, the proposed reduction of the agricultural funds could provoke the establishment of another interest group, the 'friends of agriculture' (France, Ireland, Poland, Romania, and Spain). Some observers identified such a (less formal) group already for the negotiations on the MFF 2014–2020 (Thillaye, 2016: 38). Despite the lack of coherence, such an interest formation could render compromise extremely difficult, because those countries would have to decide between their interest in farm subsidies and their position along the net-payer/ net-receiver conflict line.

To sum up, the established logic of net-payers vs. net-receivers will again play a prominent role in the negotiations for the MFF 2021–2017. In contrast especially to the negotiations for the current MFF, however, their respective strategic capabilities to act in a united manner are far less clear. This could negatively impact on the process of consensus-seeking which traditionally benefited from relatively stable preferences.

6.4.2   The Franco-German Reconciliation of Interests

The Franco-German axis very often played a decisive role in the formulation of compromise on which all Member States finally could agree. This holds especially for the 'difficult cases', such as the MFF 2007–2013, the first one which fully integrated the ten new Central and Eastern European Member States which entered the Union in 2004. In 2005, during the pre-negotiation phase, France and Germany agreed on a 'quid pro quo' that paved the way for the consensus on the new MFF. While France agreed to the German claim to fully integrate the new Member States into the MFF, Germany supported France in terms of the continuation of the 2002 reform in EU agricultural policy (Brehon and Kaiser, 2013: 53).

A Franco-German initiative could play a crucial role also for the post-2020 MFF. The victory of Emmanuel Macron in the French presidential elections in May 2017 could help to bring some of his 'pro-EU-visions' on the table of the budget talks. In this respect, the most important role certainly plays the idea to establish a special budget for the Eurozone as well as the plan to set up a European Defence Funds that could be used to provide financial means both for the procurement of military equipment as well as for the financing of military research. The Eurozone budget certainly is a much more 'radical' approach, especially because it raises questions about the link and the relation between a Eurozone budget and the MFF. Unsurprisingly, the European Commission reacted to the idea of a Eurozone budget with restraint. In its 'Reflection Paper on the Deepening of the Economic and Monetary Union' (European Commission, 2017c), the French proposal is only casually mentioned. The Commission points out that such a budget 'may rather be a long-term goal, taking into account the relationship with the general EU budget over time with an increasing number of euro area countries' (European Commission, 2017c: 26).

As for now, it is not very clear whether a Eurozone budget will be discussed in the upcoming negotiations. There was, for sure, a 'window of opportunity' that opened with the federal elections in Germany (24 September 2017). The time span of about six to nine months between October 2017 and spring/summer 2018 was, however, not used, because of the long duration of coalition formation in Germany. Because of that, the most recent agreement between France and Germany on a Eurozone budget of about 20 billion Euro is not a very strong statement, especially since both sides did not agree yet on whether it should be part of the MFF or established outside.

6.5   CONTINUITY AND CHANGE AT THE POLICY LEVEL[4]

While there are many good reasons to be sceptical of path-breaking reforms at the structural level, there are indeed indications for considerable, but incremental, change at the instrumental level. This holds especially for changes in funding of research and innovation, new rules for the distribution of funds to the Member States and a more comprehensive use of new financial instruments.

6.5.1   Changes in Funding of Research and Innovation

Compared to the large-scale funds for agriculture and regional policies, the programmes supporting research and innovation are much smaller, but significantly more vulnerable. In 2015, the European Commission set up the European Fund for Strategic Investment (EFSI), mainly by using financial resources that were available from the programme for research and innovation. In establishing EFSI, Member States, both net-payers and net-receivers, accepted a cut of major instruments in support of R&I, i.e. Horizon 2020 and the Connect Europe Facility. In this they were in line with the Commission and – in the end – with the European Parliament. Therefore, funds originally delegated to support research have become victims of new policy initiatives

---

[4]   This section mainly draws on a recent study co-authored with Heiko Prange-Gstöhl (Kaiser and Prange-Gstöhl, 2017). The data presented in that study were mainly collected by expert interviews with representatives from European institutions and national governments.

for which money was needed, but not available under MFF regulations. There is a simple reason why especially the Horizon 2020 programme is a soft target for respective outflows of funds. It is the only major EU funding programme which does not have contractually-indented commitments for the whole MFF period. Horizon2020 therefore suffered again when the European Commission proposed a new initiative to support military research on 7 June 2017. 90 million Euro were taken away from the programme to support research and innovation in defence technology. For the period after 2020, the Commission proposed even higher investments of 500 million Euro to be provided under a dedicated 'Defence Research Programme'.[5] Consequently, even if there are currently demands for contributions of up to 100 billion Euro for research after 2020, it does not necessarily mean that this money would be available for the kind of research currently funded under Horizon2020.

There are also indications that the next framework programme for research and innovation will be even more industry-driven. The establishment of the European Innovation Council (EIC) and the newly established High-Level Group supporting the EIC are clear signals for a stronger pronunciation of innovation support at the expense of research funding. This might indicate a remarkable step away from the previous paradigm in EU research and innovation policy which always argued in favour of the need to better integrate and link research and innovation. It can be assumed that for certain elements currently funded under Horizon 2020 the level of investments will be kept or even increase. This certainly holds for the European Research Council which has an undisputed track record in terms of excellence and the European added value. The situation appears to be different for the funding of large-scale collaborative research projects which could come under pressure although this funding area is already characterized by over-subscription and under-financing. In this case, a significant benefit would stem from a greater flexibility within the MFF structure that could make 'classical' research funding less vulnerable in terms of upcoming financing needs.

6.5.2   New Rules for the Distribution of EU Funds to the Member States

For some time now, there is a controversial debate about stronger conditionality to be applied for the delegation of EU subsidies. There are mainly three reasons for that. Firstly, concerns about the compliance with the rule of law in

---

[5]   'A European Defense Fund: €5.5 billion per year to boost Europe's defense capabilities', European Commission Press Release, Brussels, 07.06.2017.

Poland and Hungary provoked statements, even by EU Commissioners,[6] about the need to withdraw funds if Member States do not respect basic norms of the EU Treaty. Secondly, during the migration crisis of 2015/2016 Member States that were willing to receive refugees argued that there was a lack of solidarity in the EU, because of the refusal of some Member States to participate in a mechanism to distribute refugees across EU countries. And thirdly, there are concerns that the main recipients of cohesion and regional funds do not sufficiently address the common economic policy objectives formulated under the so-called European Semester.

Therefore, it can be assumed that conditionality will be high on the agenda of the upcoming MFF negotiations and it will be most likely one of the most controversial topics. This is because there could be a clear switch from 'soft-conditionality', based on incentives to align national and regional programmes with European policy objectives, towards ex-ante conditionality that defines conditions which have to be in place before financial resources will be delegated (Kölling, 2017). The EU will enjoy quite a prosperous economic development at least in a short-term perspective, but it has largely failed to support a coherent economic development across the Member States. This indicates that there are very good reasons to establish new rules for the access to financial means provided through the cohesion, regional- and social funds. Given the problem of coherence, it seems plausible to make payments conditional on the implementation at the national level of the 'country-specific recommendations' developed and discussed during the annual 'European Semester'. Nevertheless, conflicts over conditionality could come up not only because of the conditions itself, but also about the process of evaluation of whether conditions have been met. The reason is that the European Commission proposed to use the so-called 'reverse qualified majority voting procedure', a mechanism under which the Commission can decide on its own as long as there is no qualified majority in the Council that rejects the proposal. This decision rule will most likely provoke criticism even from Member States that, in principle, support the idea of conditionality.

6.5.3 More Comprehensive Use of New Financial Instruments

The post-2020 MFF could also delegate more resources into 'new public-private co-financing instruments' such as the EFSI. There are several activities, currently funded under the Headings 1a and 1b, which would qualify for such arrangements. That would make resources available for activities which are

---

[6] 'Brüsseler Kommissarin droht Osteuropäern mit Geldentzug', Spiegel Online, 07.03.2017.

traditionally dependent on grants, such as the support of basic and pre-market applied research. Since the structural budget balance improves in most of the Member States it would also be plausible to make a shift from grants to credit-based financial means in regional policy at least for programmes to be implemented in the more developed regions.

6.6   CONCLUSIONS

This section was based on two competing assumptions concerning the post-2020 MFF: incremental adaption to the current European challenges vs. path-breaking change in consequence of a window of opportunity that opened because of the various crisis phenomena.

The analysis has shown that the first alternative seems to be much more plausible. There is, however, a critical condition. Incremental adaption will take place only if negotiations can take place as a 'normal' policy process. There are, however, certain risks that speak against the assumption of a normal policy process. On the one hand, there are the traditional risks – such as the resurgence of the Euro-crisis or political change in key Member States – but there are, on the other hand, also the risks especially those associated to the Brexit.

One of the main insecurities is to what extent the negotiations between the United Kingdom and the EU will affect the normal EU institutional policies (such as MFF negotiations). If the UK would accept an exit bill of up to 50 billion Euro, the EU's budget negotiations could easily go on without any risk of obstruction and blockade. If, however, there is no deal between the EU and the UK until 2019, there is, of course a high risk that the remaining EU Member States will not conclude their negotiations on the post-2020 MFF on time. As discussed before, the prolongation of the current MFF in form of annual budgets for 2021 (or even longer) would certainly not be accepted by the net-contributors. A significant reduction of the post-2020 MFF's ceiling will meet resistance from the net-beneficiaries, even if it could be argued that without a Brexit deal it is not possible to agree on issues with medium- to long-term consequences. That is why, as shown above, there was only a very short-term window of opportunity for path-breaking reforms under the premise of normal politics that seems to have already closed, but there could well be another one – with much more potential to change the logic of budget bargains – if the Brexit negotiations should fail.

REFERENCES

Brehon, J.-N. and Kaiser, R. (2013), Die Vorbereitung der mittelfristigen EU-Finanzplanung – Ambivalente Rolle des institutionalisierten

Bilateralismus, in C. Demesmay, M. Koopmann and J. Thorel (eds), *Die Konsenswerkstatt. Deutsch-französische Kommunikations- und Entscheidungsprozesse in der Europapolitik.* Nomos, Baden-Baden, pp. 47–65.

Campbell, J. L., Hollingsworth, J. R. and Lindberg, L. N. (1991), *Governance of the American Economy.* Cambridge University Press, Cambridge.

Commission of the European Communities (1998), 'Financing the European Union. Commission report on the operation of the own resources system', COM(1998)560 final, Brussels, 7 October.

European Commission (2017a), 'White Paper on the future of Europe. Reflections and scenarios for the EU27 by 2025', COM(2017)2025 final, Brussels, 1 March.

European Commission (2017b), 'Reflection paper on the future of EU finances', COM(2017)358, Brussels, 28 June.

European Commission (2017c), 'Reflection paper on the deepening of the economic and monetary union', COM(2017)291, Brussels, 31 May.

European Commission (2018), 'A modern budget for a union that protects, empowers and defends. The Multiannual Financial Framework for 2021–2027', Communication from the Commission to the European Parliament, the European Council, the Council, the European Economic and Social Committee and the Committee of the Regions, COM(2018)321 final, Brussels, 2 May.

European Council (2016), 'The Bratislava Declaration', Bratislava, 16 September.

European Council (2017), 'The Rome Declaration. Declaration of the Leaders of the 27 Member States, the European Parliament and the European Commission', Rome, 25 March.

European Parliament (2006), 'European Parliament Decision on the Conclusion of an Interinstitutional agreement on budgetary discipline and sound financial management: IIA on budgetary discipline and sound financial management' (2004/2099(ACI) – 2006/2028(ACI)), P6-TA(2006)0210, Strasbourg, 17 May.

European Parliament (2018), 'The next MFF: Preparing the Parliament's position on the MFF post-2020, European Parliament Resolution' (2017/2052(INI)), Strasbourg, 14 March.

Haas, J. and Rubio, E. (2017), 'Brexit and the EU budget: threat or opportunity'. Policy Paper, no. 183, Jacques Delors Institute, Berlin, 16 January.

Hall, P. A. (1986), *Governing the Economy. The Politics of State Intervention in Britain and France.* Oxford University Press, Oxford.

High Level Group on Own Resources (2016), 'Future financing of the EU – final report and recommendations of the High Level Group on Own Resources', Brussels, December.

Kaiser, R. and Prange-Gstöhl, H. (2017), 'The future of the EU budget. Perspectives for the funding of growth-oriented policies post-2020'. Report no. 6. Swedish Institute for European Policy Studies, Stockholm, September.

Kingdon, J. W. (1984), *Agendas, Alternatives, and Public Policies*. Little, Brown, Boston, MA.

Kölling, M. (2017), *Policy Conditionality – A New Instrument in the EU Budget Post-2020? European Policy Analysis 2017/1*. Swedish Institute for European Policy Studies, Stockholm, November.

March, J. G. and Olsen, J. P. (1989), *Rediscovering Institutions. The Organizational Basis of Politics*. Free Press, New York.

Marks, G. (1993), 'Structural policy and multilevel governance in the EC', in A. Cafruny and G. Rosenthal (eds), *The State of the European Community: Volume 2*. Lynne Rienner, Boulder, CO, pp. 391–411.

North, D. (1990), *Institutions, Institutional Change and Economic Performance*. Cambridge University Press, Cambridge.

Steinmo, S., Thelen, K. and Longstreth, F. (1992), *Structuring Politics. Historical Institutionalism in Comparative Analysis*. Cambridge University Press, Cambridge.

Thillaye, R. (2016), *Can the EU Spend Better? An EU Budget for Crisis and Sustainability*. Rowman & Littlefield, London/New York.

Tsebelis, G. (2002), *Veto Players. How Political Institutions Work*. Princeton University Press, Princeton, NJ.

7. Towards a closer Intergovernmental Union? The political implications of the 2021–2027 Multiannual Financial Framework negotiations

Matteo Scotto

7.1 INTRODUCTION

Any private or public budget is the outcome of a complex process of negotiation, where actors involved state their will based on compromises related to the goals, attitudes and ambitions of each single partner. This is also the case for the European Union (EU) budget. Despite the limited relative amount of EU public spending, the EU budget has always been characterized by political disputes (Begg, 2004, 2017) that have mirrored the EU's political and economic evolution.

This chapter argues that the political debate around the EU budget composition in the 2021–2027 period (European Commission, 2018a, b)[1] mirrored the state of the European project, namely an unsteady intergovernmental Union. According to Fabbrini (2016), an intergovernmental Union occurs when Member States and national governments try to exert the largest possible control of the policy-making process by institutionalizing the principle of

---

[1] In compliance with Art. 25 of the Council Regulation 1311/2013, the Commission should have presented a proposal for a new multiannual financial framework before 1 January 2018. Nevertheless, owing to Brexit and other impediments, the Commission postponed the proposal until 2 May 2018, when the Communication 'A Modern Budget for a Union that Protects, Empowers and Defends: The Multiannual Financial Framework for 2021–2027' was published and presented to the European Parliament and EU Council of Ministers. In response the European Parliament adopted two resolutions on 14 March and 30 May and it is now working at the Committee level on a new report that will be discussed in the plenary session of November 2018. Further information on the ongoing negotiation process is available at http://www.europarl.europa.eu/factsheets/en/sheet/29/multiannual-financial-framework.

coordination rather than cooperation. Bickerton et al. (2014) talk about a form of integration without supranationalism, meaning an approach to integration that does not necessarily involve the transfer of competencies from national to supranational level (see also Bickerton et al., 2015). As the theory on new intergovernmentalism suggests, in the post-Maastricht era the intergovernmental method has been the one adopted by national governments to deal with new policy areas traditionally related to core state powers (Genschen and Jachtenfuchs, 2015). Unlike the Single Market, with the supranational institutions such as the Commission and the European Court of Justice being the catalyst of integration, in the field of domestic and foreign affairs Member States did not foresee almost any relocation of competencies to the EU level. Moreover, the governance of the Eurozone and more generally of the Economic and Monetary Union in the years of crisis saw a clear consolidation of the intergovernmental approach, with consistent literature underlying the constitutional issues related to this phenomenon (Fabbrini, 2015). The difficulties of EU28 in reaching compromises in policy areas organized according to the intergovernmental method of coordination are well known. Migration is only one example of the unwillingness of Member States of finding structural and long-term solutions to common problems. Another example is constituted by the EU budget. This chapter argues that intergovernmentalism negatively affects EU budgetary policy and it is organized as follows. First, it will discuss the EU budget from procedural perspectives, identifying the intergovernmental features of budgetary policy up to the 2021–2027 period, in particular by discussing how the EU Own Resources are organized. Second, it will analyse the political debate both on the revenue and on the expenditure side in the negotiations leading to the Multiannual Financial Framework (MFF) 2021–2027. Finally, the last section will conclude by highlighting the reluctance of many Member States to deepen the integration also with respect to the EU budget.

7.2 INTERGOVERNMENTAL FEATURES OF THE EU BUDGET

Before going into the details of the EU budget, this section will briefly frame the issue of intergovernmentalism in the current debate on European integration. Intergovernmental features have emerged both at the institutional and at the procedural level. At an institutional level one may observe the increasing involvement of national governments in the decision-making processes as a result of the weakening of supranational institutions like the Commission or the European Parliament. This may happen either by means of a formal institutionalized gathering in the EU Council of Ministers, or by means of informal meetings that normally take place among Heads of States or Ministers before or alongside official summits. For instance, informal summits of EU Heads of States have been a common praxis in the economic governance during the financial crisis and are becoming a trend also in the management of migration, as the informal summit in Brussels ahead of the European Council of 28–29 June 2018 showed. On the procedural side, one may notice that the adoption of a voting system based on unanimity or *consensus*, instead of fully or partial majoritarian systems, limits the possibility to neutralize isolated interests. In addition, Member States have recently advanced intergovernmental integration by acting beyond the EU Treaties by means of intergovernmental treaties, such the Treaty on Stability, Coordination and Governance in the Economic and Monetary Union (the so-called Fiscal Compact), or intergovernmental organizations, such as the European Stability Mechanism. In this way, national governments (especially the most influential ones) preserve their veto power to control the decision-making process. Acting beyond the Treaties, avoiding in some cases the supervision of the European Court of Justice, has caused consistent critique in the literature with many scholars addressing the Union's constitutional problems of legitimacy (Fabbrini, 2015; Pernice et al., 2017). The bigger losers of the new Union's institutional arrangement are the Commission and the European Parliament. The former has in fact lost to a large extent its pivotal role in the European integration process acting more and more as the administrative branch of the executive power in the hands of the European Council. The European Parliament, which has experienced a growth in its institutional legitimacy from Maastricht to the Lisbon Treaty, including budgetary policy, is suffering from a marginalization both in the decision-making processes of key policy areas and in the Union's political sphere of influence.

The changes in budgetary policy advanced in the Lisbon Treaty have been the most significant since the Budgetary Treaties of 1970s[2] and since the Inter-Institutional Agreement of 1988.[3] When one looks at EU budget (Benedetto, 2012), it is important to understand whether the new institutional balance after Lisbon Treaty brings into budgetary policy a real capacity to achieve outcomes and reforms that might foster a closer Union. Art. 311 TFEU sets ambitious expectations in terms of budgetary policy vis-à-vis European citizens, stating that:

> The Union shall provide itself with the means necessary to attain its objectives and carry through its policies.

---

[2]   Budgetary Treaty of 1970, entered into force on 1 January 1971, and Budgetary Treaty of 1975, entered into force on 1 January 1977. Both treaties increased the power of the European Parliament and created the European Court of Auditors.

[3]   The Delors Packages culminated with the inter institutional agreement of 29 June 1988, which reinforced budgetary discipline and set the first medium-term financial perspectives 1988–1992.

However, an increase in the voting and control power of the European Parliament in budgetary decision processes is not enough to validate a real step forward in European integration. If on the one hand the European Parliament has gained some power in the negotiation process, structural reforms of the EU budget have become harder to achieve. An intergovernmental Union cannot in fact afford to produce any losers. As every actor involved has a substantial veto power, the major risk in structurally reforming a system is to leave someone out, which in the intergovernmental negotiation is not desirable or even feasible. In this context, one may argue whether the Lisbon Treaty made a reform of budgetary policy harder to achieve and what consequences the new arrangement brings in the 2021–2027 MFF negotiation process.

7.2.1   Own Resources

Own resources collected by the EU, created already in the Decision of 1970,[4] today represent 14% of total revenue and are constituted, to a large extent, by custom duties on imports from third countries, agricultural duties and sugar and iso-glucose levies. Value-added tax (VAT)-based and gross national income (GNI)-based Own Resources are both transfers to the Union from Member States corresponding to 10.9% and 65.4% respectively, meaning two-thirds of overall revenues (see Chapter 2). This makes the EU a union not only with a very limited commitment ceiling of around 1% of EU GNI, but also a union with most of the budget resting on transfers from Member States, which are the most relevant link between the Union and the European citizens. The discussion around genuine EU Own Resources has a strong political component. Member States have always been very reluctant to grant taxation authority to the EU, given that the power of taxation is historically one of the strategic powers that legitimate state and institutional building. Since its introduction, reforming the Union's budgetary system of Own Resources has traditionally required unanimity of the Member States. Not surprisingly, harsh discussions around Own Resources began as early as the 1970s with the first enlargements, especially as regarding the accession of the UK into the European Communities. Over the years, the new accessing countries took part to the budgetary negotiation process, thus bringing diverse interests and desires and making compromises harder to reach. Yet some reforms have occurred, although they have often been races to the bottom, like the reduction of VAT

---

[4]   In the first years of European Integration the European Economic Community and the Euratom were financed only with contributions from Member States. The Own Resources Decision of 21 April 1970 introduced for the first a time a system of own resources within the European Economic Community.

levy in 2007 or the rebates and compensation in various forms allowed to large net contributors to compensate for the UK's special treatment. In relation to the EU budget, national governments succeeded in promoting a decision-making mechanism that must take into account the national interests of the Member States. According to Art. 311 TFEU,

> The Council, acting in accordance with a special legislative procedure, shall unanimously and after consulting the European Parliament adopt a decision laying down the provisions relating to the system of own resources of the Union. In this context it may establish new categories of own resources or abolish an existing category. That decision shall not enter into force until it is approved by the Member States in accordance with their respective constitutional requirements.

In other words, it is not possible to modify either the EU budget size or its structure unless every Member State is in full agreement. The European Parliament (EP) has only a consultation power, meaning that the Parliament can submit its opinion, but the Council is not legally obliged to take the opinion into account. With the Lisbon Treaty the EP gained some power on the implementation process of budgetary policy, by obtaining the right of consent over implementation measures. The fourth paragraph of Art. 311 states that:

> The Council, acting by means of regulations in accordance with a special legislative procedure, shall lay down implementing measures for the Union's own resources system in so far as this is provided for in the decision adopted on the basis of the third paragraph. The Council shall act after obtaining the consent of the European Parliament.

This means that the Council has no power to overrule the EP's opinion and a regulation can be adopted only with the consent of the EP, which can accept or reject a legislative proposal. The consent requirement of the EP was a positive novelty introduced by the Lisbon Treaty compared with former Art. 269 TEC. However, the new power concerns only the implementation side of budgetary policy in the framework of the Own Resources Decision where the EP plays a marginal role. By considering the financial provision on EU Own Resources, it emerges that the aim of national governments has been to prevent any sort of structural reform of the system. Reluctance towards structural reforms, marginalization of supranational institutions, and monopolization of decision-making processes by national governments, both formally and informally, are all evidence of the new Union intergovernmental design (see Chapter 2). In the light of permanent difficulties in the negotiation process, both interinstitutional and among Member States, it is the politically feasible that tends to prevail (Begg, 2017).

7.3   POLITICAL IMPLICATIONS OF THE MFF 2021–2027: THE INTERGOVERNMENTAL CHALLENGE

7.3.1   The Role of Intergovernmental Institutions and of Member States in the MFF Adoption

The MFF represents the cornerstone of Union's financial discipline. After the Lisbon Treaty, it was transformed from an interinstitutional agreement into a legally binding act. It establishes on a minimum of five years' basis the framework and the priorities of Union's expenditure within the limits of Union's Own Resources. By introducing Art. 312 as regarding the basic requirements of the MFF, the Lisbon Treaty confirmed the intergovernmental balance of decision-making and made the amendment of the MFF more difficult (Benedetto, 2011). Art. 312 TFEU states that

> The Council, acting in accordance with a special legislative procedure, shall adopt a regulation laying down the multiannual financial framework. The Council shall act unanimously after obtaining the consent of the European Parliament, which shall be given by a majority of its component members.

The regulation laying down the MFF, by means of a special legislative procedure, has to be agreed by unanimity in the Council and the EP is only entitled to give its consent to the regulation by a majority of votes. The consent requirement increased, as a matter of fact, the power of the EP, which can put pressure on the Council as already happened in the past. However, one can observe that in the financial provision regulating the expenditure side of EU budget, it is the intergovernmental approach that prevails, by concentrating the power to shape budgetary policy in the hands of national executives. This is well demonstrated by Art. 312 (2), according to which

> The European Council may, unanimously, adopt a decision authorizing the Council to act by a qualified majority when adopting the regulation referred to in the first subparagraph.

Art. 312 introduces a *passerelle clause* for the adoption of the MFF regulation in compliance with Art. 48 (7) TEU, which allows derogation in some policy area either from special legislative procedure to ordinary legislative procedure or from voting by unanimity to qualified majority voting, thus simplifying in both scenarios the adoption of a legislative act. Nevertheless, an agreement on the application of a *passerelle clause* is complicated to reach and requires the consent by every national Parliament, which can veto the initiative within six months. As a consequence, owing once again to a double level of intergovernmental check, the activation of the *passerelle clause* is unlikely, as Member States possibly in disagreement with the MFF regulation would never run the risk of being overrun. If ever the European Council finds a consensus on the *passerelle clause* notifying its decision to national Parliaments, every government has a second chance at home to lobby in Parliament against such decisions by fuelling the traditional anti-EU sentiment. Everything considered, this multilevel decision-making system grounded on consensus provides the Member States with the guarantee that the agreement on MFF shall produce no loser. Finally, owing to the annual ceiling on expenditure provided for with Art. 312 (3), stating that

> The financial framework shall determine the amounts of the annual ceilings on commitment appropriations by category of expenditure and of the annual ceiling on payment appropriations. The categories of expenditure, limited in number, shall correspond to the Union's major sectors of activity.

The Commission has no margin of manoeuvre, nor the flexibility to propose an extension of the budget in the Union's full interests. To sum up, as regarding MFF regulation, Member States have a *de facto* monopoly on shaping the long-term EU budget together with a veto power on provision amendments and reforms anchored in a context of rigidity in spending only adjustable by the national executives themselves. Concerning the approval of the annual budget, to which extensive literature has been dedicated (see, among others, Benedetto and Hoyland, 2007; Laffan and Lindner, 2005), Art. 314 TFEU follows basically a procedure of Co-decision giving the Council and the EP the same power. However, as well demonstrated by Benedetto, Arts 314 and 315

> entrench the current budgetary status quo. [...] amendment to the annual budget is more difficult and overall rejection is easier. Previously, the EP could reject an annual budget if it wished to push for reform or to disapprove of the Council's control over compulsory expenditure, knowing that by a three-fifths majority it could safeguard all its gains in the field of non-compulsory expenditure during the application of monthly budgets under provisional twelfths. The EP now has the ability only to cut those monthly budgets. [...] Under the new rules [Lisbon Treaty], the EP's only available tactic in the monthly budgets would have been to cut spending in areas prioritised by the governments.

Again, it appears that the legal framework created by the Lisbon Treaty on short-term budgetary policy, which is by now very visible in its application, has been organized in order to limit room for amendment and consequently to preserve the status quo settled by national governments.

7.3.2   MFF 2021–2027: Facts and Figures

On 5 May 2018, the Commission advanced the proposal for a modern EU budget that protects, empowers and defends. The aim of this subsection is to identify where, within the Commission's proposal, the intergovernmental features previously analysed will pave the way for possible political disputes that might bear negative consequences for European integration. President Juncker raised ambitions and expectations stating that the new budget would represent an opportunity to shape the future of EU27 and to enhance cohesion and solidarity. Commissioner Oettinger confirmed Juncker's statement saying that 'this budget proposal is truly about EU added value. We invest even more in areas where one single Member State cannot act alone or where it is more efficient to act together'.[5] The MFF 2021–2027 will be the first of EU 27 after the UK leave the Union and beyond Brexit it has to face crucial political challenges including migration, social problems, security, external threats, digital economy, and climate change. The final goal of Commission's proposal is to set new priorities of EU spending and proposing at the same time a revision of Own Resources to match the new objectives. The Commission proposes an overall budget up to €1.135 trillion maintaining the degree of expenditure of last MFF, which considering Brexit means a slight increase of general GNI from 1.03% to 1.11% (see Chapter 2). Moreover, exploiting the Brexit scenario, the proposal aims at simplifying the complex system of rebates by eliminating all current rebates in order to avoid further matters of complaint (see Chapter 12).

A major proposal is the adoption of a new instrument of conditionality that should make access to funds dependent on the respect of rule of law. Using the financial risks as a loophole to justify deficiencies caused by the disrespect of the rule of law, the Commission is trying to find guarantees for the respect of EU common values in times when some Member States are questioning liberal democracy in Europe. After the proposal of the Commission, the decision should be adopted by the Council by a reverse quality majority voting, thus raising the chances of success of the Commission's initiative. This is probably the strongest political take of the Commission that might trigger further political disputes. Another relevant innovation comes from EU sources of revenue, based on the work conducted by the so-called Monti Report published in December 2016 (High Level Group on Own Resources, 2016). The attempt is to introduce a basket of new Own Resources, while reducing at the same time traditional sources of revenues more exposed to political speculation

---

[5]   See   http://europa.eu/rapid/press-release_IP-18-3570_en.htm   (accessed   3 September 2018).

against the Union. With a reduction from 20% to 10% of Member States's 'collection costs' deriving from custom duties, together with a simplification of the VAT-based Own Resource, the new sources of revenue consist of a 20% share in revenues from the Emission Trading System; 3% corporate tax and a national contribution based on the amount of non-recycled plastic packaging waste in each Member States, with a potential sum up to €22 billion per year representing 12% of the total EU budget.

On the spending side, a concrete shift in expenditure has been advanced by the Commission. The Commission has decided to intervene in traditional bulky chapters of EU budget such as Common Agricultural Policy and Cohesion Policy by proposing a reduction of around 5% in alignment with a more efficient and targeted allocation of funds, designated to two policy areas, namely competitiveness and security. Concerning the former, there has been an increase of 50% of resources for innovation and research, consolidating the Horizon Europe and Euratom programmes by €100 billion and the funds dedicated to digital economy by €25 billion. New targets include a budget for the stabilization of the EMU with a Reform Support Programme (overall budget of €25 billion) to support structural reforms and accession membership to the monetary union, together with a European Investment Stabilization Function (€30 billion) to face periods of negative economic cycles and asymmetric shocks. As far as security is concerned, there has been a clear attempt to strengthen the Union's financial effort on migration and asylum policy, by increasing the spending on the protection of external borders (€33 billion for the employment of 10,000 border guards by 2027). Furthermore, there has been stronger financial support for security policy (€4.8 billion) with the creation of a defence fund of €13 billion, for supporting research in innovation of military capabilities, technologies and infrastructures. The external action service is also a beneficiary of the new EU budget with an increase of 26%.

Overall, the Commission's proposal does not present relevant changes in terms of the budget's size and the overall amount of 1.11% GNI is in line with the past. Yet, within the limited EU budget, the Commission has tried to advance substantial modifications that redefine both the sources of revenues and the allocation of funds in the light of the new political challenges the EU has to face.

7.3.3 Political Disputes and Intergovernmental Challenges

After having highlighted the intergovernmental features of EU budgetary policy and after having outlined a general overview of the Commission's proposal concerning EU budget 2021–2027, this subsection will take into consideration the possible political dispute of the current negotiation process identifying where intergovernmentalism might potentially take root more consistently. After the Commission's proposal, as explained in the introduction to this chapter, the Council has to put forward the decision by unanimity with the consent of the European Parliament, which means that the Member States have to find compromises accommodating their specific interests and within the Commissions's MFF draft.

The first problem the Commission has to face is in regard to the size of the EU budget, which presents no reduction in the level of expenditure despite the UK leaving the Union. Even though some of the largest Member States, such as Germany and France, are likely to accept increasing contributions, there is already a group of countries contesting the Commission's decision of not exploiting Brexit to make the EU budget smaller. Moreover, it is not yet clear how the Commission will manage to negotiate the votes of countries like Sweden and the Netherlands, which will represent an obstacle to the proposal for the new size of the EU budget. The same difficulties might emerge from the discussion around conditionality, the instrument the Commission put into place to secure EU funding to the respect for the rule of law. The Visegrád group (Poland, Hungary, Czech Republic and Slovakia), Bulgaria and Romania have shown some impatience concerning the new mechanism, as it could undermine the position they have recently been consolidating in Brussels. Owing to internal political transformation, sceptical EU Member States have also found it easier to find potential allies to oppose pro-European decisions in diverse negotiation tables. For this reason, it cannot be excluded that, within a system of veto, that Central European countries will find compromises with Northern European Member States, by negotiating conditionality with the EU budget size.

The new shift on the expenditure side may also represent a highly disputed political battlefield, with opposition coming not only from Member States with recent EU membership. When it comes to the agricultural policy and the Commission's proposal to reduce the budget by up to 5%, strong opposition will probably emerge from traditional beneficiaries of such policies, like France. The latter will also oppose any attempt at the re-nationalization of part of the agricultural policy for a more efficient distribution of funds. As far as cohesion policy is concerned, countries from Central Europe will be very reluctant to renounce EU funds that crucial for their economies, which means that also in this case compromises on budget reduction will not be easy to reach. Moreover, decisions over criteria for the distribution of a smaller EU budget designated to poorer regions may provoke negative competition between Central and Southern European countries, both beneficiaries of cohesion policy. The choice lies between a mechanism based on national income, endorsed by Central European members, and a mechanism that takes into account growth and unemployment rate, thus favouring Southern countries.

Other possible criteria for the assignment of funds may be the attitude towards migration and/or the numbers of migrants hosted by a country.

Investments in new policy areas like climate and environmental protection may represent potential scenarios for political disputes. As far as energy policy is concerned, for instance, tough negotiation is foreseen as regarding coal use for energy production. Within the Union there are still Member States like Poland with significant coal production for the sustainment of the economy. This will produce conflicts with countries, especially Northern European countries, which have undergone big investments to make their economies less harmful for the environment. The same scenario may come out from investments in innovation, digital economy and infrastructure. Countries which present a less developed digital economy are afraid that the new investments will reach only those countries that have the capacity to implement projects in the field of new technologies, thus criticizing a scarce progressive system of distribution of funds. With respect to security and defence, despite the large consensus gathered around the recent agreement on Permanent Structured Cooperation, there are a still few countries that do not fully agree with the strengthening of EU defence policy, with concrete risks that they will use it as a leverage for other policy areas.

Overall, in the negotiation for the 2021–2027 MFF both spending in traditional policy areas like agricultural and cohesion and expenditure in new policy areas like digital economy and innovation will represent harsh political battlefields, which the 27 Member States and the EU Institutions have to face within a negotiation process of consensus-building and cross-fire vetoes.

7.4   CONCLUDING REMARKS

The critical aspects of the Commission's proposal and the intergovernmental architecture of the EU budgetary policy are closely interconnected. The Lisbon Treaty contributed to creating a legal framework where budgetary policy is constrained by a rigidity in spending and levying new taxes and by mechanisms that prevent those ceilings to be modified. Owing to the presence of intergovernmental checks and double-checks across the budgetary procedures, the EU has adopted a short-sighted conservative system with the primary aim of preserving itself against impeding reforms of any kind. Designed without long-term perception of EU political risk, within the prudent new legal framework introduced by the Lisbon Treaty, the budgetary policy was not considered a decisive policy that might have been crucial for European integration a few years later. The self-confidence of a given historical path for European integration has brought the Member States to create a budgetary system with few capabilities to make a real difference and to adapt to social transformations in Europe.

The Commission proposal for MFF 2021–2027 was characterized by a realistic approach that took into serious consideration the reluctance of many Member States to deepen European Integration. The Commission seemed to be aware of how the decision-making system may trigger political conflicts between different groups of Member States. There were no big changes in budget size, nor strong attempts to change the *status quo*.

Given the turbulent times the EU was facing and the unsteady intergovernmental architecture, the MFF 2021–2027 did not constitute an important factor in the economic, social and political development of the EU. The conservative attitudes of the Member States hampered the capacity of the MFF 2021–2027 to represent, even symbolically, a concrete advance in the European integration process envisaged by the EU Commission.

REFERENCES

Begg, I. (2004), 'Future fiscal arrangements of the European Union', *Common Market Law Review*, 41, 775–794.

Begg, I. (2017), 'The EU's finances: can the economically desirable and the politically feasible be reconciled?' College of Europe Paper, 30 November.

Benedetto, G. (2011), 'Reform of the EU budget: does the Treaty of Lisbon make thing easier?' Centre for the Study of Political Change, CIRCAP Occasional Paper no. 25/2011.

Benedetto, G. (2012), 'Budget reform and the Lisbon Treaty', in G. Benedetto and S. Milio (eds), *European Union Budget Reform: Institutions, Policy and Economic Crisis.* Palgrave, Basingstoke, pp. 40–58.

Benedetto, G. and Hoyland, B. (2007), 'The EU annual budgetary procedure: the existing rules and proposed reforms of the Convention and Intergovernmental Conference, 2002–04', *Journal of Common Market Studies*, 45 (3), 565–587.

Bickerton, C. J., Hodson, D. and Puetter, U. (2014), 'The new intergovernmentalism: European integration in the post-Maastricht era', *Journal of Common Market Studies*, 53 (4), 703–722.

Bickerton, C. J., Hodson, D. and Puetter, U. (eds) (2015), *The New Intergovernmentalism: States and Supranational Actors in the Post-Maastricht Era.* Oxford University Press, Oxford.

European Commission (2018a), 'A new, modern Multiannual Financial Framework for a European Union that delivers efficiently on its priorities post-2020'. The European Commission's contribution to the Informal Leaders' meeting on 23 February 2018, COM(2018)98 final, Brussels, 14 February.

European Commission (2018b), 'A modern budget for a Union that protects, empowers and defends. The Multiannual Financial Framework for 2021–2027', COM(2018)321 final, Brussels, 2 May.

Fabbrini, F. (2015) 'The new architecture of EMU and the role of the courts: lessons from the crisis', in E. Dubout et al. (eds), *Union européenne et fédéralism économique.* Brussels: Bruylant.

Fabbrini, S. (2016), 'From consensus to domination: the intergovernmental union in a crisis situation', *Journal of European Integration*, 38, 587–599.

Genschen, P. and Jachtenfuchs, M. (2015), 'More integration, less federation: the European integration of core state powers', *Journal of European Public Policy*, 23, 42–59.

High Level Group on Own Resources (2016), 'Future financing of the EU'. Final report and recommendations of the High Level Group on Own Resources. Brussels, December.

Laffan, B. and Lindner, J. (2005) 'The budget', in H. Wallace et al. (eds), *Policy-making in the European Union.* Oxford University Press, Oxford.

Pernice, I., Papadopoulou, L. and Weiler, J. H. H. (eds), (2017), *Legitimacy Issues of the European Union: Lessons from the Financial Crisis.* Nomos, Baden-Baden.

PART II

Legal and economic profiles

8. The EU budget and the MFF between flexibility and unity

Peter Becker

8.1 INTRODUCTION

The Multiannual Financial Framework (MFF) 2014–2020 is the first framework that has been negotiated and decided under the legal requirements of the Treaty of Lisbon. With the Lisbon treaty, the MFF has been incorporated into primary law and enshrined in a formal regulation. The MFF provides the European Union (EU) with an instrument in its budgetary policy to strike a reliable balance between, on the one hand, predictability and the capability for multiannual planning of budgetary policy and, on the other, the need for policy adaptability and responsiveness. However, the Lisbon Treaty could not break the tendency to prolong the status quo of the Union's budgetary policy and system (see Chapter 7). Since the adoption of the first MFF (or at that time called 'Financial Perspective') in 1988 the system has developed into a well-oiled negotiating process in which most conflicts are predictable, and roles are largely known and accepted (Becker, 2012). The focus on net contributions and *juste retour* dominate the policy and increase the reluctance of Member States to even consider any significant and ambitious option for reform. Narrowly defined national interests are superseding and replacing true European interests and the need for a better budget. The participants prefer to agree on the lowest common denominator in a familiar procedure rather than becoming entangled in conflicts that an ambitious and significant initiative to modernize and reform the European budget would involve – especially given that it would contain the risk of the negotiations failing. So far, the unifying link between all actors in the negotiations is their interest in striking a compromise at the end of the process. Realizing a new MFF is still more important than negotiating a better MFF.

This unusual budgetary system and negotiation procedure ensures that the MFF negotiations end in an unchallenged consensus that guarantees seven years of budgetary stability and planning security. The flipside of this system, however, is a distinct status quo bias and a low willingness to reform

(Benedetto, 2013). The convenient but at the same time unsatisfactory stability and predictability of the MFF compromise weighs heavier than the uncertainty and insecurity of potential policy change and a fundamental reform. Around 80% of the EU budget is already fixed for seven years at the beginning of the MFF period and this means that it is very difficult for the EU to respond to unforeseen challenges. Setting the budget headings and their funding for seven years makes the MFF and the European budget in general very inflexible. Because the total volume of the MFF is set and the shares of the individual policy areas are fixed, the Union can only respond in a limited way and slowly to new political circumstances and challenges.

Budgetary stability hence means also budgetary rigidity and inflexibility. There are experiences proving that the EU is incapable of responding quickly and comprehensively to unexpected challenges, such as the insufficient financial assistance out of the EU budget to Member States worst hit by the migrant crisis. As a result, there were once more calls for making the EU budget more flexible. Therefore, an even classical point of reform of the EU's budgetary system and policy is to find a feasible relationship and interaction between the necessary ability to react quickly to new political challenges and the interest of the Member States in medium-term stability and predictability of MFF resources and spending policies.

Flexibility and predictability are two fundamental principles of budgetary policy. In principle, all actors involved in European budgetary policy can subscribe to the necessity to increase budgetary flexibility. However, this aim is closely connected with institutional powers and hence with the fundamental principles of legitimacy, transparency and scrutiny of European budgetary policy. Whereas in general the executive power is more interested in budgetary flexibility because this will increase its leeway of policy-making, the legislative power usually is interested in budgetary reliability and stability guaranteeing its budgetary monitoring and scrutiny rights. So far, the two arms of the European legislature, the European Parliament (EP) and the Council, have always combined their agreement to extend the Commission's budgetary flexibility with a parallel strengthening of their budgetary participation and control rights. It is foreseeable that this combination of budgetary flexibility and political control will also be an issue in the current negotiations on the next MFF 2021–2027.

This chapter tries to discuss this conflict and dilemma between the political necessity of budgetary flexibility and the wish for budgetary stability and predictability, hence the tension between two fundamental principles of budgetary policy. The first principle, the need for budgetary flexibility, will be discussed in the following section, which also presents the current flexibility instruments in the EU's budgetary policy. The next section then describes the second principle, the principle of unity and unitarity of the budget and its exceptions in European policy. The most fundamental exception could become a special budget for the Eurozone, which is discussed in the following section. Finally, the chapter tries to draw conclusions for European budgetary policy in general and for the negotiations on the MFF 2021–2027 in particular.

8.2 THE FLEXIBILITY OF AND INSIDE THE EUROPEAN BUDGET

Attempts to increase the flexibility of the European budget are as old as the MFF (respectively the Financial Perspective). Since the first Delors financial package, the financial perspective for 1988–1992, various flexibility elements have been successively introduced into the financial framework, such as a separate flexibility instrument since 1999 and a solidarity fund and revision clauses since 2002. In its proposal for the next multiannual financial framework 2021–2027 the European Commission also called for 'increasing flexibility within and between programmes, strengthening crisis management tools and creating a new "Union Reserve" to tackle unforeseen events and to respond to emergencies in areas such as security and migration' (European Commission, 2018b, p. 5). In its reflection paper on the future of EU finances of 28 June 2017 (European Commission, 2017b), the Commission had already mentioned these elements for increasing budgetary flexibility and in its contribution to the informal meeting of the European Council on 23 February 2018, the Commission also stressed the importance and urgency of greater budgetary flexibility: 'This will be essential to adapting to new needs and unstable geopolitical and domestic conditions' (European Commission, 2018a, p. 15). In addition, the EP in its resolution of 4 March 2018 emphasized the importance of budgetary flexibility and called for greater flexibility instruments (European Parliament, 2018, para. 26 and following).

Whereas the definition of budgetary flexibility is uncontested and all actors in the European budget negotiations agree in principle to the necessity to increase flexibility, the way to achieve this objective and the instruments to be used are strongly disputed. Flexibility in European budgetary policy is, according to the widely shared understanding, the 'ability to adjust to changing circumstances' which 'may take the shape of unforeseen and uncontrollable events' (Mijs and Schout, 2015, pp. 2–3). Budgetary flexibility shall make European funds available to react to unexpected political events like crisis and emergency situations. Hence, the primary goal of flexibility in the European budget and especially the MFF is to provide the best instruments and maximum fiscal leeway to make the MFF with its multiannual programs more responsive to political challenges. However, flexibility is more than just keeping European funds available when needed. Because any budget is the expression of political priorities and the 'life-blood of the government' (Wildavsky, 1961, p. 184), the

MFF not only sets budgetary priorities but defines also the Union's political priorities for seven years. Flexibility in budgetary policy, hence, includes also the possibility to re-define political priorities in the case of new circumstances and challenges, and then subsequently to change the spending priorities of the European budget.

A more flexible use of the MFF would therefore require the concession of greater political autonomy for the EU and especially the European Commission in interpreting the need for action and the scope of funding. The Commission will become the responsible European institution to recognize, justify and implement a change of priorities in the political framework or a European concern and, as a result, the need to reallocate budgetary resources. The Commission itself defines budgetary flexibility, 'as the margin for manoeuvre at the disposal of the Commission and the budgetary authority (BA) to meet unforeseen needs or new priorities in one or more expenditure headings, and/ or the possibility to modify the financial framework profile across different budgetary years' (European Commission, 2004, p. 1).

This means flexibility also affects the process of European budgetary policy and decision-making. Various options are feasible to enhance budgetary flexibility in the EU:

1. To reform the structure of the MFF and to reduce the number of headings, thus making it easier to shift European funds from one spending priority to another while avoiding the necessity to re-negotiate the MFF. This means, in practice, the fewer MFF-headings there are, the easier the possibility to change spending priorities.
2. To create a formal and regular MFF midterm review providing the option to adapt the MFF to new challenges in the middle of the MFF period.
3. To change the duration of the MFF, which means to increase the frequency of negotiating a MFF. The shorter the MFF duration, the more often the possibility arises to change MFF spending priorities.
4. To reform the MFF decision-making process and to skip the hurdle of unanimity. The easier and quicker the decision-making is, the easier it will be to change the MFF and to adapt it.
5. Introducing budgetary flexibility instruments in the narrow sense by making additional funds available in specific situations, either inside or outside the MFF, and by margins within the MFF spending policies.

However, the scope, degree and substance of these flexibility options vary. Some of these instruments tend to increase flexibility by reforming the decision-making process on the European budget and some elements try to increase the fiscal flexibility of the budget. Already the MFF 2007–2013 included some elements to increase budgetary flexibility, such as the possibility to revise the MFF ceilings and some special flexibility instruments.

Especially flexibility instruments in the narrow sense have always been a point of conflicting views between the Member States and the EP when negotiating the MFF. Various elements and instruments of this flexibility have been agreed and integrated into European budgetary policy and the MFF. Four new funds should, if necessary, make additional resources available above the MFF ceilings (Jones, 2010). The MFF 2014–2020 included various instruments to increase budgetary flexibility (Rubio, 2017; Núñez Ferrer et al., 2016): a special flexibility instrument; two margins, one for payments and one for commitments; the contingency margin and three special instruments outside the MFF ceilings for specific purposes (Emergency Aid Reserve, European Solidarity Fund and European Globalization Fund).

Most of these instruments and funds of budgetary flexibility remain outside the MFF and are not part of the MFF ceilings. The objective is to allow the EU in a specific political situation to mobilize additional funds above the tight expenditure ceilings. The MFF 2014–2020 foresaw several old and new instruments (legally enshrined in the MFF Regulation and the accompanying inter-institutional agreement[1]) which cannot be run by multiannual programmes and are designed to increase budgetary flexibility (Rubio, 2017). In the framework of the MFF midterm revision in 2016, these instruments and their available amounts have been reformed (Becker, 2016):

1. Emergency Aid Reserve, designed to finance specific humanitarian aid and civilian crisis operations in non-EU countries. The financial volume of the reserve was raised in 2017 in the framework of the MFF midterm revision from originally €280 million per year to €300 million/year. Unused monies can be carried over for up to one year.
2. Solidarity Fund, to provide financial aid following a major disaster in a Member State or candidate country. This aid is managed by the recipient country and will be used to rebuild basic infrastructure, emergency services, temporary accommodation or clean-up operations, or counter immediate health risks. The fund includes €500 million per year and unused funds can be carried over for up to one year.
3. European Globalization Adjustment Fund, financing specific support to facilitate the reintegration of workers into employment after they have lost their jobs because of a result of major structural changes in world trade

---

[1]   See Interinstitutional Agreement of 2 December 2013 between the European Parliament, the Council and the Commission on budgetary discipline, on cooperation in budgetary matters and on sound financial management, Official Journal of the European Union 2013/C 373/01, 20 December 2013.

patterns or as a consequence of global economic crisis. The volume of this fund is €150 million per year.

4. Flexibility instrument, providing funding for specific expenses which could not be covered by one heading of the EU budget without exceeding the expenditure in the MFF. As a consequence of the MFF midterm review this instrument has now €600 million per year at its disposal and unused funds can be carried over for up to three years.

5. Global margins for payments, to carry over unused payment appropriations and margins from one financial year to the next, although under certain conditions and within the overall ceilings set in the MFF. This adjustment is the task of the European Commission as part of the yearly technical adjustment of the budget. The upward adjustment has to be offset by a corresponding reduction of the payment ceiling in the next year in order to leave the overall MFF ceiling unchanged. Moreover, the adjustments must respect maximum limits as set in the MFF regulation (€7 billion in 2018, 11 billion in 2019 and 13 billion in 2020).

6. Global margins for commitments, which opens the possibility to use unused funds below the MFF ceilings in the years 2014–2017 to increase the commitment appropriations in 2016–2020 for measures to increase growth and employment (in particular, youth employment). The Commission calculates these margins every year in the framework of the technical adjustment of the EU budget and proposes to use the margins in its proposal for the next annual budget or an amending budget.

7. The contingency margin is a last resort instrument to increase commitment and payment appropriations up to 0.03% of EU's GNI. The Commission calculates every year the amount available for this margin and proposes to use the contingency margin in the annual budget procedure. The margin hence is an instrument to react to unforeseen circumstances.

8. Two special flexibility instruments to frontload the youth employment initiative and the European programmes for education and research (ERASMUS, Horizon, COSME) with up to €2.5 billion for the years 2014–2017.

9. The revision of structural funds to transfer unused cohesion policy allocations from 2014 to subsequent years (up to €21.1 billion), because of the delayed adoption of programmes.

Some of these flexibility instruments, such as the European Solidarity Fund or the Emergency Aid Reserve, are emergency ones and can be mobilized by the two branches of the EU budgetary authority, the EP and the Council, in case of unforeseen events like natural disasters. This means, that the incidents triggering the mobilization of these funds are not predictable and it thus is not possible to plan the financial usage of these tools.

In order to limit their application, however, the Council urged that the scope of the instruments (with the exception of the flexibility instrument) has to be clearly defined. Using these instruments in the EU's annual budgets is a problem only if the amounts actually required differ from the amounts provided for in the MFF and exceed the maximum ceilings. Hence, the binding ceilings set by the MFF are the real problem. To incorporate the flexibility tools into the MFF, it is necessary to estimate payment schedules ex ante and thus to plan them over the duration of seven years. This seems inappropriate and may not be possible.

A number of additional instruments have been added to the flexibility ones that were agreed under secondary legislation in the course of the European poly-crisis. These include the crisis instruments for stabilizing the Eurozone, such as European Financial Stability Facility (EFSF) or European Stability Mechanism (ESM), a series of regional trust funds for special foreign policy tasks, such as the Emergency Aid Fund for Africa, for the peace process in Colombia, or as a European response to the Syrian civil war (Madad Trust Fund). They also include trust funds to finance military operations in the context of security and defence policy, such as the Athena Mechanism, or to finance measures in the wake of the refugee crisis, such as the Fund for Refugees in Turkey (Carrera et al. 2018).

Most of these flexibility instruments are kept outside the MFF ceilings and according to the Parliament's interpretation can be mobilized above the expenditure ceilings. In principle, the Council and the Member States are also in favour of increased budgetary flexibility (which can increase their political room for manoeuvre, especially in unexpected situations), but they are more restrictive with respect to the question of whether these margins could be used above or outside the agreed MFF ceilings. The insistence to keep the flexibility instruments under the MFF ceilings highlights their interest in stability and in predictability of the complete MFF. This predictability reduces the flexibility of the budget and the ability to react to changing circumstances. The more the EP stressed the need for new and bigger flexibility instruments and margins, the harder the Member States fought for low MFF ceilings, especially for the payment appropriations, and for rigid multiannual spending programmes (Benedetto, 2013). Mijs and Schout argue, that in 'practice the European Parliament used the phrase "flexibility" to introduce ex-ante control mechanisms to maximize expenditure' (Mijs and Schout, 2015, p. 4). Furthermore, the Parliament always ensures that its rights of budgetary participation, monitoring and scrutiny are not hampered by an excessive reduction in the volume of the Union's budget and thus in the EU's political scope. Consequently, the EP always links its call for the inclusion of flexibility instruments in the EU budget with the application of the Community method in the adoption of the legal bases and thus with its own co-decision rights. For the Council, the

EP's demand to increase budgetary flexibility is then an attempt to extend its legislative powers. The Member States therefore see Parliament's insistence as a power game over additional legislative rights. Even if this accusation is exaggerated, it shows that the argument to make the Union's budget more flexible might also become a cause for institutional conflicts and power games between the two branches of the European budgetary authority (see Chapter 3).

As result of this struggle, the Council agreed to new flexibility instruments, but restricted the margins. The annual budgets, which have to respect the MFF ceilings, operate close to spending limits leaving only few margins for unplanned expenditure and to tackle unforeseen events (Rubio, 2017). Both the Council and the Parliament opted for special instruments outside the MFF, providing additional budgetary flexibility for European policy-making by keeping the stability and predictability of the MFF untouched. However, these instruments outside the MFF – and above the ceilings – are narrowly limited in their financial volume and constructed for one very specific political purpose. They only slightly increased the political room for manoeuvre of the EU.

In the negotiations launched for the MFF 2021–2027, the European Commission is obviously again seeking to increase budgetary flexibility and its policy room for manoeuvre. The Commission calls for a much 'more flexible and agile budget'. It proposes that the small support programmes should be combined into large instruments in order to make it easier and faster to reallocate and redistribute EU funds within and between the new multiannual programmes. In addition, reserves are to be created within the programmes. It also proposes reforming the previously limited possibility of reallocating EU funds between expenditure headings and between financial years without a ceiling for reallocations. It wants to strengthen crisis management instruments and introduce a new 'Union reserve' for unforeseen crises. Reducing the number of regulations, combined with facilitating the possibility within the programmes to re-focus existing budgetary resources more easily and quickly to new priorities, can lead to a more efficient use of EU funds and increase the EU's political flexibility and responsiveness to new challenges.

8.3   THE UNITY OF THE EUROPEAN BUDGET

Budgetary policy is an almost classical field of parliamentary policy-making, as it was the first independent parliamentary power. This parliamentary power in budgetary policy includes participating in and monitoring all steps of budgetary policy, beginning with drafting of the budget until the discharging of the executive (see Chapter 4). The two branches of the European legislative and budgetary authority, the EP and the Council, use different instruments to balance the extension of the Commission's budgetary margins with the various flexibility instruments. As a rule, the Council limits the funding of the flexibility instruments and it also tries to restrict the use of the instruments with detailed and substantive definitions of the potential areas of application. The EP, on the other hand, is always in favour of generous funding for the flexibility instruments and for a wide range of fast deployed applications. In return, however, Parliament calls for far-reaching participation in the decision-making procedures of these new instruments and appropriate involvement in control and monitoring in the case of application. Parliament always refers to its budgetary rights and the political accountability of the Commission.

The EP's budgetary power varies in four major areas of the European budgetary system. In the own resources system of revenues, the EP is consulted. In the decision process of the MFF, the EP has to give its consent. The EP co-decides the annual budgets and, lastly, it independently discharges the European Commission after the implementation of the annual budgets.

All revenues and all expenditures of the EU have to be included in one EU budget. This means that, in principle, separate, subsidiary or satellite budgets or special funds are forbidden. The Parliament's budgetary rights of participation and scrutiny, however, relate to the budget of the Union. This means, in general, that revenues or expenditures which are not included in the budget are not covered by EP's budgetary rights. The components of the EU budget thus determine the scope and the intensity of the EP's budgetary participation and scrutiny rights. The principle of budgetary unity, therefore, is closely linked with the parliamentary powers in budgetary policy. The unity of the budget is one requirement for European budgetary policy-making and financial planning, and it is certainly one precondition for parliamentary scrutiny and for EP's participation in European budgetary policy. This almost classical principle of budgetary policy is also the result of the development of creating a single European budget reaching back to the first fundamental overhaul of the budget system with the Treaty of Luxembourg 1970 (Crowe, 2017). At the beginning of European integration enshrined in Article 199 of the EEC Treaty, the principle of budgetary unity is codified today in Article 310 of the TFEU: 'All items of revenue and expenditure of the Union shall be included in estimates to be drawn up for each financial year and shall be shown in the budget'. Moreover, Article 7 of the Financial Regulation stipulates that the EU budget 'shall comprise the revenue and the expenditure of the Union, including administrative expenditure occasioned for the institutions by the provisions of the TEU relating to the Common Foreign and Security Policy, and the operational expenditure occasioned by implementation of those provisions where this is charged to the budget'. In addition, the budget has to display 'the guarantees for borrowing-and-lending operations entered into by the Union, including the European Financial Stability Mechanism and Balance of Payment Facility operations'.

However, there are some possible exceptions from the principles of unity and unitarity which either stem from history or the origins of European budgetary policy (such as the European Development Fund) or are based on the legal personality of an institution (the ECB and the EIB) and on the division of competencies between the EU and the Member States (Repasi, 2013). Exceptions are enshrined in European primary and secondary law, like the Financial Regulation, and backed by case law of the Court of Justice (Crowe, 2017, p. 22). The Treaties provide that certain policies, like defence operations and initiatives of enhanced cooperation, shall be financed directly by participating Member States. The ECSC was already aware of exceptions and the Treaty of Rome listed the European Social Fund separately alongside Community revenue and expenditure. In particular, the Treaty of Maastricht introduced and expanded this differentiation inside the EU budget system by its structure of pillars (High Level Group on Own Resources, 2016, p. 62).

Secondary law, especially the Financial Regulation, allows for assigned revenues and provides the legal basis for European trust funds, which have been used as budgetary instruments for the European reaction on the challenges of the migration and refugee crisis (D'Alfonso and Immenkamp, 2015). One of the oldest exceptions from the principle of unity, the European Development Fund (EDF), has been backed by case law of the Court of Justice in the 1990s (D'Alfonso, 2014). Others have been created recently in the framework of European crisis policy, like the ESM, which also has been justified by the European Court of Justice (Crowe, 2017, p. 440).

Hence, a complete unity of all revenues and expenditures, and all financial instruments has not yet been achieved. In contrast to the principle of unity, the fragmentation and differentiation of the Union's budget system has accelerated (Crowe, 2017). The Commission justifies this 'galaxy of financial instruments' (European Parliament, 2017a) in its reflection paper on the future of EU finances: 'This extended financial architecture has allowed the Union to mobilize additional funding but it has added to the complexity of EU finances' (European Commission, 2017a, p. 9). The Monti High Level Group on own resources argued that differentiation 'remains nonetheless a useful tool' and 'different types of differentiation can be used, with varied consequences for the EU budget, which may become more versatile and responsive, but also more complex' (High Level Group on Own Resources, 2016, p. 67).

Besides these advantages in terms of flexibility, all instruments outside the EU budget restrict the budgetary powers of the EP, i.e. the involvement and scrutiny of the EP, and thus comprise one fundament of EP's participation and contribution in budgetary policy. Therefore, it is extremely important for the EP to keep the principles of unity and completeness of the EU budget – and to reduce the exceptions (Becker, 2017). Consequently, the EP reiterates its long-standing position that the EU's budget should include all subsidiary budgets, and it asserts its scrutiny rights on these subsidiary budgets. The Parliament considered these 'shadow budgets' as a challenge for 'democratic accountability' and pushed for a budget that should become 'clearer, simpler and more coherent and better equipped to ensure sufficient transparency, accountability, performance and public understanding' (European Parliament, 2017c, para. 24).

As a kind of second-best option, the Parliament agreed that at least some instruments outside the EU budget should be included in the Commission's annual reports on the financial architecture of the Union. This improvement in interinstitutional cooperation in budgetary matters laid down in the Interinstitutional Agreement between the EP, the Council and the Commission on budgetary discipline, on cooperation in budgetary matters and on sound financial management (Inter-Institutional Agreement 2013, no. 16) states, that borrowing and lending operations, revenue, expenditure, assets and liabilities of the EDF, the EFSF, the ESM, and other possible future mechanisms, including trust funds, as well as expenditure incurred by Member States in the framework of enhanced cooperation shall be included in this annual report (European Commission, 2017d).

Thus, the exemptions from the principle of unity of the EU budget still prevail, but the consequences in terms of lack of transparency and for the EPs scrutiny rights could be minimized. Moreover, the Parliament could successfully develop its budgetary monitoring rights on flexibility instruments further. So far, the EP has no formal role in the ESM Treaty or a seat on ESM boards. However, the EP's Committee on Economic and Monetary Affairs has informal exchanges of views with the Head of the Board of Governors and the Managing Director on a regular basis. The same is true for the instruments for financing EU external policy like EU trust funds or the facility for refugees in Turkey.

To sum up, increasing the flexibility of the MFF while at the same time preserving the principle of budgetary unity and reducing the fragmentation of the budget has consequences for the budgetary powers and competences of the Council and of the EP. Consequently, they are highly disputed between these two institutions. For the Member States, the MFF negotiations are not about transparency, democratic accountability and budget scrutiny but primarily about net payments and net receipts. The overall volume of the MFF is of paramount importance for them, especially for the net payers (see Chapter 5). They struggle to limit the MFF at max. 1% of EU GNI and to include all funds outside the MFF under this overall ceiling. Including additional flexibility instruments and funds, like the EDF, into a 1% of EU GNI MFF would mean in practice that other headings would have to be reduced. At the same time the EP's legislative powers and participation in European policy-making should not be harmed by reducing the volume of the EU's budget. This is the reason why the EP demands respect for the principle of unity of the EU budget and any integration of flexibility instruments into the EU budget requires a raise of MFF ceilings, given that the financing of other EU policies and programmes should not be jeopardized. Moreover, the EP links incorporating flexibility instruments or special funds into the EU budget with the Community method for European policy-making, or more concretely with EP's co-decision rights. Hence, the EP's demand for respecting the unity of the EU budget might also be a way to enlarge its legislative powers. Subsequently, this strategy leads to reservations and partially to resistance in the Council. Member States often understand Parliament's insistence on budget unity as a function or consequence of a power game on legislative rights.

8.4   A BUDGET FOR THE EUROZONE

A special case of accelerating differentiation and fragmentation of the Union's budget is represented by the idea of creating a separate budget or a fiscal capacity for the Eurozone (see Chapter 4). The High Level Group on Own Resources (2016) and the Commission's reflection paper on the future of European finances (European Commission, 2017a) discussed this proposal. Moreover, various models, forms and functions for an additional automatic solidarity and stabilization instrument for the EMU have been discussed in the course of EU's response to the deep economic and financial crisis and in order to prepare the Eurozone and the EU for the next crisis to come (Rubio, 2012; Gros, 2012; Wolff, 2012; Enderlein et al., 2012). Although there exists a broad sympathy for automatic stabilizers or shock absorbers in the Euro area, there is still no consensus on one model or on its elements. The proposals differ widely on a variety of issues: function, purposes, tasks, financial volume, revenues, spending priorities, governance, and finally, whether fiscal capacity should be included in the EU budget (European Parliament, 2016a, b).[2] What complicates the idea even further is that the specific purposes pursued with the idea of a Eurozone budget will have different consequences. If the crucial objective is to create a mechanism of macroeconomic stabilization allowing for countercyclical policy-making, the size, the priorities of spending, and possibly, the sources of revenues and the decision-making will have to be substantially different from the current EU budget and budgetary policy. If the main objective is to create a limited fiscal capacity as European assistance to implement

---

[2]   In addition to these models or ideal types a wide range of combinations with additional elements like Eurobonds, an expanded ESM, an EMU insolvency regime, a debt redemption fund or a borrowing capacity for the Euro area and finally new organs and institutions for the Euro area have been proposed and discussed.

structural reforms in the Member States, the size of the capacity might be distinctly smaller, the spending limited and focused on national reforming, and even the revenue side of this instrument might not be that important. In addition to its size, the intended purpose of an additional Eurozone budget or a fiscal capacity will also influence the decision-making process for a rapid and decisive response in the Eurozone to tackle a crisis and the definition of demand-sided spending priorities.

In the context of the 2014–2020 MFF, the EU budget transferred European funds between the Member States and between policies, but the major purpose of these vertical transfers was not to balance economic cycles and provide buffers against asymmetric shocks but to level out divergent levels of welfare between Member States and regions with the help of multiannual programmes. If the task of a Eurozone budget were to finance countercyclical macro-economic measures in the case of asymmetric or symmetric shocks, the payments would have to be paid out immediately to obtain a stabilizing effect. Moreover, the funds available for demand-sided measures must be larger than those for the structural funds of the current cohesion policy. Countercyclical expenditures would require higher spending than gross domestic product (GDP) growth during contractions (recessions) and lower spending during expansions (Claudal et al., 2013; Bara et al., 2017; Zettelmeyer, 2017). If the capacity were to function as macro-economic buffer, the size of the current EU budget might be too small and the own resources ceiling too low for a significant capacity. However, it is still unclear where to spend and for what purposes, and the proposals on this issue are still vague. Bara et al. (2017) argue for a Euro area budget comprising three principal spending tools:

1. an investment budget to foster economic convergence;
2. a common unemployment insurance scheme; and
3. an extended ESM to protect Member States against liquidity crises.

The proposed investment budget as permanent investment flows should account for at least 2% of Euro area GDP and it should finance public investments in catching-up countries, especially in infrastructure and in human capital (i.e. R&D, innovation and education). However, it still seems uncertain how these investment priorities, financed through a Eurozone capacity, should differ from those implemented with European structural funds and cohesion policy for the EU-27.

The proposal to use a Eurozone budget as countercyclical economic policy instrument could make necessary an additional and simultaneous substantial reform on the revenue side. In general, three types of revenues to finance a EMU budget or fiscal capacity are discussed:

- contributions from national budgets of Member States in the Euro area or participating in the capacity;
- proposals for new own resources, included a European financial transaction tax or contributions from the banking sector. Some argue for seigniorage stemming from the European Central Bank and others claim that these European revenues should not be constrained by annual balanced budget requirements (Bara et al., 2017, p. 8);
- some kind of tax collection or contribution stemming from national social insurance systems, i.e. unemployment insurance; and
- a borrowing capacity, at least as an additional source of revenues.

Raising the own resources ceiling of the EU's budget requires the consensus of all Member States and the ratification by all national parliaments. The option of revenues stemming from national social insurance systems and at least a borrowing capacity option would require a treaty change with high political hurdles.

The proposal for a budget specifically aimed at the Eurozone is often combined with the idea of creating and establishing new institutions, such as a Eurozone Minister of Finance or a Eurozone Parliament. This idea is not only challenging to the unity of the EU budget but also to the unity of EU institutions. The creation of a Euro-Chamber or a Eurozone-Parliament composed of national and European parliamentarians could be interpreted as a step back for the parliamentary dimension of the EU and its budgetary policy (Maurer, 2013). Moreover, the competences and tasks of this chamber are not clear and require concrete definition and delineation to the tasks of national parliaments and the EP.

With regard to the European budget and its future, it will be of paramount importance to decide whether the budget for the Eurozone should be part of the budget of the EU or a truly separate one. Creating a Eurozone budget within the EU budget would mean solving the problem of differentiation and concentration on the Euro area Member States. On the revenue side of the budget, one option could be to assign revenues to a specific budget line and to collect these revenues from a specific group of Member States, i.e. the Member States in the Euro area only. Assigned revenues, according to Art. 21 of the Financial Regulation, need not be part of the procedure to adopt the European annual budget as laid down in Art. 314 TFEU. The contributions of the Member States would be incorporated in the EU budget. The option to collect assigned revenues had been already proposed by the Commission in its communication on a Eurozone convergence and competitiveness instrument in 2013 (European

Commission, 2013). On the expenditure side, a basic act has to assign these revenues to specific items of expenditure. This could mean establishing a new MFF heading to the benefit of only a group of Member States. Both seem possible and there are some examples for these requirements. One example of this differentiation is enshrined in the Stability and Growth Pact; revenues stemming from the corrective arm are assigned to the EFSF (Art. 10 regulation on the effective enforcement of budgetary surveillance in the Euro area).

The option to create a Eurozone budget outside the EU budget would possibly be easier and more straightforward, but it would certainly enhance institutional fragmentation and differentiation, add complexity and lack of transparency, and contradict the principle of unity. This option would imply to establish a separate budget significantly bigger than the current EU-27 one with similar spending priorities, such as investments in infrastructure and R&D reserved for Eurozone members only. All of these options and proposals pose questions for the system of revenues, expenditures and governance. It remains unclear how to distinguish revenues and expenditures from the EU budget without driving a wedge into the unity of EU budget and of EU institutions. The EP already debated broadly and decided to create a fiscal capacity inside the EU budget as a case of assigned revenues and it adopted some general principles for the capacity (European Parliament, 2017b):

1. The fiscal capacity should provide the ESM with a 'specific additional budgetary capacity', which should be part of the EU budget but above MFF ceilings.
2. It should be financed by the members of the Eurozone and participating Member States via a new source of assigned revenues. Later on, the capacity should be financed through EU own resources.
3. Three spending pillars should cover the purpose and the policy objectives:

    *   the financing of structural reforms;
    *   economic convergence as buffer against asymmetric shocks; and
    *   the absorption of symmetric shocks.

4. The governance of the new instrument should follow the community method. The institutional setup should merge the president of the Euro group with the Commissioner for Economic and Financial Affairs and so establish an additional Vice-president of the European Commission responsible for the fiscal capacity.

Moreover, the European Commission in its EMU-reform package (European Commission, 2017b) of 6 December 2017 argued for the creation of a new instrument for more stability in the Euro area within the European budget and the Union's institutional framework. This stabilization function for the

Eurozone should rapidly provide financial resources in case of big asymmetric shocks and thus prevent negative spillovers. As a budget line within the EU budget the stabilization function should:

- stay separate from existing flexibility instruments, like the European Solidarity Fund or the Globalization Adjustment Fund;
- remain financially neutral over the medium term and not lead to a permanent transfer mechanism;
- minimize moral hazard by strict, pre-defined eligibility criteria based on sound macro-economic policies;
- contribute to financial stability in Member States in crisis and be big enough to provide for a real stabilization effect. The Commission calculates a volume of 1% of GDP which could imply some form of borrowing capacity.

Without indicating its preference, the Commission listed three options for a stabilization function – a European Investment Protection Scheme, a European Unemployment Reinsurance Scheme and a rainy day fund (European Commission, 2017c). With regard to the EU budget, the most decisive precondition of these proposals is to keep a new stabilization instrument for the Euro area within the EU budget. The Commission's proposal for the MFF 2021–2027 followed this idea. To stabilize the Eurozone, a reform assistance programme as a budget line within the EU budget totalling €25 billion would assist Member States to implement structural reforms (European Commission, 2018c). The Commission also planned a European investment stabilization function to support the volume of investments with European funds in times of crisis or in the event of a sharp decline in growth, thereby stabilizing the economic cycle (European Commission, 2018d). Loans to Member States are to be secured with a maximum total of €30 billion by the EU budget. At the same time, Member States affected by a major asymmetric shock should receive interest subsidies through a special fund. This fund could later be extended by means of the European Stability Mechanism and contributions from potential beneficiaries.

To sum up, the supranational bodies have early noticed that the debate on a Eurozone budget will not only touch the existing procedures of budgetary policy-making, especially the participation and scrutiny rights of the EP, but also their role in the institutional setup of the EU (see Chapters 6 and 7). They argue therefore to keep this additional instrument inside European budgetary and institutional structures. The question of how to design, establish and implement a separate budget for the Euro area is hence above all a political question including the aspects of European policy-making, democratic legitimacy and the distribution of powers (see Chapter 5). Fiscal stabilization and risk sharing via European structures and institutions require a shift of sovereignty and powers from national to European level of policy-making, decision-making and democratic surveillance. To create this fiscal stabilization instrument inside or outside the EU budget, inside the framework of EU institutional setup or separately with new instruments, structures, institutions and procedures and even a new legal basis are not technical but highly political questions.

8.5 CONCLUSIONS: PRAGMATISM AND FLEXIBILITY

Although both the EP and the Member States in the Council agree to the necessity to increase budgetary flexibility, reforming the European budget on this point and reaching a compromise is still difficult for two reasons.

Firstly, budgetary policy is one of the oldest and classical domains of parliamentary power and therefore the EU's budgetary policy has always been a field of institutional struggles between the two pillars of European budget authority, the Council and the EP. Budgetary conflicts always include questions about the institutional design, also when the option to increase budgetary flexibility is considered.

Secondly, finding a feasible combination of predictability and flexibility is difficult under the circumstances and particularities of the European budgetary policy. For the Member States, especially for the group of net payers, the main focus, when negotiating on the MFF, is still their net payments balance and the overall volume of the MFF. Introducing new budgetary flexibility elements could mean increasing the size of the budget while not knowing if and when these additional funds will be spent and for what purpose.

These two aspects – institutional struggles and power games as well as net payments logic, burden sharing and status quo bias – make it even more difficult to reverse the trend of fragmentation and differentiation in the Union's budgetary policy. For nearly five decades (starting with the first significant overhaul of European budgetary policy with the introduction of the own resources system in 1970) the EU has been searching for the right balance between the pragmatic political necessity of budgetary flexibility and the establishment of a single European budget. Such a budget should be transparent, predictable, scrutinized, and thus legitimate.

The Treaty of Lisbon could not stop the tendencies to greater fragmentation and complexity of the European budget and of budgetary procedures and negotiations. The fragmentation of the EU budget should be the exception and a unified and universal budget should remain the norm of European budgetary policy. Nonetheless, the unity of the EU budget does not mean that all satellite budgets can be and have to be incorporated into the MFF. This is certainly true for the instruments of budgetary flexibility, like emergency funds. There seems to be a trade-off between budgetary flexibility and multiannual planning and stability. This conclusion implies that exceptions are possible and sometimes necessary. The experience of former debates shows that in general four options are conceivable:

- An *intergovernmental approach* – by outsourcing tasks of the EU and creating new institutions with their own budgets outside the European treaties the Member States tried to tackle specific political challenges swiftly while circumventing existing budget provisions and procedures.
- A *net-payers approach* – including special flexibility instruments and funds into the EU budget and the MFF while keeping the total MFF volume and the ceilings untouched means to use the principle of unity to reform the existing spending priorities at the expense of other headings. In the end, this would lead to a smaller budget.
- A *pragmatic solution* – this option would imply keeping the formal budgetary construction unchanged, and introducing additional monitoring and scrutiny procedures for instruments outside the annual budget and the MFF. In practice, this approach would mean strengthening the budgetary role of the EP as one branch of the EU budget authority and, at the same time, increasing, at least partly, budgetary fragmentation and complexity.
- *Substantial budget reform* – this option would mean including all financial instruments and funds outside the MFF in the EU budget while increasing its total volume with additional funds above MFF ceilings. New genuine own resources, as proposed by High Level Group on Own Resources (2016), could be introduced to fill this gap and to increase the Union's financial autonomy.

In general, the creation of a pure federal budget and the return to a pure intergovernmental approach seem not to be very realistic options in the negotiations on this specific topic of European budgetary policy. It seems that the current system of a complex and fragmented European budget will prevail further and last even longer. In the long term, the EU should have more room for budgetary decision-making and action. However, a much more flexible use of the MFF in a rapidly changing political environment would require the concession of greater political autonomy to the EU and to the European Commission in interpreting the need for action and the scope of funding.

REFERENCES

Bara, Y.-E., Castets, L., Ernoult, T. and Zakhatchouk, A. (2017), 'A contribution to the work on the strengthening of the euro area'. Ministère de l'Economie et des Finances, Trésor-Economics, no. 190, Paris, February.

Becker, P. (2012), 'Lost in stagnation. The EU's next Multiannual Financial Framework (2014–2020) and the power of the status quo'. SWP Research Paper 2012/RP 14, Berlin, October.

Becker, P. (2016), 'The EU budget's mid-term review with its promising reform proposals. The Commission lays the groundwork for the next post-2020 budget'. SWP Comments 2016/C 48, November.

Becker, P. (2017), 'The next Multiannual Financial Framework (MFF) and the unity of the EU budget'. European Parliament, In-depth Analysis requested by the Budget Committee, November.

Benedetto, G. (2013), 'The EU budget after Lisbon: rigidity and reduced spending', *Journal of Public Policy*, 33 (3), 345–368.

Carrera, S., Den Hertog, L., Núñez Ferrer, J., Musmeci, R., Vosyliūtė, L. and Pilati, M. (2018), 'Oversight and management of the EU trust funds. Democratic accountability challenges and promising practices'. Study requested by the CONT committee, European Parliament, Policy Department for Budgetary Affairs, February.

Claudal, N., Georges, N., Grossmann-Wirth, V., Guillaume, J., Lellouch, T. and Sode, A. (2013), 'A budget for the euro area'. Ministère de l'Economie et des Finances, Trésor-Economics, no. 120, Paris October.

Crowe, R. (2017), 'The European budgetary galaxy', *European Constitutional Law Review*, 13 (3), 428–452.

D'Alfonso, A. (2014), 'European Development Fund. Joint development cooperation and the budget: out or in?' European Parliamentary Research Service (EPRS) In-Depth Analysis, Brussels, November.

D'Alfonso, A. and Immenkamp, B. (2015), 'EU trust funds for external action. First uses of a new tool'. European Parliamentary Research Service Briefing, Brussels, November.

Enderlein, H., Delors, J., Schmidt, H., Bofinger, P., Boone, L., De Grauwe, P., Piris, J.-C., Pisani-Ferry, J., João Rodrigues, M., Sapir, A., Vitorino, A., Fernandes, S. and Rubio, E. (2012), 'Completing the Euro. A road map towards fiscal union in Europe'. Report by the Tommaso Padoa-Schioppa Group, Notre Europe Institute Jacques Delors, Paris, June.

European Commission (2004), 'Working document of the Commission Services. Subject: flexibility within the multiannual financial framework, Multiannual Financial Framework 2007–2013', Fiche no. 3, Brussels, 24 March.

European Commission (2013), 'Towards a deep and genuine economic and monetary union. The introduction of a convergence and competitiveness instrument', COM(2013)165 final, Brussels, 20 March.

European Commission (2017a), 'Reflection paper on the future of EU finances', COM(2017)358 final, Brussels, 28 June.

European Commission (2017b), 'Further steps towards completing Europe's economic and monetary union: a roadmap', COM(2017)821 final, Brussels, 6 December.

European Commission (2017c), 'New budgetary instruments for a stable Euro Area within the Union Framework', COM(2017)822 final, Brussels, 6 December.

European Commission (2017d), 'Annual report on the EU financial architecture (point 16 of the Inter-Institutional Agreement)', Brussels 20 November.

European Commission (2018a), 'A new, modern Multiannual Financial Framework for a European Union that delivers efficiently on its priorities post-2020'. The European Commission's contribution to the Informal Leaders' meeting on 23 February 2018, COM(2018)98 final, Brussels, 14 February.

European Commission (2018b), 'A modern budget for a Union that protects, empowers and defends. The Multiannual Financial Framework for 2021–2027', COM(2018)321 final, Brussels, 2 May.

European Commission (2018c), 'Proposal for a regulation on the establishment of the Reform Support Programme', COM(2018)391 final, Brussels, 31 May.

European Commission (2018d), 'Proposal for a regulation on the establishment of a European Investment Stabilisation Function', COM(2018)387 final, Brussels, 31 May.

European Parliament (2016a), 'Committee on Budgets, Committee on Economic and Monetary Affairs, working document on a budgetary capacity for the Eurozone', Brussels, 19 February.

European Parliament (2016b), 'Committee on Budgets, Committee on Economic and Monetary Affairs, working document 2 on a budgetary capacity for the Eurozone', Brussels, 17 March.

European Parliament (2017a), 'Committee on Budgets, the Galaxy of Funds and Instruments around the EU Budget', workshop, http://www.europarl.europa.eu/committees/en/budg/events-workshops.html?id=20170118WKS00261.

European Parliament (2017b), 'Resolution of 16 February 2017 on budgetary capacity for the Euro area' (2015/2344(INI)), Böge-Berès report, P8_TA(2017)0050, Brussels, 16 February.

European Parliament (2017c), 'Discharge 2015: EU general budget – European Commission, European Parliament decision of 27 April 2017 on discharge in respect of the implementation of the general budget of the European Union for the financial year 2015', Section III – Commission (2016/2151(DEC)), P8_TA(2017)0143, Brussels, 27 April.

European Parliament (2018), 'Resolution of 14 March 2018 on the next MFF: preparing the Parliament's position on the MFF post-2020', P8_TA-PROV(2018)0075, Brussels, 14 March.

Gros, D. (2012), 'The false promise of a Eurozone budget', CEPS Commentary, Brussels, 7 December.

High Level Group on Own Resources (2016), 'Future financing of the EU. Final report and recommendations of the High Level Group on Own Resources', Brussels, December.

Jones, F. (2010), 'Flexibility in the Multiannual Financial Framework 2007–2013: revisions and use of instruments', European Parliament, Directorate General for Internal Policies, Policy Department D: Budgetary Affairs, Note, Brussels, October.

Maurer, A. (2013) 'From EMU to DEMU: the democratic legitimacy of the EU and the European Parliament', IAI Working Paper 13/11, April.

Mijs, A. and Schout, A. (2015), 'Flexibility in the EU budget. Are there limits?', Clingendael report, December.

Núñez Ferrer, J., Le Cacheux, J., Benedetto, G. and Saunier, M. (2016), 'Study on the Potential and limitations of reforming the financing of the EU budget', Brussels, 3 June.

Repasi, R. (2013), 'Legal options for an additional EMU fiscal capacity'. European Parliament, Policy Departement C: Citizens' Rights and Constitutional Affairs, Note, Brussels.

Rubio, E. (2012), 'Eurozone Budget: 3 functions, 3 instruments'. Notre Europe Jacques Delors Institute, Tribune, Paris, 15 November.

Rubio, E. (2017), 'The next Multiannual Financial Framework (MFF) and its flexibility, European Parliament, in-depth analysis requested by the Budget Committee', November.

Wildavsky, A. (1961), 'Political implication of budgetary reform', *Public Administration Review*, 21, 183–190.

Wolff, G. (2012), 'A budget for Europe's Monetary Union', Bruegel Policy Contribution, Issue 2012/22, Brussels, December.

Zettelmeyer, J. (2017), 'Rethinking economic policy – a better fiscal framework for the Eurozone', in Schellinger, Alexander and Phillip Steinberg (eds), *The Future of the Eurozone. How to Keep Europe Together: A Progressive Perspective from Germany*. Bielefeld, pp. 123–144.

9. The European framework for monitoring and control of the EU budget

Elsa Perreau

9.1 INTRODUCTION

Accountability has been an important concern since the inception of the European Union (EU) budget. Bovens (2007: 452) defines accountability as 'a relationship between an actor and a forum, in which the actor has an obligation to explain and to justify his or her conduct, the forum can pose questions and pass judgment, and the actor may face consequences'. The concept of accountability relates to democratic, hierarchical, legal and financial accountability, which is the focus of this chapter. Hojlund (2015: 38) defines financial accountability as: 'related to budgetary execution and financial controls that an organisation can be subject to'.

This chapter will first provide an overview of the budget monitoring and control system in the EU. Monitoring will be defined as followup during the implementation, and control is understood as happening mainly ex-post, i.e. after the implementation of the budget. The chapter will look at the main principles for control and monitoring and the institutional architecture of the control system of the EU. It will then look at the challenges inherent to monitoring and control and at those arising in the Lisbon era and regarding monitoring and control of the EU budget. The latter include the increased complexity and fragmentation of the EU budget.

9.2 THE ARCHITECTURE FOR MONITORING AND CONTROL OF THE EU BUDGET

As it is important to develop an understanding of the architecture for monitoring and control within the EU, this section will look at the principles of monitoring and control of the EU budget, and the potential risks to the EU budget, and it will provide an overview of the institutional architecture of the EU financial control system.

9.2.1   Principles and Treaty Base for Monitoring and Control

Article 310 of the Treaty on the Functioning of the European Union (TFEU) states the six principles governing the EU budget: unity, universality, equilibrium, annuality, specification, and sound management (see Chapter 11). The Financial Regulation (FR) stipulates three main principles on sound financial management: the principle of economy, the principle of efficiency, and the principle of effectiveness. The principle of economy implies that resources are 'made available in due time, in appropriate quantity and quality and at the best price', efficiency relates to the link between inputs (resources) and outputs (results), and effectiveness refers to 'the attainment of the specific objectives set and the achievement of the intended results' (FR, Article 30(2)). Monitoring and control of the budget are embedded in the concept of sound financial management. The FR defines control as a process that looks not only at sound financial management, but also at the reliability of reporting, the safeguarding of assets and information, prevention, detection, correction and followup of fraud and irregularities, and at the adequate management of the risks relating to the legality and regularity of the underlying transactions (FR Article 2). The definition of the FR is quite broad regarding control and it also includes the reliability of accounts, their regularity and their legality.

9.2.2   The Risks to Good Financial Management of the EU Budget

The European Court of Auditors (ECA) identifies the four following risks to good financial management of EU funds: (a) the funds are not spent according to the rules or for their intended purpose (legality and regularity); (b) expenditures are not accounted for properly (reliability of the accounts); (c) the funds are not spent following sound financial management principles (economy, efficiency and effectiveness); and (d) benefits from the use of the funds do not materialize and the EU budget does not produce EU added value (European Court of Auditors, 2014b). These risks, in cases where they materialize, can impact the proper delivery of EU policies and result in losses damaging to the EU and Member States' reputations.

Errors in the management of the budget, i.e. when a payment made is neither legal nor regular, happen for various reasons. For example, the payment might have been made to beneficiaries that are not eligible for EU funding, or to fund expenditure that should not be financed by the EU budget. Poor performance or poor financial management is usually due to weaknesses in the processes before and during the implementation of the budget, such as broad objectives for the funding resulting in difficulties in measuring effectiveness, or poor assessment of the needs ex-ante. The framework for monitoring and control of the EU budget is designed to address these risks and ensure that they do not materialize or that corrective measures can be taken.

9.2.3 The Institutional Architecture of the EU's Control System

According to the ECA, management and control are based on an institutional framework where the European Commission and other implementing bodies assume the executive role, the European Parliament and the Council provide democratic oversight, and the ECA is the EU's auditor (European Court of Auditors, 2014a). These institutions interact to form the control system of the EU as shown in Figure 9.1. The treaties name the ECA as the EU's external auditor and the European Commission as responsible for the implementation of the budget. The European Commission reports on its activities to the European Parliament and the Council who also receive the audits of the ECA about the European Commission's activities.

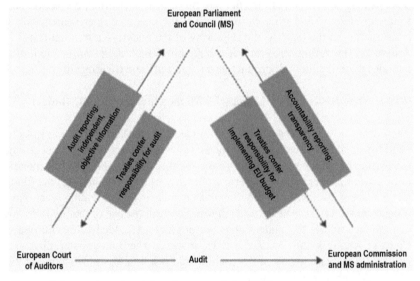

Figure 9.1   *Accountability framework for EU's management and financial controls*

Source: European Court of Auditors (2014) Gaps, overlaps and challenges: a landscape review of EU accountability and public audit arrangements, Luxembourg: Publication Office of the European Union. P14.

This framework for control is based on two levels: internal control undertaken by the European Commission and external scrutiny undertaken by the ECA, the European Parliament and the Council.

9.2.3.1 Internal control

The FR defines the role of the internal auditor as to assess the 'suitability and effectiveness of internal management systems and the performance of departments in implementing policies, programmes and actions by reference to the risks associated with them' and 'the efficiency and effectiveness of the internal control and audit systems applicable to each budgetary implementation operation' (FR, Article 99(1)). The internal control framework of the European Commission is designed so that the European Commission can take responsibility for the implementation of the budget in view of the discharge procedure (European Court of Auditors, 2014a).

There are two main features in the EU's internal audit architecture. First, the Internal Audit Service (IAS) holds the centralized internal audit function. It provides independent and objective assurance and consulting services to the European Commission with a view to improving European Commission operations. Between 2001 and 2015, each Directorate General (DG) had its own Internal Audit Capabilities that held decentralized audit functions at the DG level. The role of the Internal Audit Capabilities was to develop and establish audit procedures, risk-based strategies and annual plans at the DG level and to coordinate with the IAS. Since 2015, the internal audit function of the European Commission has been centralized in the IAS. Second, the Audit Progress Committee oversees audit matters in the European Commission and reports to the College of Commissioners once a year. It has no management powers and mainly plays a preventive role: it identifies issues that the European Commission needs to address and ensures followup of audit recommendations related to the European Commission's work.

Internal control in the European Commission is required to follow up on the recommendations made by the ECA in its audits and special reports. The IAS and other DG services maintain RAD (Recommendation, Action, Discharge) applications to monitor the implementation of audit recommendations and audit findings relevant to their service. These applications support internal control and ex post control in the European Commission (European Court of Auditors, 2016). In a report on European Commission followup on audit recommendations, the ECA examined the recommendations it made to the European Commission in its special reports between 2009 and 2012 and found that the European Commission had fully implemented most of them. The ECA notes improvements in the followup system but still highlights shortcomings (European Court of Auditors, 2016). Information management on recommendations is still a challenge because the status of audit recommendations is not always available, and it may not be accurate because the implementation level may be overestimated. Moreover, the European Commission and the ECA categorize it differently. Finally, there is a lack of followup on actions that Member States are supposed to carry out in order to improve financial management (European Court of Auditors, 2016). The ECA emphasizes the importance of having an effective system for followup on audit recommendations noting that 'an improved followup system would provide sufficient reliable and pertinent information on improvements resulting from the Court's audit recommendations and thus contribute to the sound financial management of the EU budget' (European Court of Auditors, 2016: 17).

9.2.3.2 External scrutiny

External scrutiny, also known as external control, mainly takes place after the implementation of the EU budget. This section will examine the role of the main actors involved in the external scrutiny of the EU budget, namely the ECA, the European Parliament and the Council.

The above-mentioned ECA is the EU's external auditor. It was created by the 1975 Brussels treaty and installed in 1977. It only became an EU institution with the 1993 Maastricht treaty and since then it has been required to publish an annual statement of assurance on the reliability of the accounts and the legality and regularity of the transactions in the accounts. With the Amsterdam treaty in 1977, the ECA was given extended competences to cover the second and third pillars of EU activities (namely foreign and security policy and justice and home affairs). Progressively, the ECA increased its prerogatives and now has competence to examine the accounts of all EU revenue and expenditure (Article 287 TFEU). The ECA has extensive investigative powers defined by the FR. The ECA provides annual reports, special reports and the statement of assurance, which constitute the raw material for parliamentary and administrative accountability.

In its activities, the ECA adheres to the International Standards for Supreme Audit Institutions that identify three types of audits: financial audit covering the reliability of financial reporting; compliance audit that covers the regularity and legality of the finances; and performance audit that assesses sound financial management. The first two types of audit looking at reliability, regularity and legality are more traditional than performance audit that evaluates efficiency. However, it does not make much sense to separate the different types of audits because they are necessarily intertwined. The ECA's performance audits usually reflect compliance as well, mainly because compliance and performance are strongly linked in the implementation of the budget (Caldeira, 2013). The role of the ECA is not limited to acting as the external auditor of the Union. It also defines itself as the EU's 'financial watchdog', looking at potential risks linked to the EU budget, providing guidance to improve financial management and transparency, with the overall purpose of strengthening the democratic legitimacy and sustainability of the EU (Eca.europa.eu, 2018). The ECA is considered as the 'financial conscience'[1] of the Union and plays a very central role in the financial accountability system of the EU, embracing the IAS, the Budgetary Control (CONT) Committee of the European Parliament and national audit authorities (Laffan, 2003).

Despite its name, the ECA has no judicial powers and cannot impose penalties or give orders to European institutions and bodies. The ECA's powers are limited because its opinions are not binding. In the end, the ECA's influence remains largely dependent on whether the controlling bodies, the European Parliament and the Council take into account its remarks (Sanchez Barrueco, 2015).

The other two actors of budgetary control are the European Parliament and the Council. Budgetary powers are shared between the two institutions, but the European Parliament assumes the essential responsibility for political control over the implementation of the budget. The CONT committee of the European Parliament is in charge of the scrutiny of the implementation of the EU budget. The discharge procedure is its main tool for control. Article 319 TFEU as further detailed in the Financial Regulation sets out the procedure. Each year in May, the European Parliament takes a decision on the discharge for the year *n* − 2. Granting discharge was initially a competence of the Council in the Treaty of Rome (1957). The treaty of Luxembourg (1970) made it a shared competence between the European Parliament and the Council and progressively it became a competence of the European Parliament after the Brussels Treaty (1975) (D'Alfonso, 2014).

The decision to grant the discharge marks the final approval of the implementation of the EU budget and allows the accounts of the financial year under scrutiny to be closed. The discharge aims to verify compliance (whether the budget was implemented in accordance with the relevant rules) and performance (the principles of sounds financial management) (D'Alfonso, 2014). The discharge procedure involves four main institutions. The European Commission gives an account to the ECA which provides audits to the Council and the European Parliament. The European Parliament takes the discharge decision on the basis of reports from the CONT Committee and the ECA statement of assurance and annual report and after having received a recommendation from the Council. In the end, the Council's control role is limited to drafting the recommendation, which is not legally binding but requires the European Commission to follow up. Since the Treaty of Lisbon, the procedure

---

[1] The expression was first used by Hans Kutscher, President of the European Court of Justice at the swearing-in ceremony of the ECA in 1977.

also includes a report produced by the European Commission on the results achieved with the EU budget. However, in 2012, the ECA noted that the first report provided by the European Commission was vague, short on substance and added little value (European Court of Auditors, 2012). Most EU bodies, agencies and joint undertakings are subject to the discharge procedure, as stated in the rule 94 of procedure of the European Parliament, even though article 319 TFEU only mentions the discharge of the European Commission. In total, the European Parliament votes on 52 reports during the plenary for one given year (Europarl.europa.eu, 2018). Some EU bodies are also accountable to their governing boards. When funds are made available from sources other than the EU budget, there are exceptions to the discharge procedure. This is, for example, the case of the European Investment Bank. Its discharge is granted by its governing board and it is audited by an independent auditor. The discharge procedure can also be seen as the moment in the EU budget cycle when financial accountability interacts with political accountability as this is the assessment of the implementation of the budget by a democratically elected institution (Laffan, 2003). Failure to grant the discharge has strong political significance. The European Parliament refused to grant discharge in 1984 and in 1998. In 1998, this contributed to the events leading to the resignation of the European Commission in 1999 (D'Alfonso, 2014).

The role of the European Parliament used to be limited to ex-post control of the budget through the discharge procedure. However, the CONT committee has gradually increased its prerogatives and now monitors the implementation of the budget constantly through review of European Commission documents on budget implementation or studies it produces. Concerns about sound financial management have not always been as present as today. The evolution in the roles of the European Parliament and the ECA over their years of existence responded to increasing needs for financial accountability and to ensure value for money (Laffan, 2003).

9.3   CHALLENGES IN TERMS OF MONITORING AND CONTROL OF THE EU BUDGET: FRAGMENTATION AND COMPLEXITY IN THE LISBON ERA

The architecture for monitoring and control described above faces various challenges as the EU budget has evolved over the years. In recent years, the EU budget has been increasingly characterized by its fragmentation and its complexity. This section examines the different aspects of this complexity and its effects on monitoring and control mechanisms. It first looks at the inherent complexity of the EU budget resulting in complex monitoring and control mechanisms. It then looks at the trends in recent years that have increased further the existing complexity and fragmentation of the EU budget. Finally, it balances the requirements for sound financial management and the necessary flexibility.

9.3.1   The Inherent Complexity of EU Budget Management

The EU budget, as the financial tool to implement the many EU policies, provides for instruments corresponding to specific policy objectives such as grants, loans, guarantees, subsidies, direct budget support to third countries and so on (see Chapter 3). Every year thousands of projects and activities are implemented with EU funding. Beneficiaries are very diverse and can be Member States, individuals, companies, universities, civil society organizations or governmental organizations. Implementing the EU budget involves many actors in the EU institutions as well as in the Member States and sometimes third countries as well. Moreover, control takes place on a yearly basis even though many activities are carried out over several years. There is consequently a significant difference between the commitments and the payments for a given year. The environment for monitoring and control of the EU budget is already complex because of the nature of the EU.

The responsibility for sound financial management in the implementation of the budget lies with the European Commission. However, there are several methods to implement the EU budget. The chosen option necessarily affects its monitoring and control. There are four different methods for management of the EU budget: centralized (by the European Commission), shared (with Member States), decentralized (by third countries) and joint with international organizations (Sanchez Barrueco, 2015). The management of the budget is considered direct when the budget is managed by the European Commission, EU delegations or EU executive agencies. As a result, the responsibility for monitoring is relatively diffuse: all of the actors involved in the management of funds have a role in monitoring at their level and this also has implications for the control mechanisms. The ECA observes that the way the budget is managed (direct, indirect, or shared management) has limited impact on the regularity of the accounts (European Court of Auditors, 2017). However, the ECA notes that the management mode 'determines the control, audit and accountability arrangements put in place' (European Court of Auditors, 2014b:15).

The Member States manage about 80% of the budget under the shared management procedure for implementation of the EU budget (Ec.europa. eu, 2018). Under shared management, Member States have responsibility for managing expenditure programmes and schemes, executing payments to beneficiaries and protecting the financial interests of the EU. There is asymmetry between the responsibilities of the European Commission and Member

States in terms of control and the actual share that they implement. While the European Commission implements only a small share of the EU budget, it holds responsibility for the overall sound financial management (Sanchez Barrueco, 2015). The treaties require Member States to 'cooperate with the Commission to ensure that the appropriations are used in accordance with the principles of sound financial management' (Article 317 TFEU), which makes them 'bystanders' for financial accountability (Sanchez Barrueco, 2015).

There are a number of checks that bind Member States when implementing the EU budget. Member States must comply with EU rules when spending the EU budget. This means that the EU rules need to be known at the local, regional and national level and possibly integrated into national rules. Member States also provide annual accounts and management declarations on the use of EU funds. They provide a summary of audits reports and controls carried out. Member States may also issue national declarations, a statement of assurance produced by the Ministry of Finance, but only s few Member States do it and their contribution to financial transparency and accountability can be questioned (Sanchez Barrueco, 2015). Despite the existing framework binding the Member States, there might be room for breaches in accountability (Sanchez Barrueco, 2015).

The European Commission largely depends on the system of management and audit at the level of Member States. It assumes that funds have been managed according to sound financial management principles, unless it finds evidence suggesting otherwise (Sanchez Barrueco, 2015). It can impose financial corrections and recovery of funds if it observes that a Member State is not performing as it should to protect the financial interests of the EU. Recovery means that the beneficiary needs to repay the funds. Financial corrections are imposed when Member States do not detect and correct the irregularities in expenditure. However, the myriad instruments and regulations related to funds managed by Member States create complexity and different degrees of European Commission oversight, and this does not contribute to the effectiveness of financial corrections. Moreover, the procedure for financial corrections is very long and it does not necessarily produce effects (Sanchez Barrueco, 2015).

The role of the ECA is also slightly different when the management of EU funds is decentralized. In this case, the ECA is required to cooperate with the Supreme Audit Institution (SAI) of Member States (Article 287(3) TFEU). This cooperation is meant to help the ECA perform its tasks. However, it is not certain that the ECA effectively relies on audit work performed by SAIs. EU budget implementation is subject to many provisions for monitoring and control. However, the ECA notes that 'challenges remain for streamlining frontline governance, accountability and audit processes carried out at Member State level' (European Court of Auditors, 2014a: 7). Member States have different audit systems, and some are more effective than others in identifying and correcting errors. There is room for national audit authorities to be more involved in the control of EU funds management. Further, 'the lack of common standards for auditing the execution of the EU budget at European and national level is clearly a major gap in hampering international cooperation' (Sanchez Barrueco, 2015: 82). Besides, managing authorities at the national level are responsible both to their national authorities and to the European Commission, which sometimes creates overlaps in terms of control and audit of the funds. One action or one authority may be audited several times by national authorities. This is due to national requirements and to the audit system of the EU, given that the funds come from the EU budget.

Indirect management of EU funds also occurs when the European Commission delegates implementation to third countries or to international organizations. In its annual report 2012, the ECA identified challenges in two specific areas related to delegated management. The first one relates to budget support, where the ECA notes that its audit of regularity 'cannot go beyond the stage at which aid is paid to the partner country' (European Court of Auditors, 2014a: 25). As a result, accountability relies mainly on the partner country's audit and control arrangements. The Court also observed that 'for EU expenditure under budget support, EU multi-donor actions and similar cooperation in instruments, the complex system of rules and procedures [...] means that the risks to regularity are high' (European Court of Auditors, 2014a: 25).

The European Commission relies on the audit system of the United Nations (UN) when it funds multidonor actions. In 2009, the ECA published a very critical special report on the funds channeled through UN organizations. It observed that 'the process for deciding to implement aid through the UN does not demonstrate that this is the most efficient and effective option' (European Court of Auditors, 2009: 29) and that 'monitoring arrangements do not provide adequate information on the robustness of financial procedures and on the achievement of objectives' (European Court of Auditors, 2009: 30). The same report also observed that it was challenging for the ECA to be able to audit the use of EU funds channeled through the UN. On this basis, the ECA formulated several recommendations, and most of them were implemented (European Court of Auditors, 2016). Other studies also confirm that there have been improvements in the monitoring and control system of funds channeled through the UN (Blomeyer & Sanz, 2016: 116).

When the funds are managed in partnership with others, accountability relies on external audit as well as the governance structure of the partner, and the EU's own system for accountability and audit. The partners of the EU need to have sufficient and reliable audit and control systems. Ideally, there would be a single audit system so that overlaps and gaps are avoided.

**9.3.2   An Increased Number of Instruments and Mechanisms for
            Funding**

In addition to the challenges resulting from the various methods for implementation of the EU budget, Crowe (2017) identifies four tendencies in the
Lisbon era that contribute to increased complexity and fragmentation of the
EU budget. First, the financial troubles of 2007 gave rise to intergovernmental
budgetary mechanisms to address the crisis. Second, the more recent migration
crisis of 2015 gave rise to hybrid instruments that combine Member States
and EU budget contributions. Third, there was increased use of instruments
financed only by participating Member States. Finally, there was internal
fragmentation and complexity within the budget owing to the shift from
a policy-driven budget to a demand-driven budget. There are also challenges in
terms of accountability and audit arrangements depending on how EU bodies
are funded (fully funded by the EU budget or partially). The main examples
illustrating the budget's fragmentation and complexity that developed between
2007 and 2017 are the responses to the financial crisis of 2007 and more
recently to the migration crisis in 2015 (Crowe, 2017; Mijs and Schout, 2015).
This section will examine the various trends of increased complexity and fragmentation of the EU budget and their implications for financial accountability.

9.3.2.1   Coordinated actions
Coordinated actions between Member States and the EU usually take the form
of instruments or intergovernmental agreements within or outside the EU
framework in order to act upon a specific issue. Coordinated action occurs for
various reasons and corresponds to situations when the European Commission
is coordinating policy implementation but does not fund it entirely. Many EU
policies, such as the Cohesion policy, are funded by Member States and the
EU at the same time and pursue the same policy objectives. This results in the
existence of parallel lines of accountability because many EU policies require
cooperation with Member States in order to achieve common objectives (e.g.
Europe 2020). The European Commission is accountable to the Council and
to the European Parliament and it can be audited by the ECA. National authorities are accountable to national parliaments and they can be audited by the
national SAI. According to the ECA, coordinated action 'may rely on a fragmented system of parliamentary scrutiny and public audit' (European Court of
Auditors, 2014a: 6). The ECA notes that accountability for coordinated actions
remains fragmented and that 'there are many separate programmes, projects
and actions serving similar or complementary objectives, to which different
management and control rules apply' (European Court of Auditors, 2014b:
16). Coordinated action also includes the intergovernmental tools that were
put in place to face the financial crisis. Most of them have specific accounta-

bility and audit arrangements. Even though they may not be funded by the EU budget, they are closely interrelated with EU institutions and EU bodies and require comprehensive scrutiny and public audit.

9.3.2.2   Hybrid instruments

Hybrid budgetary instruments are instruments that combine funding from the EU budget and funding from Member States or other actors. Several hybrid instruments were created to address the refugee crisis. These were mainly created to attract more funding and to provide rapid *ad hoc* assistance to third countries. These include the creation of trust funds, which has been possible since 2013. Trust funds are managed by the European Commission, combine funds from the EU budget and participating states and operate outside the EU budget (Blomeyer & Sanz, 2017). They are subject to the discharge procedure and the regular procedure for monitoring and control that covers the instruments they fund. Another example of a hybrid structure is the EU Facility for refugees located in Turkey. This completely *ad hoc* mechanism was created to address the migration crisis affecting the EU in 2015. Its role is basically to collect funding and to allocate it to the relevant budgetary or non-budgetary instruments for funding. Hybrid instruments were created as flexible tools to respond to fast-moving events. However, these hybrid tools can also be seen as means to circumvent the regular budgetary procedures (Crowe, 2017).

9.3.2.3   Multispeed Europe

Multispeed Europe implies policies that are implemented by only a limited number of Member States. It presents challenges to financial accountability and it creates a complex policy architecture, leading in turn to parliamentary scrutiny and audit issues. Actions taken under intergovernmental agreements in general bypass the EU's institutional and procedural system of checks and balances.

9.3.2.4   Special instruments

Special instruments refer to the instruments that can be mobilized to respond to unforeseen events. They basically are above the MFF ceiling and they imply the use of limited financial amounts in peculiar circumstances that do not allow the expenditure of other funds (Crowe, 2017). They are represented by the Flexibility Instrument, by the Emergency Aid Reserve and by the European Solidarity Fund, among others.

9.3.2.5   Financial instruments

The increasing use of financial instruments is an example of demand-driven budget implementation. They create a greater complexity and pose risks to accountability because of the absence of clear links between the funds and the outcomes of the projects implemented. This concern was raised by the President of the ECA when presenting the ECA's annual report 2015 (Lehne, 2016). Back in 2011, the ECA had already pointed out the challenges resulting from the use of financial instruments in terms of 'accounting of the use of EU funds, their supervision, the ownership of the financial instrument, the capacity of Commission services to manage relatively complex financial instruments' (European Court of Auditors, 2011: 8). In 2014, it noted that it was still too early to assess whether the implementation of new rules would address the identified challenges (European Court of Auditors, 2014a).

The emergence of new instruments subject to different provisions in terms of monitoring and control and parliamentary oversight has led to increased complexity in the EU budgetary framework in terms of implementation as well as accountability. This complexity is illustrated by the many instruments and budgetary tools and their sometimes very different settings: partially funded by the EU, with the participation of some or all Member States and with different modes for implementation and different accountability procedures (Crowe, 2017). In its annual report on the budget 2016, the ECA noted that budgetary arrangements continued to increase complexity in the EU budget. It observed that, after the various crises that had affected the EU (the financial crisis and the migration crisis mainly), 'the number of entities and instruments involved in financing the implementation of EU policies and programmes has increased considerably', which 'makes it more difficult to manage, audit and report on EU spending effectively, or to obtain a comprehensive overview' (European Court of Auditors, 2017: 17). The ECA concluded: 'We note that a continuation of this trend risks undermining the accountability and transparency of the EU budget' (European Court of Auditors, 2017: 17). Having many different accounting and audit arrangements may lead to disproportionate levels of scrutiny, gaps and overlaps (European Court of Auditors, 2014a).

This complexity is not only problematic in terms of budgetary control and monitoring. More complexity and fragmentation tend to create more risks and democratic oversight becomes more challenging. Moreover, it adds to the overall perceived complexity of the EU in the eyes of its citizens, which in turn can decrease general public scrutiny of the use of the budget, often considered essential to sound democratic governance. Crowe summarizes the situation as follows: 'Revenue ultimately drawn from Union citizen-taxpayers to support Union policies is processed according to different procedures, involving different institutional actors and governance structures, different levels of transparency and parliamentary oversight and different auditing and discharge procedures, depending on the mechanism for which the funds are raised' (Crowe, 2017: 449).

9.3.2.6 Finding the balance between sound monitoring and control and the necessary flexibility of the EU budget

The Lisbon era is also characterized by the emphasis on flexibility in the management of the EU budget. Mijs and Schout (2015: 2) define budgetary flexibility as 'the ability of the budget to adjust to changing circumstances'. There are two main aspects related to flexibility and sound monitoring and control of the EU budget. First, there is a need to find the balance between allowing for more flexibility in budget spending and ensuring sound financial management. In this case flexibility refers to the rapid and targeted disbursement of funds to address specific circumstances. Second, there is also a balance between sound financial management and the necessary flexibility for the implementation of the EU budget. Here, flexibility refers to the necessary adaptation of the EU rules to the specificities of each context in which the budget is implemented. This also means ensuring sound financial management without increasing too much the administrative burden for managing authorities and implementing bodies. It is important to ensure that the flexibility guaranteed by new instruments allows for sound financial management and proper audit and control arrangements. While flexibility can be considered necessary to respond to emerging challenges, it may come at the expense of sound control and monitoring mechanisms, whether ex-ante or ex-post. In this regard, the EU response to the migration crisis is a good example. Several observers of the situation have expressed doubts about the soundness of financial management in this context (den Hertog, 2016 in Blomeyer & Sanz, 2017).

The second aspect of flexibility is more relevant in the context of this chapter and refers to the administrative burden created by the monitoring and control requirements. In 2014, the ECA observed that 'excessively complicated rules on spending or control requirements may delay implementation and contribute to negative image of the EU' (European Court of Auditors, 2014b: 25). While budgetary monitoring and control comprise a very important aspect of the EU funding, increased complexity in the requirements and the governance arrangements may lead beneficiaries to consider whether applying for EU funds is worth the hassle of administrative procedures. This is an issue that is often raised regarding the EU cohesion policy where managing authorities and intermediary bodies often declare that they have difficulties in implementing fully the guidelines of spending the EU budget or even the simplification options proposed by the European Commission (Council of European Municipalities and Regions, 2016).

In 2014, the ECA published a landscape review of the risks to the financial management of the EU budget and listed the specific areas where risks are significant. These include the eligibility rules and conditions to receive EU support. National managing authorities sometimes add eligibility conditions to the EU rules and the control systems may not be sufficient to verify eligibility.

This may create several layers of rules and lead to different interpretations and inconsistencies from one country to another. Moreover, Member States have varying levels of capacity to manage the implementation of EU funds. Administrative capacity varies greatly among the EU Member States in terms of skills and resources and this also plays a role in the monitoring and control systems. Recently, the EU has been taking steps to reduce the administrative burden and to simplify the EU rules in the framework of the Better Regulation Agenda.

9.4   CONCLUSIONS

The monitoring and control framework of the EU budget is structured around four EU institutions: the European Commission, the European Parliament, the Council and the ECA. Financial control takes place internally within the European Commission. The European Parliament, the Council and the ECA are responsible for external scrutiny via the discharge procedure and the ECA's role of auditor.

The budgetary framework governing the implementation, monitoring and control of EU finances is characterized by complexity and fragmentation, a tendency that accelerated in the Lisbon era with the creation of many instruments and their corresponding monitoring and control arrangements. These added to the already inherent complexity of the EU budget owing to the nature of the EU itself. While the risks regarding monitoring and control of the EU budget are real, there is also an important balance to find between sound financial management and the possibility of flexible implementation of the EU budget (see Chapter 8). The Better Regulation agenda aims at reducing burdens and inconsistencies. However, many further steps are necessary to improve the EU budget monitoring and control system.

Finally, the monitoring and control of the EU budget are primordial for financial accountability. Yet they does not guarantee the appropriate measure of results achieved. Some results rely on non-budgetary instruments such as regulatory instruments. In this regard, to ensure the coherence of EU policies and EU budget use as well as the complementarity between budgetary instruments and non-budgetary instruments, evaluation covering all these aspects is necessary. Over the past years, the Better Regulation Agenda advocated for putting evaluation at the heart of EU policy-making. A lot remains to be done to achieve EU objectives effectively combining non-budgetary tools and sound budgetary management.

REFERENCES

Blomeyer & Sanz (2016), 'Turkey: how the pre-accession funds have been spent, managed, controlled and the monitoring system?' Study for IPOL Department D. European Parliament, Brussels.

Blomeyer & Sanz (2017), 'The budgetary tools for financing the EU external policy'. Study for IPOL Department D. European Parliament, Brussels.

Bovens, M. (2007), 'Analysing and assessing accountability: a conceptual framework', *European Law Journal*, 13 (4), 447–468.

Caldeira, V. (2013), Speech at the Hearing of the Committee on Budgetary Control of the European Parliament, Brussels, 25 September.

Council of European Municipalities and Regions (2016), 'Cohesion policy: simplification and cutting red tape in European Structural and Investment Funds'. Position paper, January.

Crowe, R. (2017), 'The European budgetary galaxy', *European Constitutional Law Review*, 13 (3), 428–452.

D'Alfonso, A. (2014), 'Discharge procedure for the EU budget, Political scrutiny of budget implementation'. European Parliament Research Service, Brussels.

Eca.europa.eu (2018). *Mission and Role|European Court of Auditors*. https://www.eca.europa.eu/en/Pages/MissionAndRole.aspx (accessed 5 February 2018).

European Court of Auditors (2009) 'Special Report 15: EU Assistance implemented through the United Nations: decision-making and monitoring'. Publication Office of the European Union, Luxembourg.

Europarl.europa.eu. (2018). 'Discharge procedure: how Parliament scrutinises the EU budget'|News|European Parliament. http://www.europarl.europa.eu/news/en/headlines/eu-affairs/20150427STO46470/discharge-procedure-how-parliament-scrutinises-the-eu-budget (accessed 5 February 2018).

European Court of Auditors (2011) 'Opinion No 7/2011 on the proposal for a Regulation of the European Parliament and of the Council laying down common provisions on the European Regional Development Fund, the European Social Fund, the Cohesion Fund, the European Agricultural Fund for Rural Development and the European Maritime and Fisheries Fund covered by the Common Strategic Framework and laying down general provisions on the European Regional Development Fund, the European Social Fund and the Cohesion Fund and repealing Regulation (EC) No 1083/2006', Official Journal of the European Union.

European Court of Auditors (2012) 'Opinion No 4/2012 on the Commission's evaluation report on the Union's finances based on results achieved established under Article 318 of the Treaty on the Functioning of the European Union', Official Journal of the European Union.

European Court of Auditors (2014a) 'Gaps, overlaps and challenges: a landscape review of EU accountability and public audit arrangements'. Publication Office of the European Union, Luxembourg.

European Court of Auditors (2014b) 'Making the best use of EU money: a landscape review of the risks to the financial management of the EU budget'. Publication Office of the European Union, Luxembourg.

European Court of Auditors (2016) '2014 Report on the follow-up of the European Court of Auditors' special reports'. Publication Office of the European Union, Luxembourg.

European Court of Auditors (2017) '2016 EU audit in brief'. Publication Office of the European Union, Luxembourg.

Hojlund, S. (2015), 'Evaluation in the European Commission. For accountability or learning?', *European Journal of Risk Regulation*, 6 (1), 35–46.

Laffan, B. (2003) 'Auditing and accountability in the European Union', *Journal of European Public Policy*, 10 (5), 762–777.

Lehne, K. (2016), 'Speech by Klaus-Heiner Lehne, President of the European Court of Auditors', presentation of the ECA's 2015 annual report Committee on Budgetary Control of the European Parliament, European Parliament, 13 October.

Mijs, A. and Schout, A. (2015) 'Flexibility in the EU Budget, are there limits?' Clingendael Report. The Hague: Netherlands Institute of International Relations Clingendael.

Sanchez Barrueco, M. (2015), 'The contribution of the European Court of Auditors to the EU financial accountability in times of crisis', *Romanian Journal of European Affairs*, 15 (1), 70–85.

10. Growth, competitiveness and the EU budget

Luca Zamparini

10.1 INTRODUCTION

Competitiveness and growth represent two of the most important issues related to all economic systems. The linkages between these two issues are very important in order to understand long-term development and also convergence among different regions pertaining to larger economic areas, such as the European Union (EU). Providing the possibility to increase both competitiveness and growth not only increases the living standards of citizens, but also increases the approval rating of an institution such as the EU (see Chapter 5).

Competitiveness can be interpreted with respect to either private firms or economic systems. In the former case, it involves the ability to use inputs efficiently to produce goods and services that are competitive in a local or global economic environment. When economic systems (such as a local region, a country or the EU) are considered, competitiveness represents an important factor to maintain high standards of living and sustainable gross domestic product (GDP) growth based on the gains in productivity related both to physical and to human capital. In order to achieve such gains, it is important to create an economic environment that is prone to the diffusion of product and process innovation, to the catching-up of most advanced practices and technologies by firms, and on the substitution of firms and sectors that are no longer competitive with innovative and modern ones. These results can only be obtained through investments that target, among other things, human capital, strategic physical and immaterial infrastructures, climate change and environment, and the development of efficient institutions and markets. As highlighted in work by Molle (2014), the main drivers of competitiveness are then represented by: (a) industrial structure; (b) innovation; (c) physical and immaterial accessibility; (d) environmental quality; (e) human resources; and (f) good governance. A report by the European Investment Bank (2016) has stated that the EU's competitiveness is based on three levels: (a) the capability of firms to either generate or adapt to change; (b) the enabling environment;

and (c) the achievements in terms of trade performance, productivity growth and economic well-being. Preconditions for these three levels are the structural reforms, the removal of the barriers to investment and the integration of the EU single market. All of the factors that were mentioned both in Molle (2014) and in European Investment Bank (2016) provide a clear link between competitiveness and economic growth.

Growth is one of the most important themes in economic research. It has been considered since the early works of Adam Smith and David Ricardo. Modern growth theory dates to the period between 1939 and 1956 with the seminal works by Harrod (1939), Domar (1946) and Solow (1956). The former two models emphasized the role of investments and adapted the Keynesian theory to the long term. The latter model, which is still very influential, considered the saving rate, the growth rate of population and the production function to analyse the concept of conditional convergence[1] as the main explanation for heterogeneities among countries in the GDP per capita. The Solow model also highlights that continuing improvements in technology are necessary to sustain GDP per capita increases. The models that followed this line of research considered technological progress as the exogenous variable that may explain sustained GDP per capita growth rates for decades.

Since the mid-1980s, growth theory has been characterized by a renewed interest that was sparked by the works of Romer (1986) and Lucas (1988), aiming at analysing the determinants of long-run growth. In this line of research, the role of investments in research and development, the diffusion of technological advances and the role of human capital (Mankiw et al., 1992) are all considered. The result was the proposition of the theory of endogenous growth.

Sections 10.2 and 10.3 will consider the evolution of the EU GDP, the EU GDP per capita since the inception of the first financial perspective covering the period between 1988 and 1992 and the competitiveness in the EU and in the EU regions. Section 10.4 will then analyse the role of the EU budget for growth and competitiveness between the first financial perspective that covered the period between 1988 and 1992 and the Multiannual Financial Framework (MFF) for the period between 2014 and 2020. The last section will propose some concluding remarks.

---

[1]   According to the concept of conditional convergence, each country converges to a long-run stable level of GDP per capita that depends on its structural economic characteristics (i.e. infrastructure, education and financial system).

10.2 THE EVOLUTION OF EU GDP AND GDP PER CAPITA

Tables 10.1 and 10.2 present the data related to average growth rates of GDP and GDP per capita for the current EU28 countries in the following periods: (a) first financial framework (Delors Package I) between 1988 and 1992; (b) second financial framework (Delors package II) between 1993 and 1999; (c) the Agenda 2000 period between 2000 and 2006; (d) the 2007–2013 MFF; and (e) the years between 2014 and 2017, part of the 2014–2020 MFF.

Several considerations emerge from the analysis of Table 10.1. First, very few countries display a relatively stable pattern of average growth rates of the GDP in the considered periods (Austria, Belgium, Luxembourg and Malta). For all of the other countries, it is possible to notice large relative variations in the average growth rates. The averages of all of the considered countries has been markedly positive in three out of five periods. In the 1988–1992 period, several Eastern Europe countries (Bulgaria, Czech Republic, Hungary, Poland and Romania) underwent negative average growth rates of their GDPs. The 2007–2013 period saw eight countries displaying negative averages (Croatia, Cyprus, Denmark, Greece, Hungary, Italy, Portugal and Spain). It was also characterized by an overall average below 1% because of the world recession starting in 2008 and the ensuing debt crisis for some of the EU countries in 2011. The coefficient of variation[2] displays a very high value in the first considered period (1988–1992) and then decreases in the two ensuing periods (1993–1999 and 2000–2006). This decrease may be the outcome of the convergence among countries in those 14 years. The remarkable increase of the coefficient of variation between 2007 and 2013 witnesses the different reactions to the two crises occurring in those periods and, mostly, the impact of the debt crisis in Greece, Italy, Portugal and Spain. Among Eastern Europe countries, Bulgaria, Poland and the Slovak Republic fared much better than the others. Croatia and Hungary show negative average growth rates in this period. The years between 2014 and 2017 were marked by an important decrease of the coefficient of variation. Ireland has been by far the best performing country with an average growth rate of 11.71%. Greece and Italy have been the worst performing countries (with 0.39 and 0.86% respectively).

---

[2]   The coefficient of variation is a measure of the dispersion of data with respect to their mean. It is computed as the ratio between the standard deviation of distribution and the absolute value of the mean. The higher the value of the coefficient of variation is, the higher the dispersion of the observations.

Table 10.1   *GDP growth rates for EU countries*

	Average 1988–1992	Average 1993–1999	Average 2000–2006	Average 2007–2013	Average 2014–2017
Austria	3.41	2.45	2.24	0.98	1.60
Belgium	2.94	2.21	2.18	0.99	1.47
Bulgaria	−3.44	0.04	5.75	1.99	3.11
Croatia	—	3.36[a]	4.43	−0.69	2.05
Cyprus	6.83	4.15	4.00	−0.06	1.96
Czech Republic	−6.06	1.99	4.39	0.89	3.73
Denmark	1.09	2.81	2.05	−0.02	1.86
Estonia	—	5.10[a]	8.05	0.53	2.87
Finland	0.35	3.89	3.24	0.15	1.07
France	2.93	2.07	2.08	0.63	1.26
Germany	3.98	1.41	1.36	1.06	1.96
Greece	2.38	2.40	4.15	−3.79	0.39
Hungary	−3.06	2.09	4.24	−0.36	3.45
Ireland	4.95	7.90	6.14	0.44	11.71
Italy	2.39	1.50	1.49	−1.05	0.86
Latvia	—	5.12[a]	8.33	0.13	2.90
Lithuania	—	4.94[a]	7.05	1.99	2.94
Luxembourg	6.81	4.44	4.03	1.92	3.50
Malta	6.77	5.05	2.71	2.44	7.35
Netherlands	3.24	3.54	2.07	0.49	2.26
Poland	−2.25	5.39	3.75	3.68	3.64
Portugal	4.67	2.83	1.39	−0.77	1.75
Romania	−10.84	1.31	5.61	1.89	4.70
Slovak Republic	—	4.37	4.99	3.15	3.33
Slovenia	—	4.30[a]	3.97	0.08	3.35
Spain	3.44	2.75	3.77	−0.62	2.78
Sweden	0.73	2.75	3.23	1.04	3.16
UK	1.67	3.12	2.84	0.63	2.28
Average of all considered countries	1.50	3.33	3.91	0.63	2.97
Coefficient of variation	2.92	0.49	0.49	2.29	0.73

Note: [a] Average 1996–1999.
Source: Author's elaboration based on World Development Indicators Data by the World Bank.

Table 10.2   *GDP per capita growth rates for EU countries*

	Average 1988–1992	Average 1993–1999	Average 2000–2006	Average 2007–2013	Average 2014–2017
Austria	2.70	2.18	1.74	0.62	0.64
Belgium	2.58	1.95	1.73	0.15	1.04
Bulgaria	−2.52	0.60	6.92	2.65	3.79
Croatia	—	4.05[a]	4.81	−0.08	2.85
Cyprus	4.75	2.43	2.68	−2.03	2.07
Czech Republic	−6.01	2.04	4.45	0.51	3.54
Denmark	0.92	2.39	1.74	−0.48	1.17
Estonia	—	5.99[a]	8.53	0.84	2.92
Euro area	2.78	1.82	1.67	−0.05	1.59
Finland	−0.09	3.53	2.95	−0.32	0.74
France	2.44	1.67	1.35	0.11	0.83
Germany	3.25	1.15	1.31	1.38	1.32
Greece	1.58	1.90	3.80	−3.72	0.86
Hungary	−3.03	2.28	4.48	−0.10	3.74
Ireland	4.85	7.07	4.20	−0.68	10.59
Italy	2.32	1.47	1.18	−1.55	0.73
Latvia	—	6.14[a]	9.49	1.52	3.84
Lithuania	—	5.72[a]	8.20	3.47	4.10
Luxembourg	5.62	3.06	2.65	−0.09	0.99
Malta	5.39	4.26	2.05	1.71	5.00
Netherlands	2.52	2.94	1.58	0.10	1.77
Poland	—	5.28	3.95	3.71	3.68
Portugal	4.83	2.44	0.96	−0.68	2.16
Romania	—	1.51	6.50	2.76	5.23
Slovak Republic	—	4.11	5.05	3.04	3.21
Slovenia	—	4.39[a]	3.79	−0.29	3.26
Spain	3.19	2.30	2.38	−1.32	2.81
Sweden	0.10	2.43	2.86	0.24	1.94
UK	1.39	2.84	2.31	−0.13	1.54
Average of all considered countries	1.88	3.10	3.63	0.39	2.69
Coefficient of variation	1.56	0.53	0.65	4.27	0.76

Note: [a] Average 1996–1999.
Source: Author's elaboration based on World Development Indicators Data by the World Bank.

By taking into account the demographic dynamics, it is possible to consider the GDP per capita growth rate in Table 10.2. Its analysis leads to similar considerations to the comments for Table 10.1.

The average of all considered countries and the coefficient of variation evolve in a similar manner. Moreover, the average growth rates of GDP per capita were positive for all of the considered countries in the 1993–1998, 2000–2006 and 2014–2017 periods. However, in the 2007–2013 period the averages were negative for 13 out of the 28 sampled countries (Croatia, Cyprus, Denmark, Finland, Greece, Hungary, Ireland, Italy, Luxembourg, Portugal, Slovenia, Spain and the UK).

In general, it seems to emerge that in periods of crisis there is a large heterogeneity in the performances of the countries belonging to the EU. The EU budget cannot represent a useful tool to tackle idiosyncratic recessions/crises in some EU countries, given its low relative dimension with respect to the EU GDP and its lack of marked flexibility (see Chapter 8). Moreover, as stated in Nuñez Ferrer and Katarivas (2014), most of the funds are managed by local and national administrations which have very specific priorities and plans. The EU budgetary impacts are then positive in some cases but very ineffective in other ones, also in terms of competitiveness of the EU regions. This latter issue will be discussed in the following subsection.

10.3   THE COMPETITIVENESS IN THE EU AND IN THE EU REGIONS

The report by the European Investment Bank (2016) mentioned in the introduction has also provided an analysis of the degree of competitiveness in the EU. It has emerged that the EU performs worse than the US, Japan and South Korea in most of the indicators related to the innovation environment (availability of scientists and engineers, capacity for innovation, company spending on research and development, government procurement of advanced technological products, quality of scientific research institutions and university–industry collaboration in research and development), especially in many Southern and new Member States. The reasons for this weak performance are twofold. On the one hand, there are some structural deficiencies (inefficient exploitation of knowledge created elsewhere, weak industry–science links and poor commercialization of research results). On the other hand, in the 2010s the increasing competition of emerging economies and US and the slow recovery from the crises mentioned in Section 10.2 also played an important role. The European Investment Bank (2016) report also indicated the key strategic sectors in which the EU is lagging behind the other competitors (life sciences, semiconductors and software), while it has an advantage in other sectors (energy, solid waste and water technologies and transport equipment). Moreover, it should be taken

Table 10.3   *Annual private/public investment for technological innovation and adaptation (€ billion)*

	Required	Actual	Gap
Transport equipment	55	30	25
Machinery and equipment, including information and communications technology and electronics	75	40	35
Life sciences/pharmaceuticals	40	15	25
Renewable energy and eco-innovation			20
Others			25
Adoption of latest generation technology in advanced manufacturing sector	320	230	90
Total gap			220

Source: Author's elaboration based on European Investment Bank (2016).

into account that another source of competitiveness is the adoption of the latest generation technology in the advanced manufacturing sector, especially in the countries that have traditionally depended on basic manufacturing and services, such as the Central and Eastern Europe ones. In order to catch up in the weak sectors and to maintain the competitive advantage in others, the report provides an estimation of the gap between the current and the required investment, summarized in Table 10.3.

Another dimension of competitiveness is represented by the creation of an enabling environment. This requires human capital, strategic infrastructures in transport, logistics, energy, water and waste management. As far as human capital is concerned, there is the need to increase both the capital expenditure, related to the infrastructure (including ICT equipment), and the operational one that is mostly related to the teaching and administrative staff. The investments for the strategic infrastructures for transport and logistics should mainly address the urban movement of goods and people (which affects more than 70% of EU population), the completion of the internal market to achieve seamless and efficient transport systems, and the improvement of the international gateways (especially ports and airports). The energy sector is another relevant one for EU competitiveness. Investments should be directed to upgrade energy networks, increase energy efficiency in buildings and industry and foster power generation, with an emphasis on renewable sources. Telecommunications should be improved by widening the reach of broadband and by increasing data centre capacity and cyber-security. Lastly, water and waste management should be upgraded in terms of water security (including flood risk management), compliance and rehabilitation of Europe's water infrastructure, enhancement of waste management and material recovery,

Table 10.4   Annual investments for an enabling environment for competitiveness (€billion)

	Required	Actual	Gap
Operating expenditure to match US investments in education	880	790	90
Energy efficiency savings in building and industry	112	42	70
Compliance and rehabilitation of Europe's water infrastructure	75	30	45
Ensuring sufficient capacity in interurban traffic	80	40	40
Modernizing urban transport to meet global benchmarks	80	40	40
Reaching global benchmark for broadband services	75	45	30
Additional needs for resilient and efficient urban infrastructure	40	13	27
Matching US data centre capacity	50	25	25
Upgrading energy networks (gas and electricity)	64	47	18
Water security, including flood risk management	15	2	13
Power generation, including renewables	53	41	12
Capital expenditure to match US investments in education	80	70	10
Matching US investments in cyber-security	35	25	10
Enhancing waste management/materials recovery	8	3	5
Total gap	1,647	1,213	435

Source: Author's elaboration based on European Investment Bank (2016).

and additional needs for resilient and efficient urban infrastructure. Table 10.4 summarizes the actual expenditure (2015), the required one and the investment gap to achieve an enabling environment comparable with other world regions. The items are ordered by decreasing absolute value of investment gap.

It emerges that the overall annual investment gap is equal to €435 billion (given by the difference between a required expenditure of €1647 billion and an actual one of €1213 billion). The two issues that require the largest increases in investment are the operating expenditure to match US investments in education and energy efficiency savings in building and industry.

By considering that the overall EU budget for 2015 was equal to €145billion, it is evident that an increase in the EU budget and a set of measures to foster private investments are necessary to enhance the EU competitiveness. A proposal by Griffith-Jones and Cozzi (2016) considers a three-fold approach to increasing public EU investments for competitiveness relying on: (a) an expansion of lending by the European Investment Bank, financed by an increase in the capital provided by Member States; (b) the use of funds of the EU budget to mitigate the investment risks of the private sector; and (c) the creation of a new European fund for investment to be used for long-term, large-scale infrastructure projects related to energy, ICT and transport. However, more prominence should be given to regulations and fiscal laws leading to higher private investments.

After considering the situation at the EU level, it is also important to take into account the regional dimension of competitiveness. The European Commission (Annoni et al., 2017) has proposed a competitiveness index for the EU regions based on the Global Competitiveness Index of the World Economic Forum in 2010, 2013 and 2016. This index aims at providing a measure of economic and social development for the regions of the EU and at fostering medium- and long-term plans. The main pattern that emerges from the three editions of the regional competitiveness index is a polycentric one with the best performing regions represented by the metropolitan and capital areas in many EU countries (Finland, France, Germany, and Spain among others). In some cases, the regions neighbouring the best performing ones are also characterized by a high degree of competitiveness. In other cases (i.e. in Spain), the situation is marked by the lack of spillover effects and by the fact that the regions adjoining the best performing ones are much less competitive. The most competitive regions are characterized by higher GDP per capita and by higher rates of net migration (the difference between in-migration and out-migration). These heterogeneous results pave the way for an active approach to regional policies by the European Union (see Section 10.4). A paper by Glaeser (2012) has highlighted that there are three possible rationales for the implementation of different spatial policies. A first debatable reason is related to the possibility that barriers to mobility may be a response to the negative externalities that characterize areas with high population densities. However, the economic literature is not conclusive in this respect as positive externalities may compensate for negative externalities in denser areas. A second reason is related to the mission statement of the EU with respect to equity. By helping poorer regions, it is possible to help a large share of poor EU citizens. A third argument considers the possibility of generating net positive spillovers for the people and firms located in the subsidized regions.

Despite the varying theoretical findings and empirical evidence, raising the degree of convergence among regions represents an important factor in the development of the EU. The next section will consider how the budgets related to the various financial perspectives and multiannual financial frameworks have tackled the issues related to growth and competitiveness in the EU.

10.4   THE ROLE OF THE EU BUDGET FOR GROWTH AND COMPETITIVENESS

The role of the EU budget for growth and competitiveness can, first, be ascertained by the historical analysis of the expenditure commitments of the EU

Commission in the past decades. Tables 10.5 and 10.6 provide a breakdown of these commitments from 1991 to 2018.

Table 10.5 contains the EU Commission expenditure divided by heading for the 1991–2003 period. In that period, there were nine main lines that represented: (a) European Agricultural Guidance and Guarantee Fund (EAGGF); (b) structural operations, structural and cohesion expenditure, other agricultural and regional operations, transport and fisheries; (c) training, youth, culture, information and other social operations; (d) energy, Euratom nuclear safeguards and environment; (e) consumer protection, internal market, industry and innovation technology; (f) research and technological development; (g) cooperation with developing and other non-Member countries (external actions); (h) expenditure in support of community operations; and (i) common foreign and security policy.

It emerges that expenditure on agriculture issues has always represented more than 50% of the overall budget and it has also been characterized by an almost continuous upward trend. It is also important to take into account that the expenditures on structural issues, cohesion, regional operations, transport and fisheries have ranked second in the whole period and have displayed the largest relative increase.

On the other hand, less than €1 billion have been spent yearly on the heading referring to training, youth, culture and information and less than 5% of the overall budget has been destined for research, technological development and industry, and innovation technology. This demonstrates the low interest of the EU in long-term growth investments. A very marginal sum was devoted to common foreign and security policy in the 1995–2003 period.

In 2004–2018, it has been possible to observe a more detailed division of main headings of the EU Commission expenditure commitments (see Table 10.6 where the list of entrances in the table is coherent with the structure presented in the EU budget publications).

For the whole period, the largest expenditure heading is represented, similarly to the period considered in Table 10.5, by agriculture and rural development. Boulanger and Philippidis (2015) have proposed a model trying to estimate the effects of a possible 50% cut in agriculture-related expenditure in the EU budget. It appears that this cut would have a limited impact on third countries and on the EU agricultural output. However, an effect of this cut would be an impact on intra-EU trade balances, real incomes and income transfers where some countries (i.e. Netherlands and Germany) would gain and others (i.e. France, Poland and Romania) would lose from these expenditure reductions. This limits the possibility of observing a remarkable change in the situation unless the legal arrangements to modify the budget are drastically changed.

Table 10.5 *EU Commission expenditure divided by heading (billions of Ecus until 1998 and billions of Euros since 1999)*

	1991	1992	1993	1994	1995	1996	1997	1998	1999	2000	2001	2002	2003
EAGGF Guarantee section	32.52	36.04	35.05	37.46	38.42	41.33	41.31	40.94	40.94	41.93	43.80	44.48	44.76
Structural operations, structural and cohesion expenditure, other agricultural and regional operations, transport and fisheries	14.27	17.62	20.71	21.53	23.73	26.01	26.63	28.59	30.66	31.96	31.77	32.29	33.33
Training, youth, culture, information and other social operations	0.38	0.51	0.47	0.54	0.63	0.82	0.78	0.71	0.74	0.72	0.79	0.89	0.88
Energy, Euratom nuclear safeguards and environment	0.21	0.23	0.24	0.17	0.19	0.19	0.20	0.18	0.20	0.19	0.19	0.19	0.25
Consumer protection, internal market, industry and innovation technology	0.28	0.25	0.30	0.46	0.65	0.67	0.73	0.78	0.88	1.01	1.06	1.12	1.17
Research and technological development	1.74	1.95	2.35	2.56	2.79	3.10	3.16	3.00	2.99	3.60	3.61	3.75	3.65

	1991	1992	1993	1994	1995	1996	1997	1998	1999	2000	2001	2002	2003
Cooperation with developing and other non-Member Countries (external actions)	2.23	2.27	2.99	3.35	4.16	4.65	4.78	4.51	4.28	5.48	6.20	7.39	7.69
Expenditure in support of community operations	0.20	0.15	—	—	—	—	—	—	—	—	—	—	—
Common foreign and security policy	—	—	—	—	0.08	0.07	0.03	0.02	0.23	0.03	0.04	0.04	0.05
Repayments, guarantees and reserves	1.30	0.89	—	0.32	1.87	0.93	0.45	0.44	0.35	0.20	0.21	0.34	0.37

Source: Author's elaboration based on the EU budgets for the considered years that were retrieved from https://eur-lex.europa.eu/budget/www/index-en.htm (last accessed 25 August 2018).

Table 10.6   EU Commission Expenditure commitments divided by heading (billions of Euros)

	2004	2005	2006	2007	2008	2009	2010	2011	2012	2013	2014	2015	2016	2017	2018
Economic and financial affairs	0.48	0.45	0.47	0.47	0.40	0.43	0.45	0.52	0.61	0.56	0.23	0.37	2.53	3.09	2.34
Enterprise	**0.31**	**0.34**	**0.39**	**0.52**	**0.59**	**0.66**	**0.80**	**1.06**	**1.15**	**1.14**	**2.50**	**2.51**	**2.26**	**2.46**	**2.36**
Competition	0.08	0.09	0.10	0.07	0.08	0.09	0.09	0.09	0.10	0.09	0.10	0.10	0.10	0.11	0.11
Employment and social affairs	**10.84**	**11.59**	**11.93**	**11.43**	**11.48**	**11.19**	**11.25**	**11.40**	**11.58**	**12.00**	**13.80**	**13.09**	**12.92**	**13.81**	**14.52**
Agriculture and rural development	**48.76**	**53.72**	**55.45**	**52.44**	**53.70**	**54.68**	**57.78**	**57.29**	**58.59**	**59.00**	**58.05**	**58.05**	**61.99**	**57.54**	**58.16**
Energy and transport[a]	1.35	1.42	1.46	0.98	1.92	2.74	4.87	1.55	1.66	1.74	2.87	3.28	4.06	3.78	4.01
Environment	0.32	0.32	0.34	0.35	0.40	0.46	0.46	0.47	0.49	0.50	0.41	0.43	0.44	0.47	0.50
Research	**3.22**	**3.36**	**3.52**	**3.56**	**4.04**	**4.66**	**5.14**	**5.33**	**5.93**	**6.86**	**6.28**	**6.66**	**5.74**	**6.19**	**6.89**
Information society	1.18	1.24	1.42	1.43	1.49	1.51	1.62	1.54	1.68	1.81	1.62	1.72	1.78	2.01	2.13
Direct research	0.31	0.37	0.33	0.35	0.36	0.37	0.38	0.39	0.41	0.42	0.42	0.40	0.40	0.40	0.40
Fisheries	0.93	1.03	0.92	0.89	0.95	0.98	0.99	1.00	1.03	0.91	0.94	1.08	1.09	1.11	1.13
Internal market	0.07	0.07	0.07	0.06	0.06	0.07	0.07	0.09	0.10	0.10	0.11	0.11	0.08	0.09	0.09
Regional policy	**26.81**	**27.10**	**28.63**	**34.68**	**35.98**	**37.90**	**38.90**	**40.38**	**42.05**	**43.38**	**33.16**	**35.34**	**35.98**	**38.61**	**39.81**
Taxation and customs union	0.11	0.12	0.13	0.11	0.12	0.13	0.14	0.14	0.14	0.15	0.16	0.16	0.16	0.18	0.18

	2004	2005	2006	2007	2008	2009	2010	2011	2012	2013	2014	2015	2016	2017	2018
Education and culture	**0.95**	**1.05**	**1.00**	**1.22**	**1.33**	**1.40**	**1.50**	**2.43**	**2.70**	**2.76**	**2.57**	**2.89**	**2.82**	**3.37**	**3.85**
Press/communication	0.17	0.19	0.20	0.20	0.21	0.21	0.22	0.27	0.26	0.26	0.24	0.24	0.20	0.21	0.21
Health and consumer protection	0.47	0.52	0.55	0.53	0.55	0.62	0.68	0.69	0.69	0.63	0.61	0.61	0.58	0.56	0.60
Freedom, security and justice	0.51	0.57	0.59	0.61	0.71	0.92	1.06	1.21	1.26	1.29	1.19	1.17	—	—	—
Migration and home affairs	—	—	—	—	—	—	—	—	—	—	—	—	**1.84**	**3.46**	**2.64**
External relations	3.53	3.56	3.47	3.38	3.92	4.01	4.21	4.31	4.82	4.89	0.72	0.76	0.78	0.74	0.84
Trade	0.08	0.08	0.08	0.07	0.08	0.08	0.08	0.11	0.10	0.11	0.12	0.12	0.11	0.11	0.12
Relations with ACP[b]	1.18	1.24	1.26	1.22	1.32	1.87	1.65	1.54	1.50	1.57	—	—	—	—	—
Development and cooperation	—	—	—	—	—	—	—	—	—	—	4.95	5.04	3.14	3.70	3.49
Enlargement	**1.28**	**1.35**	**2.07**	**1.05**	**1.10**	**1.08**	**1.02**	**1.12**	**1.09**	**1.06**	**1.51**	**1.53**	**3.75**	**4.51**	**3.96**
Humanitarian aid	0.51	0.51	0.51	0.75	0.77	0.80	0.82	0.88	0.90	0.92	0.99	1.01	1.03	1.05	1.19
Fight against fraud	0.05	0.06	0.06	0.06	0.07	0.08	0.08	0.08	0.08	0.08	0.08	0.08	0.08	0.08	0.08
Commission's policy coordination and legal advice	0.20	0.21	0.21	0.17	0.18	0.19	0.19	0.19	0.19	0.20	0.20	0.19	0.20	0.23	0.24

	2004	2005	2006	2007	2008	2009	2010	2011	2012	2013	2014	2015	2016	2017	2018
Commission's administration	0.67	0.65	0.66	0.92	0.97	0.97	0.98	1.02	1.02	1.04	1.01	1.00	1.01	1.07	1.13
Budget	1.48	1.39	1.16	0.52	0.27	0.28	0.07	0.07	0.07	0.07	0.10	0.07	0.07	0.08	0.08
Audit	0.01	0.01	0.01	0.01	0.01	0.01	0.01	0.01	0.01	0.01	0.01	0.01	0.02	0.02	0.02
Statistics	0.12	0.13	0.13	0.12	0.12	0.13	0.14	0.15	0.13	0.08	0.13	0.13	0.14	0.14	0.14
Pensions	0.84	0.91	0.95	1.00	1.09	1.16	1.21	1.28	1.33	1.42	1.50	1.57	1.65	1.80	1.90
Language services	–	–	–	0.36	0.37	0.38	0.39	0.39	0.40	0.40	0.40	0.39	0.39	0.41	0.40
Energy	–	–	–	–	–	–	–	0.70	0.72	0.73	0.96	1.06	1.53	1.64	1.64
Justice and consumers	–	–	–	–	–	–	–	–	0.22	0.22	0.20	0.21	0.26	n.a.	0.26
Climate action	–	–	–	–	–	–	–	–	–	–	0.12	013	0.14	n.a.	0.16
Reserves	0.61	0.56	0.65	4.43	1.82	0.93	1.29	0.98	1.45	0.94	0.46	0.47	2.65	n.a.	0.52

Notes: [a] Only transport since 2011; [b] African, Caribbean and Pacific States.
Source: Author's elaboration based on the EU budgets for the considered years that were retrieved from https://eur-lex.europa.eu/budget/www/index-en.htm (last accessed 25 August 2018).

The second largest expenditure heading is related to regional policy. The commitments for this issue have grown from €26.81 billion in 2004 to €39.81 billion in 2018, increasing by about 50%. This is a very important development of the EU budget, also considering the discussion in Section 10.2. Another two headings that should foster long-term growth and competitiveness are those related to employment and social affairs and to research. In 2018, the EU Commission allocated €14.52 billion and €6.89 billion to these areas, respectively. Moreover, it more than doubled its commitment on research between 2004 and 2018. Two other important headings deal with education and culture, and enlargement. Two new headings were included in 2014 (Development and cooperation replacing Relations with African, Caribbean and Pacific States) and in 2016 (Migration and home affairs replacing Freedom, security and justice) and have, to some extent, reduced the rigidity of the EU budget (see Chapter 8).

10.5   CONCLUDING REMARKS

The present chapter has provided an analysis of growth, competitiveness and of the role of the EU budget with respect to these two important economic issues. It has emerged that the largest share of the expenditure has been constantly directed towards agricultural policy. However, since the mid-2000s, a larger emphasis has been put on regional policy and on research, as important factors of growth and competitiveness. Moreover, in the mid-2010s, two new headings explicitly referring to migration and to development and cooperation were inserted in the EU budget. The 2021–2027 MFF may start from these changes and determine a reform of the EU budget. A paper by Begg (2017) analysed the possibility of three different scenarios: the base/status quo scenario, a moderate reform and a radical reform. The elements leading to a base scenario are related to several issues. The first is the conflicts between net contributors and net recipient Member States which may keep the overall EU budget expenditure at about 1% of the EU GDP. The agreement on the increase in spending is problematic given that the largest share of the EU budget revenues is represented by national contributions (see, among others, Benedetto, 2017; Chapters 3 and 5). Secondly, the agricultural and cohesion policy will receive the majority of EU commitments. Thirdly, it is not possible to reduce administrative expenditures. In this context, a moderate reform scenario would not be able to induce a relevant change in the economic function of the EU budget. A radical reform scenario would imply that, in the short term, the EU budget should serve as a tool of macroeconomic stabilization (see Dullien and Schwarzer, 2009). Moreover, in the long term, it should be more focussed on investments fostering growth and competitiveness. A possible strategy to achieve this goal may be to align it with the quinquennial mandates of the

European Parliament and the Commission (see Chapter 2), in order to reduce the degree of Member States' control.

REFERENCES

Annoni, P., Dijkstra, L. and Gargano, N. (2017), 'The EU regional competitiveness index 2016'. European Commission working paper 02/2017.

Begg, I. (2017), 'The EU budget after 2020', *European Policy Analysis*, 9, 1–11.

Benedetto, G. (2017), 'Institutions and the route to reform of the European Union's budget revenue, 1970–2017', *Empirica*, 44, 615–633.

Boulanger, P. and Philippidis, G. (2015), 'The EU budget battle: assessing the trade and welfare impacts of CAP budgetary reform', *Food Policy*, 51, 119–130.

Domar, E. D. (1946), 'Capital expansion, rate of growth, and employment', *Econometrica*, 14 (2), 137–147.

Dullien, S. and Schwarzer, D. (2009), 'Bringing macroeconomics into the EU budget debate: why and how?', *Journal of Common Market Studies*, 47 (1), 153–174.

European Investment Bank (2016), *Restoring EU Competitiveness*. EIB, Luxembourg.

Glaeser, E. (2012), 'The challenge of urban policy', *Journal of Policy Analysis and Management*, 31 (1), 111–122.

Griffith-Jones, S. and Cozzi, G. (2016), 'Investment-led growth: a solution to the European crisis' in M. Jacobs and M. Mazzucato (eds), *Rethinking Capitalism: Economics and Policy for Sustainable and Inclusive Growth*. Wiley-Blackwell, Chichester, pp. 119–133.

Harrod, R. F. (1939), 'An essay in dynamic theory', *The Economic Journal*, 49, 14–33.

Lucas, R. (1988), 'On the mechanics of economic development', *Journal of Monetary Economics*, 22 (1), 3–42.

Mankiw, G., Romer, D. and Weil, D. (1992), 'A contribution to the empirics of economic growth', *Quarterly Journal of Economics*, 107 (2), 407–437.

Molle, W. (2014), 'Competitiveness, EMU and cohesion experiences in the past (2000–2013); assessment of the present (2014–2020) and lessons for the future (2020 and beyond)', *International Journal of Management and Economics*, 44, 39–50.

Nuñez Ferrer, J. and Katarivas, M. (2014), 'What are the effects of the EU budget: driving force or drop in the ocean?', *Center for European Policy Studies Special Report*, 86, April.

Romer P. (1986), 'Increasing returns and long run growth', *Journal of Political Economy*, 94 (5), 1002–1037.

Solow R. (1956), 'A contribution to the theory of economic growth', *The Quarterly Journal of Economics*, 70 (1), 65–94.

11. The relevance of the EU budget for the structural balances of Member States

Maurizia Pierri

11.1 INTRODUCTION

The EU annual budget lays down all the expenditure and revenue of the European Union relating to a financial year and it is responsible for the financing of the EU programs and actions in all of its areas of intervention. The formation of the budget is governed not only by the principles of the Treaty, but also by the Financial Regulation (art. 322 of the Treaty on the Functioning of the European Union, TFEU) that establishes 'the procedure to be adopted for establishing and implementing the budget and for presenting and auditing accounts'. It appears that the EU budget is inadequate to the Union's activities and competences. Furthermore, the financing of the Union is not based on direct contributions but on the level of prosperity of the Members States. This mechanism should exclude tensions between Members. However, some of them complain of being 'net-payers', i.e. not being recipients of direct or indirect funds arising from European programs whose extent corresponds to what they contribute to the EU (see Chapter 5).

According to the financial regulation (reg. EU, Euratom no. 966/2012 of the European Parliament and Council, 25 October 2012, in GUUE L 298, 1), to the application rules adopted by the Commission (reg. EU delegate no. 1268/2012, in GUUE L 362, 1) and to the provisions (as already mentioned) of the TFEU, the European budget, as in almost all Member States, is regulated by a set of accounting principles:

1. Principles of unity and of budgetary accuracy – no revenue shall be collected and no expenditure accomplished unless present in a line of the budget; all operations are subject to the approval of the competent authority).

2. Principle of annuality – the appropriations (commitment and payment) entered in the budget shall be authorised for a financial year between 1 January and 31 December. Exceptions are possible for Union programs or actions intended to be realized in a multiannual space of time. The annual budget can be corrected if additional resources are needed to cope with the effects of unexpected needs, such as the consequences of a natural disaster in one Member State.
3. Principle of universality – total revenue aims at covering total payment appropriations.
4. Principle of specialty – appropriations should be earmarked for specific purposes by title and chapter and the chapters must be further subdivided into articles and items. Budgetary authorisation must be given in a specific way for certain expenditure; a certain degree of flexibility (see Chapter 8) is possible in the management of the budget, so that surpluses are reported in the next financial year; outstanding credits should not be accumulated, but divided into supporting causes.
5. Principle of unit of account.
6. Principle of transparency.
7. Principle of sound financial management, which implies economy, efficiency and effectiveness.
8. Principle of equilibrium – revenue and payment appropriations must be in balance; total expenditure must remain within the limits of resources.

The approval of the community budget requires a complex procedure (articulated in two stages, one of which is activated only in the case of disagreement between the Council and the European Parliament) that involves various EU institutions. In the first phase, the proposed budget is defined by the Council on the basis of a draft drawn up by the Commission. By 5 October of the year preceding the financial year which the budget relates to, the Council proposes this statement to the European Parliament.

The Parliament has three possibilities: (a) approving the budget with no amendments and/or modifications; (b) making some amendments, on behalf of a majority of its members, or proposing some modifications, by an absolute majority; or (c) rejecting the proposal, on behalf of the majority of its members and with two-thirds of the votes.

In case of (b), the Council has 15 days to decide on the amendments, by a qualified majority, and to give its opinion on the proposals made by the Parliament. The Parliament, within 15 days of the new draft budget, can amend or reject the modifications made by the Council to its own amendments, acting by a majority of its members and three-fifths of the votes cast or reject *in toto* the budget and require the submission of a new project, for 'important reasons' acting by a majority of its members and two-thirds of the votes cast.

The guarantee of legitimacy of the accounts of all revenue and expenditure entered in the Community budget is ensured by the control of the European Court of Auditors (see Chapter 9). Once the procedure is completed, the President of the Parliament is responsible for ascertaining the definitive adoption of the budget.

Several authors have considered the principles governing Europe's revenues, the annual and multiannual budget and the procedures needed for their approval (see, among others, Villani, 2013; Adam and Tizzano, 2017). Among the principles that govern the EU Budget, the one that will be discussed in this chapter is the *golden rule* (principle of equilibrium). Such principle was not widely adopted by Member States but it has been progressively implemented given the EU requirements (Tereanu et al., 2014). The political decisions in fiscal policy with respect to the level and nature of taxation and to the use of tax revenues remained a competence of Member States. This determined a considerable difference in countries' behavior and so a partial ineffectiveness of the golden rule (Fabbrini, 2013; Lledò et al., 2017).

The second section deals with the issue of the regulatory framework of the budgets in Eurozone countries, highlighting the complexity of the regulatory system at European level, because of the simultaneous presence of standards deriving from treaties both external and stipulated within the Union law, regulations and directives. This set of rules is for monetary policy but fiscal policy remains in the sovereignty of individual states, so achieving stability is linked to the virtuous behavior of each country. The balanced budget rule is also brought to bear on state budgets, owing to an international treaty (the so-called Fiscal Compact) that provides for the incorporation into each country's law (preferably at constitutional level) of the rule of the balanced budget. The compliance with the principle of balance guaranteed by prior scrutiny and the corrective arm of European institutions, as well as a series of deadlines, which are useful to monitor the progress of accounts within the Eurozone countries (Giupponi, 2014).

The third section analyzes the monitoring procedures by the European institutions on the appropriateness of the budgetary accounts of individual states, emphasizing the distinction between nominal and structural balance that will be better considered in Section 11.4. This section will discuss how (a) the possibility of including the rule of balanced budget even at subconstitutional level, (b) the difference between nominal and structural balance and (c) the ambiguous identification of justification causes for the violation of the stability standards determine a considerable difference in countries' behavior and so a partial ineffectiveness of the golden rule.

11.2   THE REGULATORY FRAMEWORK OF THE BUDGETS IN EUROZONE COUNTRIES

Despite the adoption of a single currency, the political decisions related to fiscal policy, to the level and nature of taxation, and to the use of tax revenues remained a competence of the Member States (Barnes et al., 2016; Amick et al., 2017). Even though the economic literature has always emphasized that the adoption of a single currency involves consistent fiscal policies between the countries of the area, the EU is not a federal state. Consequently, transferring fiscal policy to a supranational level would have violated the principle of representative democracy, 'no taxation without representation' (see Chapter 4), and would have met the resistance of the Member States unwilling to surrender such an important part of their sovereignty (Delledonne, 2012; Luciani, 2013). On the other hand, the Treaties (i.e. the Maastricht Treaty but the provisions are still present in the TFEU) oblige Member States to coordinate economic policies. They also give the EU the task of promoting such coordination, through a recommendation adopted by the Council. The Treaties also provide preventive measures and corrective ones on Member States' budgets. In the former case, there is a multilateral surveillance (art. 121 TFEU) by the Council and the Commission who can intervene by issuing warnings. In the latter case, a corrective procedure (art. 126 TEU) can be triggered by the Council, after a proposal of the Commission, in the event of an excessive deficit.

The EU treaty framework has not been sufficient to ensure financial sustainability in Eurozone countries, so a few years after the approval of the Treaty of Maastricht in 1996, the Stability and Growth Pact was signed in Dublin and afterwards a number of measures were introduced in different regulatory acts that would guarantee stability (Regulations 1466 and 1467 of July 1997). These measures have had no effect on the ownership of powers in the field of public finance but on their implementation, by imposing a series of obligations and prohibitions and identifying a process intended to verify compliance. The sovereign debts have shown the inconsistency between the European monetary policy and the fiscal indiscipline of some Member States. In fact, the discipline of treaties makes a counter-cyclical use of the budget and the increase in available resources impossible (Grasso, 2012). Moreover, the crisis highlighted the lack of solidarity mechanisms between Member States, especially in the case of the Greek debt crisis. A package of measures outside the Union law was approved, and the mechanism of financial solidarity was subsequently introduced by an international agreement, the *European Financial Stability Facility* and only in 2011, in order to overcome the objections to the incompatibility of the latter instruments with the principle of no bail-out. In 2012, an international treaty finally established the European Stabilisation Mechanism, which replaced the mechanism of financial solidarity and the European Financial Stability Facility. The Treaty also required the Member States to apply and to entrench, preferably with constitutional provisions, within one year from the date of its implementation, some rules, the most important of which are certainly the balanced-budget clauses.

To sum up, the current situation in the European budgetary regulation, in which the golden rule is inserted, is extremely complex, resulting as it does from a system of different legal sources:

1. the Treaty on the Functioning of the European Union, and in particular articles 121 (multilateral surveillance on the economic policies of the Member States), 126 (procedure for pursuing excessive public deficits), 136 (special scheme for the Eurogroup) and Protocol no. 12 of the Treaty of Lisbon (on the excessive deficit procedure);
2. secondary laws – two regulations of 1997, modified in 2005, better known as the Stability and Growth Pact, amended yet again in 2011 by some regulation of the so-called Six Pack (reg. EU 1175/2011 and reg. EU 1177/2011), reg. EU 1173/2011, also part of the Six Pack, and the regulation of the Two Packs intended only for the Members of Euro-area; finally two application acts of Protocol no. 12 of the Treaty of Lisbon, i.e. a regulation (479/2009/EC) and a directive (dir. 85/2011/EU);
3. an international treaty that falls outside the European Union (the Fiscal Compact).

The following section will discuss the control over Member States, especially with respect to the golden rule of a balanced budget.

11.3 THE CONTROL OVER MEMBER STATES AND THE GOLDEN RULE OF A BALANCED BUDGET

Member States are incorporated into a system of strict controls, managed by the Commission and by the Council (while the role of the European Parliament is limited to so-called economic dialogue), articulated by procedures which considerably condition their margin for action (Asatryan et al., 2017):

1. A preventive measure (so-called preventive arm), linked to the Stability and Growth Pact, based on the concept of prudent budgetary policy that should encourage the implementation of the medium-term objectives (MTO), which is a three-year program aimed at achieving a structural deficit (so relating to structural and not nominal balance) lower than 0.5% in the Eurozone countries and 1% in the others. Annual adjustments, taking into account exceptional circumstances or structural reforms, are allowed to those Member States that do not reach their MTO. This legal framework

is characterized by a certain flexibility, because it takes into account not only economic fluctuations but also national structural interventions. The countries that have reached their MTO must contain the expenditure within their gross domestic product (GDP) growth rate defined as 'prudent' and evaluated on the basis of a 10-year projection. The rules of 'good spending' stipulate that the increase in revenue of countries in a favorable economic climate should be used to reduce debt. Compliance to the rules by countries can be established when evaluating the budgetary plans presented by the Member States in the framework of programs for the Stability and Growth Pact. If the assessment has a negative outcome, the Commission can intervene with a 'warning' or, in particularly serious cases, the Council may issue a recommendation to adopt corrective measures which must be observed under penalty of the opening of a monitoring procedure. Precautionary surveillance also concerns the macroeconomic aspects: the Six Pack, in fact [reg. (EU) 1174 and 1175 2011] has proposed that the Commission should consider a series of macroeconomic indicators and verify that they do not exceed the thresholds of alert and thereafter draw up the list of states that are at risk of imbalance. The forecasts on the trend of the macro-economic indicators must be drawn up by independent authorities, through transparent procedures (according to the provisions of the Two pack).

2. A corrective control (so-called corrective arm), which is deployed when, despite preventive measures, the deficit of a country exceeds 3% or is in violation of the debt rule, i.e. its progressive reduction, evaluated very strictly, especially after the changes to the original stability and growth pact. The Member States whose debt exceeds 60% of GDP must take measures to reduce it annually according to prearranged deadlines, whose quantitative rule requires a reduction of the debt by a twentieth part per year for the share in excess of the parameter of 60%. Violation of this rule (defined debt rule and introduced into the Stability and Growth Pact by the Six Pack) does not automatically lead to the opening of an excessive deficit procedure because the final assessment takes into account a number of risk factors, such as the structure of the debt and the rate of growth in national GDP. Anyway, there are two benchmarks for the implementation of art. 126 TFEU: deficit and debt, but, for both of these, exceeding the parameter does not automatically lead to the beginning of the procedure because there are bailout clauses that take into account the decrease and/or proximity to the threshold of 3% for the deficit. In any case, before beginning the corrective procedure, the Commission must take into account a number of factors, among which are investment costs related to the implementation of structural reforms or to growth policies (see Chapter 10). Only after this evaluation does the Council, on a proposal from the Commission, start the

procedure for excessive deficit, which obliges the recipient state to agree on a program (of economic and budget partnership) containing binding commitments to be submitted to the Council for approval. The breach of these undertakings determines the subordination to sanctions imposed by the Council unless a qualified majority of Member States overturns them. The Commission, in fact, shall decide the penalties.

The European Union's complex economic governance is mainly achieved in the context of the European Semester, which is a temporally regular cycle of procedures so designed as to allow both the coordination of the policies of the Member States of the Eurozone ex ante and the subsequent observance of the assumed commitments.

11.4 STRUCTURAL BALANCE AND NOMINAL BALANCE: THE IMPLEMENTATION OF THE FISCAL RULES IN SOME EUROZONE COUNTRIES

The Treaty on Stability, Coordination and Governance in the Economic and Monetary Union (also known as the Fiscal Compact) (Title III of the Treaty) stipulated the introduction of a permanent numerical budget rule, a so-called debt brake, into national law by the beginning of 2014 (Roux, 2012). While the specific design of the budget rule was left to the individual states, the Fiscal Compact defined a number of general requirements on the contracting parties, the most important of which is to define a balanced budget rule (similarly to the 'Medium-term objective' in EU law) with 0.5% GDP as the lowest limit of structural deficit (if public debt is significantly lower than 60% of GDP, this lower limit is set at 1% of GDP) into national law, preferably at constitutional level. The Fiscal Compact defined some cornerstones of the budget rule. To make compliance with the budget rule highly legally binding, the corresponding law would be monitored by an independent supervisory institution, i.e. a fiscal council that was supposed to evaluate in particular the consolidation progress and the circumstances that end, trigger or prolong emergency situations.

Some empirical studies have shown that the budget rules can support fiscal consolidation. However, the impact of the Fiscal Compact on public finances is not straightforward, because several legal ambiguities and loopholes exist. The most important are: (a) the constitutional anchoring of the Fiscal Compact provisions is only recommended, but not mandatory; (b) the cyclical component of the public deficit can only be estimated; (c) the exceptions for emergency situations are rather loosely defined; (d) a violation of the budget rule does not necessarily trigger the 'automatic' correction mechanism; and (e) any non-compliance with the advice given by the independent fiscal council is required to be explained by the government.

A comparative analysis of the Fiscal Compact implementation and in particular of the balanced budget rule demonstrates that these ambiguities and loopholes determine a certain heterogeneity in government regulations, which did not comply with all the Fiscal Compact requests. Moreover, Member States used the discretionality provided by the Compact to implement rather weak budget rules, without explicitly violating the provisions (Dickmann, 2012; Kutasi, 2012). Almost no rule of national budget has fully complied with the Fiscal Compact provisions: the countries often meet in excess certain requirements (for example the correction mechanism) while they neglect others (e.g. constitutional implementation).

Even if a numerical limit of the structural deficit was implemented in 10 of the 18 Euro area Member States, in most countries the new budget rules were implemented as simple laws. Only Italy, Spain and Slovenia have enshrined the budget rule in their respective constitutions. Germany had already implemented a new constitutional budget rule in 2009 (Gesetz zur Änderung des Grundgesetzes – Artikel 91c, 91d, 104b, 109, 109a, 115, 143d of 29 July 2009). France, after the opinion of the Conseil Consititutionelle, had adopted an organic law. The next subsections will consider the above-mentioned Member States to ascertain how the new constitutional rules were devised in order to bind the primary legislation. Homogeneities and differences will be particularly emphasized.

11.4.1   France

In France, the constitutional revision of 23 July 2008 had already inserted in the art. 34 of the Constitution the objective of budget balance for the government, stating that the multiannual guidelines of public finances are defined by the planning laws (Lombard, 2012).

Given the issues related to the requirement for reviewing the text of the Constitution, in order to authorise the ratification of the Treaty, the French President, François Hollande, called for a judgment of the *Conseil constitutionnel* in July 2012. Such judgment was expressed with the Decision of 9 August 2012 (case no. 2012-653DC). In its decision the *Conseil* stated that a prior constitutional revision was not required and it considered the strengthening of the existing legal framework through a simple organic law sufficient. The legislative text was approved by the two Chambers of Parliament in November 2012. The new organic law was promulgated on 17 December 2012, after the pronunciation of the *Conseil constitutionnel* on its compliance with the relevant provisions of the constitutional text (Magnon, 2012).

The Organic Law no. 2012-1403 provides, in particular, three main innovations in the planning and management of public accounts:

- The determination of a medium-term objective of all general government accounts.
- The establishment of an independent body, the *Haut Conseil des finances publiques*, with the task of giving its opinion on the forecasts of the country's growth and on the coherence of the annual draft laws with the multiannual aims established by the economic planning law.
- The provision of a correction mechanism to operate in the event of significant over-expenditure in public accounts compared with the strategic course indicated by the planning law: the *Haut Conseil des finances publiques*, taking into account the exceptional circumstances which justify the 'substantial over-expenditure' detected, has the task of publicly alerting the Parliament and the Government. Once confronted with the *Haut Conseil* alarm, the Government is obliged to explain the reasons for these discrepancies from the multiannual guidelines for structural balance defined by its planning laws and, if necessary, must promptly propose to the Parliament the necessary and appropriate corrective measures to bring the accounts back onto the planned course.

11.4.2 Germany

Before the two constitutional federalist reforms of 2006 and 2009, the principle of a balanced budget was mentioned in art. 110, paragraph 1 of the *Grundgesetz*. It was established that revenue and expenditure in the budget should be balanced. This principle was made effective with the amendment of art. 109 (already modified in the first phase of the reform), the introduction of the new art. 109a and the amendment of art. 115 (Bifulco, 2011).

With the first federalist reform (*Föderalismus reform* I) on 28 August 2006, the new paragraph 5 of art. 109 (separation of powers between the Federation and the *Länder*; principles in budgetary matters) set out the joint responsibility of the Federation and the *Länder* for compliance with the obligations of Germany in relation to the European stability treaty. It stipulates that the sanctions for breach of the provisions on compliance with budgetary discipline, as referred to in art. 104 of the Treaty establishing the European Community, are applied to an extent of 65% to the Federation and by 35% to the *Länder*.

Among the modifications of art. 109 introduced with the second federalist reform (*Föderalismus reform* II) on 29 July 2009, the new subparagraph 3 is particularly important. It imposes as a general rule, to both the Federation and the *Länder*, the balance of the budget without resorting to a loan. With this arrangement, which in fact introduces a brake to debt (*Schuldenbremse*), the so-called golden rule is exceeded, i.e. the possibility of resorting to a loan in order to finance capital expenditures, previously laid down in art. 115 of the Basic Law and in the constitutions of several *Länder*. The new constitutional provisions lay down that, in order to comply with the criteria established at Community level, the budgets of the Federation and the *Länder* should be in equilibrium, drawing upon public debt – allowed only to the Federation and not to the *Länder* – for a maximum of 0.35% of GDP. Derogations are admitted to the general principle only in the case of natural disasters or exceptional situations of emergency which depart from state control and seriously undermine its financial capacity. In these cases a plan should be adopted to return to the parameters established as soon the exceptional circumstances cease.

In compliance to the principles laid down by the new wording of art. 109, art. 115 (recourse to credit) was also changed. In the presence of cyclical developments that deviate from normal conditions, especially in circumstances where the federal budget requires resort to a public debt exceeding the established parameters, the deviations of the actual recourse to credit from the maximum allowed threshold are recorded in a special control account. Amounts that exceed the threshold of 1.5% of GDP must then be reduced, taking into account the evolution of the cyclical economic situation. In situations resulting from natural disasters or extraordinary emergencies, the exemption should be authorised by a decision adopted by the *Bundestag* with an absolute majority.

The limits laid down in the new provisions contained in arts 109 and 115 are complemented by a system designed to prevent excessive indebtedness, i.e. a mechanism of cooperative early warning. A new art. 109a was therefore introduced according to which, in order to avoid an emergency budget, a bicameral federal law (so-called *Zustimmungsgesetz*, a law which necessarily requires the consent of the *Bundesrat*) may be issued with provisions that relate to: (a) the continuous control of the budgetary management of the Federation and the *Länder* as part of a joint body (Stability Council – *Stabilitätsrat*); (b) the conditions and procedures for the establishment of an imminent emergency budget; and (c) the principles governing the development and implementation of rehabilitation programs aimed at preventing budget emergencies.

In implementation of art. 109, on 10 August 2009 the appropriate federal law of execution was adopted in order to establish a Council of stability and to avoid budget emergencies (*Gesetz zur Errichtung eines Stabilitätsrates und zur Vermeidung von Haushaltsnotlagen – Stabilitätsratsgesetz – StabiRatG*). This law has been in force since 1 January 2010.

During 2012 the German Parliament had to face several problems relating to the serious international financial and economic crisis, particularly in the Eurozone.

With the second law of implementation of a package of measures to stabilise the financial market (*Zweites Gesetz zur Umsetzung eines*

Maßnahmenpakets zur Stabilisierung des Finanzmarktes – Zweites Finanzmarktstabilisierungsgesetz – 2. FMStG) on 24 February 2012, the reopening of the Stabilization Financial Fund was decided (i.e. a rescue fund set up by the previous act in 2008 in the new stabilization Institute of the financial market – *Finanzmarktstabilisierungsanstalt* – with headquarters in Deutsche Bundesbank). The conditions for recourse to stabilization measures aimed at ensuring the solvency of financial institutions headquartered in Germany and to prevent a general paralysis of credit have also been revised and improved.

After the judgment of the Constitutional Court on 12 September 2012, which allowed the participation of Germany in the European Mechanism of stability and to the Fiscal Compact, the new law on financial participation in European Mechanism for stability (*Gesetz zur finanziellen Beteiligung am Europäischen Stabilitätsmechanismus – ESM-Finanzierungsgesetz, ESMFinG*) was promulgated on 13 September, together with the law of ratification of the so-called Fiscal Compact (*Gesetz zu dem Vertrag vom 2. März 2012 über Stabilität, Koordinierung und Steuerung in der Wirtschafts- und Währungsunion, ESMVG*), both approved by the Bundestag at the end of June.

In line with recent positions expressed by the Constitutional Court on measures to preserve the financial stability of the European Monetary Union and similarly the law on the European Stabilization Fund, the new law on participation in the European Mechanism of Stability defines in some detail the competences of the *Bundestag* and its components (Budget Commission and the Special Committee).

After the consent denied by the *Länder* within the *Bundesrat* in December 2012 to the federal government bill laying down rules governing the application of Fiscal Compact in the national context (already approved by the *Bundestag* on 20 November 2012), the parliamentary groups of majority submitted to the *Bundestag* on 13 January 2013 a new draft law with a homonymous title and substantially similar to the Government one, which later became the Law on the National Implementation of the Fiscal Compact Treaty (*Gesetz zur innerstaatlichen Umsetzung des Fiskalvertrags, FiskVtrUG*) on 15 July 2013. The key point of the new framework consists of having fixed a maximum limit to the structural deficit of 0.5% of GDP with the modification of section 51 of the law on the budget principles. The stability Council ensures compliance with this provision, assisted by a new independent Committee established with the introduction of the new section 7 of the already cited Law on the Stability Council, of 10 August 2009.

11.4.3   Italy

In Italy, the draft constitutional law which contained the principle of a balanced budget was definitively approved on 18 April 2012, as the constitutional law no. 1/ 2012 (Bergonzini, 2014).

The constitutional law, reforming arts 81, 97, 117 and 119 of the Constitution, has introduced the principle of balanced budget, by connecting it to a constraint of debt sustainability for all public authorities, in compliance with economic–financial rules concerning the European legal system.

In particular, the principle of equilibrium is contained in art. 81, which lays down, in the first paragraph, that the state guarantees the balance between revenue and expenditure of its budget, taking account of the different stages in the economic cycle. The second subparagraph of art. 81 affirms that it is possible to derogate from the general rule of budgetary balance, making recourse to indebtedness, only during downturn phases of the economic cycle or after the occurrence of exceptional events that, for art. 5 of the constitutional law, may consist of serious economic recessions, financial crises and serious natural disasters.

In order to isolate and to make extraordinary the recourse to debt connected to exceptional events, the second subparagraph of art. 81 stipulates that it shall be authorized with deliberations in accordance of the two Chambers on the basis of a compounded procedure, which provides for a vote by an absolute majority of the respective components.

The new third paragraph of art. 81 provides that every law – including the budget law – considering new or higher expenditures must indicate the related revenues.

The new sixth subparagraph of art. 81 affirms that a special law approved by the absolute majority of both Chambers is necessary for: (a) the definition of budget law content; (b) the fundamental norms and criteria aimed at ensuring the balance between revenue and expenditure of the budget; and (c) the sustainability of the debt of the body of general government.

This implementation Law of the rule of a balanced budget was approved at the end of the parliamentary term (law no. 243/2012, published on 15 January 2013). The obligation to ensure the balance of the budgets and the sustainability of public debt, in coherence with the legal system of the European Union, is extended to all general government by art. 97 of the Constitution.

As regards the budgetary discipline of territorial entities, the constitutional law introduces some changes to art. 119 of the Constitution, in order to specify that the financial autonomy of local authorities (municipalities, provinces, metropolitan cities and regions) is assured in accordance with the balance of their respective budgets. The principle of compliance of these institutions to the economic and financial constraints deriving from the European Union legal system becomes part of the Constitution.

An amendment to the sixth paragraph of art. 119 states that the recourse to borrowing – which the existing constitutional framework allows only when needed to finance investment expenditure – is subject to the contextual definition of repayment plans and to the requirement that the complex of local authorities of each region respect the budget balance.

In addition, the constitutional law has changed art. 117 of the Constitution, by inserting the field of standardisation of public budgets among the subjects on which the State has exclusive legislative competence.

The Law which implements the principle of standardised balanced budget also regulates the institution of an independent body in the two Chambers with audit and analysis tasks on trends in public finance and assessment of compliance with the budgetary rules (Bilancia, 2012; Boggero and Annichino, 2014; Ciolli, 2014).

11.4.4   Slovenia

Slovenia has amended its constitution in May 2013 in order to implement the Fiscal Compact Budget Rule. The revised art. 148 of the Slovenian constitution stipulates that revenues and expenditures of the general government have to be balanced over the medium term or they have to generate a surplus. The public budgets had to be gradually adjusted such that the new budget rule was met from 2015 onwards. Law on Fiscal Rule (Official Gazette of RS, no. 55/15) defined the method and timing of the principle of medium-term balance implementation, in order to balance revenues and expenditures without borrowing, and the criteria for determining the exceptional circumstances and the manner of their occurrence. Implementation of the Fiscal Rule Act is defined in the Public Finance Act. The Fiscal Rule Act, published on 24 July 2015, which defines in detail the principle of the medium-term fiscal balance, calls for the gradual reduction of the structural government deficit. Reduction of the structural deficit must be carried out in accordance with the dynamics envisaged by the Stability and Growth Pact.

11.4.5   Spain

The obligation of a balanced budget rule was introduced for the first time under Spanish law with the reform of art. 135 of the Constitution, published and entered into force on 27 September 2011 (*Reforma del artículo 135 de la Constitución Española*). This reform provides that all public authorities comply with the principle of budgetary stability (art. 135, paragraph 1) and that the state and the autonomous communities may not incur a structural deficit that exceeds the margins set by the European Union (paragraph 2). An organic law fixes the maximum limit of the structural deficit in the state and in the Autonomous Communities according to their respective GDP. Even the local authorities must keep a balanced budget (paragraph 2). In addition, the State and the Autonomous Communities must be authorized by law to the issuance of public debt (paragraph 3).

To implement the new constitutional precepts, in compliance with the constitutional provisions contained in art 135, the Organic Law on budgetary stability and financial sustainability (*Ley Orgánica 2/2012 de Estabilidad Presupuestaria y Sostenibilidad Financiera*) was approved on April 27th 2012 and it is in force since May 1st 2012. It repealed the previous legislation, assuming the form of a single text for the stability of the budget and the financial sustainability. The law established the limits of deficit and debt, the exceptions, the mechanisms for correcting deviations and the tools to enforce the responsibility of every public administration in the event of a failure. It should be applied to all the public sector (i.e. the general government, comprising in turn the central administration – State and members of the central administration – the autonomous communities, the local authorities and administrations of social security, as well as public entrepreneurial and commercial companies, bodies and other bodies governed by public law and dependent on general government).

All institutions should submit a budget which has to be in balance or in surplus, without incurring in structural deficits. However, the State and the Autonomous Communities (but not local ones) may have – after approval by an absolute majority of the Congress of Deputies – a structural deficit in exceptional situations: natural disasters, serious economic recession or extraordinary emergency situations that are beyond the control of the administrations and significantly affect their financial situation or economic/social sustainability. In addition, public expenditure may not increase above the reference rate of growth of GDP in the medium term of the Spanish economy. The limit of the debt of the general government, may not exceed 60% of national GDP expressed in nominal terms (or established by European regulations). The public administration that exceeds the ceiling will not be able to carry out operations of net financial debt. The state and the Autonomous Communities must be authorized by law to issue public debt or obtain credit.

Chapter IV of the law contains preventive, remedial and enforcement measures. Among the preventive measures, an automatic mechanism is established to ensure that any administration does not incur in deficit at the end of each financial year and that a threshold of debt of 95% on the maximum to avoid exceeding the predetermined limits. In the same framework, the law also introduces an alert mechanism, consisting of the sending of a statement by the Government to the defaulting administration that, within a month, is required to adopt the necessary measures. The law also provides for measures of automatic correction. The failure of the objective of budgetary stability, of the objective of public debt or of public spending, entails the submission of a business plan that allows correction within the following year. In the case of a deficit for exceptional circumstances, a plan of rebalancing is submitted, with indication of the appropriate measures to address the budgetary implications arising from these circumstances.

The government can send a committee of experts to evaluate the economic and budgetary situation of the affected administration. If an autonomous community fails to comply with the obligations provided for in the case of a deficit, the Government, in accordance with art. 155 of the Constitution, requires the President of the Community to fulfil that obligation. Otherwise, with the approval of an absolute majority of the Senate, it shall adopt the necessary measures to oblige the Community to its enforcement. Similar measures are envisaged for local authorities, for which the possibility of the suppression of the institution is also contemplated.

11.5 CONCLUSIONS

By considering in general how Member States have applied in their national law systems the necessity of the balanced budget, there emerges a remarkable heterogeneity of governmental regulations. The rules on the balanced budget of almost all countries provide for exceptions that allow deviations in emergency situations. The clauses of escape of most countries coincide with the provisions of the Fiscal Compact, but in some cases include additional exceptions. Moreover, governments may invoke exceptional circumstances in almost all countries without parliamentary approval. The latter is only required in Austria, Spain and Italy, and Italian and Spanish laws require an absolute majority. In Germany this approval is only required by the rule of constitutional budget at federal level.

A correction mechanism for significant deviations from the rule of the budget which are not justified by emergency situations was only implemented in the national legislation of some countries (Austria, Cyprus, Spain, Finland, France, Ireland, Italy, Latvia, the Netherlands and Portugal), while in others it is not foreseen (Germany and Slovenia). In Germany, as discussed in Subsection 11.4.2, the automatism of the correction relates to constitutional rule of the budget of the Federal Government ('brake of debt').

The laws adopted by various Member States provide for the creation of an independent tax council at national level in order to check the conformity with the new rule of the budget and the correction mechanism (Austria, Germany, Spain, Finland, France, Ireland, Italy, Latvia and Portugal), while in some states the monitoring will be carried out by already existing institutions (Finland and Luxembourg) or by independent authorities (e.g. Belgium, Greece, The Netherlands). A principle of 'comply or explain' should ensure that national governments do not ignore the assessments of their tax council, as required by the Fiscal Compact, but only six governments are obliged to explain and justify their actions if they differ from the opinion of their fiscal council (Spain, Finland, France, Ireland, Italy and Portugal).

The limit of the structural deficit and the potential of the corrective measures should consider both national and subnational administrations. This is particularly important for countries with a federal structure. However, only five countries (Austria, Spain, Italy, Luxembourg and The Netherlands) have established a sub-national allocation of the limit of deficit, and the German law has also set specific limits of deficit for the federal level and for the various *Länder*.

REFERENCES

Adam, R. and Tizzano, A. (2017), *Manuale di diritto dell'Unione Europea*. Giappichelli, Torino.

Amick, J., Chapman, T. and Elkins, Z. (2017), 'On constitutionalizing a balanced budget'. Presentation at the conference *Liberal Democratic Constitutions During Severe Financial Crises* (Lisbon, May 2017), pp. 1–36.

Asatryan, Z., Castellón, C. and Stratmann, T. (2017), 'Balanced budget rules and fiscal outcomes: evidence from historical constitutions'. ZEW (Discussion Paper no. 16-034), pp. 1–40.

Barnes, S., Botev, J., Rawdanowicz, L. and Stráský, J. (2016), 'Europe's new fiscal rules', *OECD Economics Department Review of Economics and Institutions*, 7 (1), art. 2, 1–20.

Bergonzini, C. (2014), 'Il c.d. "pareggio di bilancio" tra costituzione e l. n. 243 del 2012: le radici (e gli equivoci) di una riforma controversa', *Studiumiuris*, 3, 15–22.

Bifulco, R. (2011), 'Il pareggio di bilancio in Germania: una riforma costituzionale postnazionale?', *Rivista AIC*, 3, 1–6.

Bilancia, F. (2012), 'Note critiche sul c.d. "pareggio di bilancio"', *Rivista AIC*, 2, 1–6.

Boggero, G. and Annichino, P. (2014), '"Who will ever kick us out?": Italy, the balanced budget rule and the implementation of the fiscal compact', *European Public Law*, 2, 247–261.

Ciolli, I. (2014), 'The balanced budget rule in the Italian constitution: it ain't necessarily so … useful?', *Rivista AIC*, 4, 1–21.

Delledonne, G. (2012), 'Financial constitutions in the EU: from the political to the legal constitution?', *Sant'Anna Legal Studies Stals Research Papers*, 5, 1–29.

Dickmann, R. (2012), 'Le regole della governance economica europea e il pareggio di bilancio in costituzione', *federalismi.it*, 4, 1–55.

Fabbrini, F. (2013), 'The fiscal compact, the "golden rule," and the paradox of European Federalism', *Boston College International and Comparative Law Review*, 36 (1), 1–87.

Giupponi, T. F. (2014), 'Il principio costituzionale dell'equilibrio di bilancio e la sua attuazione', *Quaderni costituzionali*, 1, 51–78.

Grasso, G. (2012), *Il costituzionalismo della crisi*. ESI, Napoli.

Kutasi, G. (2012), 'Budgeting with rules and advisory institutions in the EU', *Délkelet Európa – South-East Europe International Relations Quarterly*, 3 (1), 1–10.

Lledó, V., Yoon, S., Fang, X., Mbaye, S., and Kim, Y. (2017), 'Fiscal rules at a glance'. International Monetary Fund, March, pp. 1–82.

Lombard, M. (2012), 'Le futur rôle de régulateur financier du Conseil constitutionnel', *Actualité juridique-Droit administratif*, 31, 1717–1718.

Luciani, M. (2013), 'Costituzione, bilancio, diritti e doveri dei cittadini', Astrid Rassegna, no. 3/2013, p. 1 ss.

Magnon, X. (2012), 'La ratification du traité sur la stabilité, la coordination et la gouvernance dans l'Union économique et monétaire (TSCG) peut ne pas exiger de révision constitutionnelle préalable', *Revue française de droit constitutionnel*, 92, 554–854.

Roux, J. (2012), 'Le Conseil constitutionnel et le traité sur la stabilité, la coordination et la gouvernance au sein de l'Union économique et monétaire', *Revue trimestrielle de droit européen*, 4, pp. 855–876.

Tereanu, E., Tuladhar, A. and Simone, A., (2014), 'Structural balance targeting and potential output uncertainty'. IMF Working Papers, no. 14/107, International Monetary Fund, pp. 1–30.

Villani, U. (2013), *Istituzioni di diritto dell'Unione europea*, Cacucci, Bari.

12. Brexit and the EU Budget

Margit Schratzenstaller

12.1 INTRODUCTION[1]

The debate about the implications of Brexit for the EU budget was led in the run-up to the negotiations about the Multiannual Financial Framework (MFF) of the EU for the period 2021 to 2027. It almost exclusively focused on the volume of the EU budget and on the national contributions EU Member States would have to expect after the UK, as (measured in own resource payments in absolute terms) the third largest contributor to the EU budget, had left the EU. This debate followed the argumentation pattern well-known from past negotiations about the MFF: when determining the benefits derived from the EU and the EU budget, respectively, Member States primarily consider their individual net positions, i.e. the difference between payments into the EU budget and transfers received out of it. In contrast, indirect benefits from membership in the Single Market and from EU expenditures exceeding Member States' contributions to the EU budget by far,[2] are almost completely neglected. This *juste-retour* logic prevents Member States from perceiving the Brexit shock as an opportunity to fundamentally reform the structure of the EU's expenditures and revenues: an opportunity most prominently stressed by the Monti Report on the future of EU funding released at the beginning of 2017 (HLGOR, 2016).

Departing from the hypothesis that Brexit may act as a catalyst for fundamental reforms within the EU budget aiming at strengthening the added value of EU expenditures and revenues, the chapter first sketches the cornerstones of such far-reaching reforms. It then focuses on the financial impact of Brexit

[1] The research leading to these results has received funding from the European Union's Horizon 2020 research and innovation programme 2014–2020, grant agreement No. 649439. The author is grateful to Andrea Sutrich for careful research assistance.

[2] For an estimation of the benefits Member States derive from European integration see Felbermayr et al. (2018).

on the EU budget. Against this background, the chapter undertakes a brief first assessment of the European Commission's proposals for the 2021–2027 MFF.

12.2 OPTIONS TO STRENGTHEN ADDED VALUE OF THE EU BUDGET[3]

The EU is facing various long-term challenges, which include digital change, the recent and imminent rounds of enlargement, structural problems of the southern countries and persisting regional divergences, demographic change, climate change, energy transition and refugee migration. The 2014–2020 MFF determined a structure of the EU budget that was broadly considered to be inadequate to cope with these challenges (e.g., HLGOR, 2016; Núñez Ferrer et al., 2016). It also contributed little to central EU initiatives and strategies, such as the Europe 2020 Strategy aiming at 'smart, inclusive and sustainable growth', the 2030 Agenda for Sustainable Development, the EU Action Plan for the Circular Economy or the efforts to combat tax avoidance and evasion.

It is obvious that the general approach for the 2021–2027 MFF would also depend on which one of the five integration scenarios sketched in the European Commission's 'White Paper on the Future of Europe' (European Commission 2017a) would be pursued eventually. According to the European Commission's 'Reflection Paper on the Future of EU Finances', released mid–2017 (European Commission, 2017b), all scenarios except the 'Doing less together scenario' would require structural shifts in EU expenditure, albeit to differing extents and, sometimes, in different directions; and they would also imply the need to introduce new own resources, or at least other revenue sources. However, as stressed by Haas and Rubio (2017b), considering the deficiencies in the current EU budget within the existing institutional and political framework of the EU, there are strong arguments in favour of an overhaul of the MFF with fundamental changes for the EU budget with a longer-term perspective, regardless of which of the future integration scenarios is envisaged. Such a fundamental reform should include EU expenditures as well as revenues.

12.2.1   Options to Strengthen Added Value of EU Expenditures

As a general principle, EU expenditures should only target policy areas in which Member States' uncoordinated actions would be insufficient owing to free riding, coordination problems and cross-border issues, or policy areas in which common European interests are at stake. Indeed, it is not an easy

---

[3]   This section draws heavily on Schratzenstaller (2017).

task to assess, measure and quantify the European added value of specific policies (Heinemann, 2016). One central criterion to identify European public goods with a European added value is whether action at the EU level results in a higher value compared with separate national actions; another is whether expenditure has a cross-border element (European Commission, 2011).

Indeed, some restructuring of EU expenditure towards areas creating EU added value has been taking place in the more recent past (Núñez Ferrer et al., 2016). However, the EU budget in its current structure still provides too little 'true' European public goods and thus too little added value (Bertelsmann Stiftung, 2017). Heinemann (2016) shows that EU funds still finance too many projects, creating local added value only, supporting a *juste retour* perspective of Member States trying to maximize national benefits from EU expenditure in return for their contributions.

Despite some long-term shifts in spending priorities, the 2014–2020 MFF was still dominated by the common agricultural policy, which was consuming a decreasing, but still substantial share of overall expenditure (Schratzenstaller, 2013). This share went down from 42% in the MFF 2007 to 2013 to 39% in the 2014–2020 MFF. Cohesion policy made up for another 34% of EU spending, compared with 36% in the preceding MFF. An increasing, but still moderate, share of 7.3% is dedicated to the European research framework programme Horizon 2020. Another 2% was spent on trans-border infrastructure (Connecting Europe Facility). Only about 2% of overall expenditure was dedicated to development assistance within the regular EU budget,[4] and Schengen-related spending (asylum, migration, borders and internal security) amounted to only 1% of the 2014–2020 MFF (Schratzenstaller, 2017).

12.2.2   Common Agricultural Policy

Expenditure for agricultural policy today is mainly preserving existing, conventional production structures within the 'first pillar', prioritizing large agricultural units (Bonfiglio et al., 2014). The more sustainability-oriented 'second pillar' of agricultural expenditures, which could actively support organic farming and rural employment in smaller units, amounts to about 24% of overall agricultural spending. Past research suggests that the effectiveness of EU agricultural policy in reducing agriculture's climate impact is limited (Darvas and Wolff, 2018). After several reforms common agricultural policy still tends to have regressive effects on regional and personal income distribution (Núñez Ferrer and Kaditi, 2007; Núñez Ferrer et al., 2016).

---

[4]   In addition, another €30 billion are foreseen within the European Development Fund outside the MFF.

Accordingly, overall expenditure on agricultural policy should be reduced and the second pillar should be strengthened, thus contributing to a European decarbonization strategy. Moreover, agricultural subsidies should be targeted more towards the less wealthy Member States, so that they would also contribute to cohesion goals (Núñez Ferrer et al., 2016).

12.2.3 Cohesion Policy

Structural and cohesion policy focuses too strongly on a traditional infrastructure policy favouring material (large-scale) infrastructure, too often lacking a European added value (Heinemann, 2016). Moreover, funds are not redistributed to the 'poorer' Member States in a focused and targeted way. The empirical evidence suggests that EU cohesion policy is indeed effective in the most underdeveloped European regions (Gagliardi and Percoco, 2017), while the positive effect decreases with increasing development (Becker et al., 2018). Therefore, cohesion funds should be shifted from the 'richer' to the 'poorer' Member States and regions, respectively, thus producing European added value as the whole EU benefits from macroeconomic stability and growth in the cohesion countries.[5] They should also be coupled more strongly with climate and employment goals as well as a proactive migration and integration policy (e.g. education programmes).

12.2.4 Research and Cross-border Infrastructure

Expenditure for research, which has been shown to have a particularly large effect on growth and productivity (Núñez Ferrer et al. 2016), and for infrastructure should be increased significantly, with a specific focus on environmentally and socially relevant aspects and requirements (see Chapter 10). This includes the European research framework programme as well as investment in education, which should be expanded and particularly support the mobility of pupils, students and (young) workers. Expenditure on sustainability oriented infrastructure should be increased significantly, giving priority to trans-border transport infrastructure, as another element of a European decarbonization strategy.

---

[5] Núñez Ferrer and Katarivas (2014) show that cohesion policy benefits all EU Member States economies.

12.2.5   External Action

Too little funding is made available to make a substantial EU contribution
to development assistance in general and to an internationally coordinated
approach to the mitigation of the worldwide 'refugee and migrant crisis'
in particular. In 2017, Official Development Assistance by the EU and its
Member States amounted to 0.5% of gross national income (GNI), thus still
lagging considerably behind the target of 0.7% of GNI.[6] Thus funds should be
increased significantly to help the EU to reach internationally agreed official
development assistance targets.

12.3   OPTIONS TO CREATE EU ADDED VALUE BY A REFORM OF THE EU SYSTEM OF OWN RESOURCES

Along with substantial reforms in EU expenditures, the EU system of own
resources needs to be overhauled fundamentally. The current EU system of
own resources certainly has its merits: it provides steady, predictable and
reliable revenues; it guarantees a balanced budget; and it is based on the subsidiarity principle as Member States can decide freely about the distribution of
the financial burden among individual taxpayers. Nonetheless, the financing
system has been attracting various criticisms over recent decades. These
relate to its non-transparency and complexity, but particularly to the fact that
the EU system of own resources does not contribute to central EU strategies
and policies (Schratzenstaller et al., 2017). Over recent decades, 'true' own
resources have been continually declining in importance, leaving national
contributions (GNI- and value-added tax (VAT)-based own resources) as the
by far dominating revenue source for the EU.[7] In 2016, the VAT-based own
resource accounted for 11% of overall EU revenues and the GNI-based own
resource for 66.3%, while traditional own resources contributed a rather small
share of 13.9% only.

The introduction of sustainability-oriented tax-based own resources, partially substituting Member States' national contributions, can strengthen
the contribution of the EU system of own resources to central EU policies
(Schratzenstaller, 2017). Such a partial substitution of national contributions
would enable Member States to cut more harmful taxes at the national level,

---

[6]   http://www.oecd.org/development/financing-sustainable-development/
development-finance-data/ODA-2017-detailed-summary.pdf.

[7]   See for a detailed overview over the evolution of the EU system of own resources
Schratzenstaller et al. (2016).

particularly the high taxes on labour, and would thus allow a fiscally neutral, but sustainability-enhancing tax shift. To meet additional revenue needs – to cover the Brexit gap[8] or to expand the EU budget volume – tax-based own resources appear as a preferable option compared with raising national contributions.

Obvious candidates for sustainability-oriented tax-based own resources are those taxes that cannot be enforced effectively at the national level owing to tax competition based on highly mobile tax bases and/or tax subjects. The case for assigning Pigovian taxes to the EU level is strengthened further if tax rates owing to cross-border externalities not considered by national governments are set at suboptimal levels (Jones et al., 2012). In addition, unilateral tax measures aimed at reducing cross-border externalities (e.g. externalities caused by emitting greenhouse gases) may alleviate the pressure on other countries to implement unilateral tax measures themselves as they can act as free-riders (Auerswald et al., 2011). Following the reasoning of Keen et al. (2012), it can be argued that the revenue from taxes levied on tax bases characterized by international spill-overs (e.g. CO_2 emissions) should be used to finance a supranational budget as it can hardly be assigned to specific countries.

Table 12.1 contains several candidates for sustainability-oriented tax-based own resources, including taxes on flight tickets, net wealth, nuclear power and financial transactions; a share of a common (consolidated) corporate tax base and a surcharge on national fuel tax rates; and revenues from a border carbon adjustment for the European Emission Trading System.[9]

12.4 EXPECTED FINANCIAL IMPACT OF THE BREXIT

At the time of writing, no agreement had been reached yet on the final financial settlement including the budgetary arrangements related to the future UK–EU partnership. Such an agreement, comprising all areas affected by Brexit, was envisaged by the end of October 2018. The UK was expected to leave the EU in March 2019. Afterwards there would be a transitional period until the end of 2020, when the 2014–2020 MFF would expire. The status of UK–EU Brexit negotiations implied a twofold financial impact of Brexit, comprising the one-off 'Brexit bill' or 'divorce bill' and the permanent 'Brexit gap'. Any financial impact of the withdrawal of the UK with regard to the 2014–2020

---

[8]   For details regarding the Brexit gap see Section 12.5.
[9]   These sustainability-oriented candidates for tax-based own resources are explored in the H2020 EU project 'FairTax' (www.fair-tax.eu).

Table 12.1   *Sustainability-oriented tax-based own resources to finance the EU budget*

Study	Potential tax-based own resource	Reference year	Member States involved	Details	Potential revenues, billion, €
Krenek and Schratzenstaller (2017)	Carbon-based flight ticket tax	2014	EU28	Carbon price €25–35 per tonne carbon emissions	4–5
Dellinger and Schratzenstaller (2018)	Nuclear power tax	2014	EU14 (Member States producing nuclear power)	1 cent per kW electricity produced and tax on windfall profits for carbon price of €25	8–19
Krenek and Schratzenstaller (2018)	Net wealth tax	2014	EU20 (Member States for which HFCS data are available)	1% on household net wealth above €1 million; 1.5% on household net wealth above €1.5 million	156
Krenek et al. (2018)	Border carbon adjustment	2021	EU28	Carbon price €54 per tonne carbon emissions embodied in imports	27–84
Nerudová et al. (2017)	Financial transaction tax	2016	EU10 ('Coalition of the Willing')	0.1% on equity; 0.01% on derivatives	4–33
Nerudová et al. (2019)	Supplement to surcharge on national fuel tax	2014	EU28	0.03 € to 0.20 € per litre fuel	13–86
Nerudová et al. (2016)	CCCTB-based own resource	2015	EU28	National corporate tax rates of 2015 applied on CCCTB	202

Source: Own compilation.

MFF was not to be expected, as the UK in principle had agreed to fulfil its respective commitments.

12.4.1 The 'Divorce Bill'

In December 2017, an agreement was reached between the UK and the EU on the principles of financial settlement until the termination of the current MFF and post-2020 (Negotiators of the European Union and the United Kingdom Government, 2017). Besides the transitional phase until the termination of the 2014–2020 MFF, the agreement set out the methodological approach of how to determine the size of the 'divorce bill', but did not mention any estimates.

Based on this joint UK–EU report, British officials estimated the UK's divorce payment at £35–39 billion (€39.7–44.2 billion) (The Institute for Government, 2018). This sum was to cover the UK's share of outstanding liabilities, resulting from earlier commitments due after the current MFF period, i.e. after 2020, as well as from future commitments jointly undertaken by EU Member States during the UK's membership, for example regarding pensions to EU civil servants. Payments would probably start in 2019 and would be terminated only in 2064. Darvas and Wolff (2018) point out that the agreement clarifies all relevant aspects, with one exception: it does not explain whether the UK's post-2020 financial obligations will be determined based on the country's rebate-adjusted or non-rebate-adjusted historical contributions. The authors therefore estimate the exit fee for the UK at €36 billion based on the country's non-rebate-adjusted historical share and at €23 billion based on the rebate-adjusted share.

12.5   THE 'BREXIT GAP'

In addition to the one-off 'divorce bill', the withdrawal of the UK from the EU will cause a structural funding gap (Haas and Rubio, 2017a). Owing to the country's size (the UK makes up 17% of EU GNI), the UK has a considerable weight in the EU budget. Table 12.2 contains average contributions to and transfers received from the EU budget as a percentage of GNI as well as in absolute terms by Member States for the period 2014–2016. Over these three years, the UK contributed 13% of total own resources (traditional own resources plus VAT- and GNI-based own resources) on average, which corresponds to a yearly average of about €17.4 billion. The country's yearly operating budgetary balance amounted to about €7.6 billion.

The 'Brexit gap' resulted from the fact that the UK was one of 11 net-contributor countries (on average for the years 2014–2016) to the MFF (see Table 12.2). For the period 2014–2016, the UK's net contribution (measured as the difference between the national contribution and the transfers received from the EU) reached −0.32% of GNI (Table 12.3). During the first 3 years of the 2014–2020 MFF, the UK had been the sixth largest net contributor in relation to national GNI.

Table 12.2   Average expenditure and revenue by Member State, 2014–2016

	Total own resources[a]	Total national contribution[b]	Traditional own resources (TOR)[c]	Expenditures[d]	Operating budgetary balance[e,f]
			Average 2014–2016 as percentage of GNI		
EU-28	0.93	0.80	0.13	0.87	-
Germany	0.89	0.77	0.13	0.35	-0.44
The Netherlands	1.05	0.71	0.34	0.33	-0.42
Sweden	0.84	0.73	0.11	0.36	-0.40
Belgium	1.35	0.90	0.45	1.72	-0.35
France	0.96	0.88	0.07	0.59	-0.33
UK	**0.74**	**0.61**	**0.13**	**0.31**	**-0.32**
Austria	0.87	0.80	0.06	0.52	-0.31
Finland	0.93	0.87	0.06	0.62	-0.28
Denmark	0.90	0.78	0.12	0.54	-0.27
Italy	0.98	0.88	0.11	0.70	-0.21
Luxembourg	0.96	0.91	0.05	5.20	-0.01
Ireland	1.00	0.85	0.15	1.00	0.10
Cyprus	1.11	1.00	0.12	1.28	0.22
Spain	1.01	0.88	0.13	1.13	0.22
Croatia	0.99	0.88	0.10	1.63	0.71
Portugal	0.98	0.91	0.07	2.07	1.12
Malta	1.08	0.94	0.14	2.34	1.29
Slovenia	1.06	0.89	0.17	2.30	1.36
Estonia	1.05	0.92	0.13	2.99	2.00
Poland	1.03	0.90	0.13	3.41	2.48
Czech Republic	1.04	0.89	0.15	3.51	2.59
Slovakia	0.96	0.83	0.13	3.51	2.65
Greece	0.95	0.86	0.08	3.61	2.71
Latvia	1.04	0.92	0.13	3.79	2.81
Lithuania	1.10	0.89	0.21	3.93	2.99
Romania	0.95	0.87	0.09	4.23	3.33
Hungary	1.01	0.89	0.12	5.33	4.41
Bulgaria	1.08	0.93	0.15	5.61	4.63

	Total own resources[a]	Total national contribution[b]	Traditional own resources (TOR)[c]	Expenditures[d]	Operating budgetary balance[e,f]
	Average 2014–2016 in million Euro				
EU-28	134,157	115,013	19,143	125,516	0
Germany	27565	23642	3922	1,0860	−13,560
The Netherlands	7,079	4,812	2,268	2,221	−2,814
Sweden	3,835	3,320	515	1,624	−1,809
Belgium	5,588	3,712	1,877	7,110	−1,426
France	21,250	19,645	1,605	13,074	−7,382
UK	**17,368**	**14,221**	**3,146**	**7,165**	**−7,567**
Austria	2,918	2,713	205	1,767	−1,032
Finland	1,951	1,817	134	1,308	−583
Denmark	2,473	2,140	334	1,491	−752
Italy	16,142	14,409	1,733	11,542	−3,479
Luxembourg	316	299	17	1,717	−4
Ireland	1,873	1,599	274	1,870	187
Cyprus	191	171	20	220	37
Spain	10,907	9,535	1,372	12,276	2,416
Croatia	426	381	45	703	305
Portugal	1,732	1,605	127	3,641	1,963
Malta	92	80	12	199	110
Slovenia	405	341	65	876	518
Estonia	209	183	26	595	398
Poland	4,164	3,632	532	13,811	10,062
Czech Republic	1,594	1,360	234	5,381	3,973
Slovakia	732	634	98	2,689	2,030
Greece	1,674	1,529	145	6,385	4,789
Latvia	255	224	31	926	687
Lithuania	394	320	75	1,414	1,076
Romania	1,492	1,355	137	6,614	5,208
Hungary	1,060	930	130	5,598	4,631
Bulgaria	470	405	65	2,443	2,016

Source: European Commission (2017c). [a] Sum of National Contribution and Traditional Own Resources. [b] Total National Contribution: VAT- and GNI-based own resources. [c] Sugar levies and customs duties. [d] Transfers received from the EU budget. [e] National contribution (VAT- and GNI-based own resources) minus transfers received from the EU (excluding administrative expenditure and traditional own resources. including UK and other corrections). [f] (−) Net contributing country.

Table 12.3 *Net positions, EU28, 2014–2016 (average), in percentage of GNI*

	Operating budget balance (revised) as percentage of GNI[a]			
	2014	2015	2016	Average 2014–2016
Germany	−0.49	−0.43	−0.40	−0.44
The Netherlands	−0.56	−0.39	−0.30	−0.42
Sweden	−0.45	−0.41	−0.33	−0.40
Belgium	−0.40	−0.37	−0.28	−0.35
France	−0.36	−0.28	−0.36	−0.33
UK	**−0.25**	**−0.46**	**−0.24**	**−0.32**
Austria	−0.41	−0.29	−0.23	−0.31
Finland	−0.43	−0.27	−0.14	−0.28
Denmark	−0.29	−0.26	−0.28	−0.27
Italy	−0.30	−0.20	−0.14	−0.21
Luxembourg	0.26	−0.29	0.03	−0.01
Ireland	−0.03	0.15	0.16	0.10
Cyprus	0.67	−0.18	0.18	0.22
Spain	0.08	0.40	0.19	0.22
Croatia	0.40	0.50	1.20	0.71
Portugal	1.85	0.53	0.99	1.12
Malta	2.33	0.35	1.30	1.29
Slovenia	2.14	1.48	0.51	1.36
Estonia	2.46	1.20	2.37	2.00
Poland	3.45	2.28	1.75	2.48
Czech Republic	2.04	3.72	2.04	2.59
Slovakia	1.35	4.04	2.53	2.65
Greece	2.88	2.77	2.47	2.71
Latvia	3.34	3.10	2.04	2.81
Lithuania	4.37	1.50	3.12	2.99
Romania	3.07	3.26	3.64	3.33
Hungary	5.62	4.36	3.34	4.41
Bulgaria	4.43	5.31	4.17	4.63

Source: European Commission (2017c). (−) Negative net position. [a] National contribution (VAT- and GNI-based own resources) minus transfers received from the EU (excluding administrative expenditure and traditional own resources including UK and other corrections).

12.5.1   The Size of the Brexit Gap

The exact size of the Brexit gap will depend on various factors, which are highly uncertain at the time of writing, particularly the modalities of Brexit ('hard' or 'soft Brexit') and the future UK–EU financial arrangements. Also, the volatility of the UK's yearly contributions makes an exact estimation of the future funding gap caused by Brexit difficult (Haas and Rubio, 2017b). Haas and Rubio (2017a) undertake a simple estimation based on the figures for the 2014–2020 MFF, neglecting these uncertainties by assuming that the UK will completely cease to contribute to the EU budget after its withdrawal ('hard Brexit'). Based on yearly payments of the UK of €17.4 billion[10] on average for the period 2014–2016 and yearly transfers to the UK from the EU of €7.2 billion, the structural gap resulting from Brexit would amount to €10.2 billion annually. Table 12.4 shows the impact of such a hard Brexit scenario on Member States' net balances.

The funding gap caused by Brexit would be decreased in a 'soft Brexit' scenario in which UK–EU financial relations would be shaped according to the relations several non-EU European countries have established with the EU. One option is the Norwegian model: Norway, as a non-European Economic Area member, currently pays a direct contribution to the EU budget to participate in certain EU programmes. According to estimations based on the figures for 2014 and 2015 provided by Chomicz (2017), such an arrangement would reduce UK gross payments to more than one-sixth of the current level, while net payments would even be decreased by 85%. An alternative option is the Swiss model: Switzerland is a European Free Trade Association, but not a European Economic Area member, so that its relations to the EU are based on bilateral agreements. This model would imply a reduction of gross contributions by more than one-tenth and of net contributions by 95.3% (Chomicz, 2017). Both models would imply considerably reduced UK payments to the EU budget and would thus decrease the Brexit gap only moderately.

In contrast, a 'hard Brexit' scenario, in which the UK would cease all direct payments to the EU budget, would entail increasing customs revenues of Member States from trade with the UK, the bulk of which would be transferred into the EU budget and would thus somewhat reduce the Brexit gap (Núñez Ferrer and Rinaldi, 2016; Haas and Rubio, 2017b).

---

[10]   This sum corresponds to the UK's total own resource payments and includes the UK's national contribution (consisting of GNI- and VAT-based resources, about 80% of overall UK payments) and customs duties collected by the UK (about 20% of overall UK payments).

Table 12.4   The impact of a €10 billion increase in contributions on Member States' net balances ('Hard Brexit')

Country	Change in net balance (EUR million)	Brexit change as percentage of national contribution
Germany	−3756	15.92
France	−1359	6.97
Italy	−1014	7.03
Netherlands	−815	19.32
Spain	−661	7.09
Sweden	−553	16.94
Austria	−413	15.33
Belgium	−252	6.72
Poland	−248	6.74
Denmark	−178	8.23
Finland	−136	7.60
Ireland	−134	8.36
Greece	−110	7.92
Portugal	−106	6.71
Czech Republic	−100	7.36
Romania	−98	7.23
Hungary	−64	6.81
Slovakia	−49	7.82
Bulgaria	−28	6.85
Croatia	−28	7.42
Luxembourg	−23	7.56
Slovenia	−23	6.79
Lithuania	−22	6.79
Latvia	−14	6.69
Estonia	−12	6.34
Cyprus	−10	5.68
Malta	−5	6.43

Source: Haas/Rubio (2017A).

12.5.2   Scenarios to Cope with the Brexit Gap

Three possible scenarios are conceivable to cope with this Brexit gap. In the first scenario, the spending level is maintained in the EU27, i.e. current expenditures are reduced by the UK's receipts from the EU budget and EU27 countries compensate for the Brexit gap by increased contributions. In the second scenario, the Brexit gap is covered by the introduction of new own resources. A third scenario foresees a reduction of EU expenditures corresponding to the Brexit gap. The country-specific impact of these scenarios differs according to Member States' net positions as well as to the structure of the payments they receive from the EU budget.

12.5.2.1 Scenario 1: the current spending level is maintained in the EU27
If it is assumed that the spending level is maintained in the EU27 (i.e. that the volume of the current MFF 2014–2020 is reduced by the amount of EU transfers to the UK), net positions of all Member States would deteriorate, as EU revenues would have to be increased through additional GNI-based own resource payments of Member States. The authors' calculations show that in this scenario net balances of all Member States would be worsened by Brexit (Table 12.4). Moreover, those net contributor countries that were enjoying a 'rebate on the rebate' or other forms of payment relief limiting their contributions to the EU budget would be burdened over-proportionately, as the UK rebate, as well as the rebates granted to selected net-contributor countries, would be assumed to be abolished after the UK's withdrawal.

12.5.2.2 Scenario 2: new own resources are introduced
A second possible scenario would be to substitute for the loss of contributions from the UK by introducing new own resources to avoid an increase in national contributions from Member States. As Núñez Ferrer and Rinaldi (2016) correctly argue, the EU cannot face a revenue shortfall in a narrow sense, as it is able to exploit new revenue sources. In such a scenario in which the EU generates additional own resources, net positions would remain constant.

12.5.2.3 Scenario 3: EU expenditure is decreased
A third scenario is a reduction in EU expenditure corresponding to the structural funding gap caused by the UK's withdrawal (Haas and Rubio, 2017a). In this case Member States' contributions (apart from the impact of the rebates on the UK rebate, which would lead to a redistribution of the financial burden) would hardly be affected. However, net positions would deteriorate, particularly for the recipients of transfers from agricultural and cohesion funds as the largest spending items.

12.6 THE POSSIBLE IMPACT OF BREXIT ON THE SYSTEM OF CORRECTIONS

Brexit can also be expected to end the current system of corrections, alleviating the relative financial burden for several net-contributor countries and causing the other Member States to pay more into the EU budget to finance the rebate granted to the UK. Based on the so-called Fontainebleau Agreement, the UK abatement was introduced in 1984, providing for a reduction of UK contributions by 66% (about €6 billion) of the difference between UK contributions to and receipts from EU abatable expenditure (see Chapter 2).

Since 1999, Austria, Germany, the Netherlands and Sweden have paid only 25% of the 'normal share' of additional national contributions necessary to compensate for the UK rebate (so-called rebate on the rebate). Additionally, Germany, the Netherlands and Sweden have been granted a halving of the call-up rate for the VAT-based own resources to 0.15% for the duration of the MFF 2014–2020. Denmark, the Netherlands and Sweden receive annual reductions in their GNI-based contributions of €130 million, €695 and €185 million, respectively. Austria has benefitted from a reduction in its GNI-based contribution of €30 million in 2014, €20 million in 2015 and €10 million in 2016.[11] This system of corrections contributes to the non-transparency and complexity of the EU system of own resources (HLGOR, 2016). Additionally, it is problematic from an ability-to-pay perspective. Member States' contributions to the EU budget are largely proportionate to their respective GNI (Begg, 2017); owing to the various corrections the effective distribution of the financial burden deviates from national ability to pay measured by national GNI.

Brexit creates the necessary preconditions to terminate this system of corrections and to reduce the complexity and non-transparency of the system of own resources accordingly. The elimination of all rebates would entail a significant re-distribution of the financial burden within the EU (Körner, 2018). Those countries who currently benefit from a rebate on the UK rebate will face an increase of their shares in the overall financial burden post-2020. Based on the figures for 2014–2016, Germany, the Netherlands, Sweden and Austria would pay additional annual contributions of about €2 billion together. France, Italy, Spain, Belgium, Poland and Finland on the other hand would profit most from the elimination of all rebates, with a total alleviation of their financial burden of about €1.6 billion per year. Altogether, the share of all Member States in total payments to the EU budget would increase after Brexit. However, relative shares of rebate countries would rise above and those of non-rebate countries would rise below average.

12.7   THE PROPOSAL OF THE EU COMMISSION FROM MAY 2018

The proposals launched by the European Commission on 2 May 2018 (European Commission 2018a–f) went in the direction of reforms enhancing

---

[11]   For details see Schratzenstaller et al. (2016).

the EU budget's European added value. At the same time, it is obvious that the European Commission's reform approach remained within the limits of political feasibility, thus representing a pragmatic approach instead of actual far-reaching deep reforms of EU expenditure and revenues. To address the long-term challenges the EU was facing and to close the Brexit gap, the European Commission proposed an expansion of the EU budget volume, financed by new own resources and increased national contributions and by cuts in existing expenditure programmes.

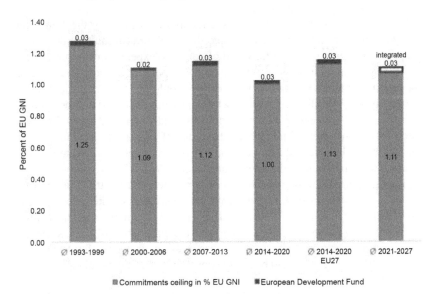

Figure 12.1   The size of the EU budget as a percentage of gross national income (GNI)

Source: European Commission 2018a. 2014–2020 estimated commitments (UK expenditure excluded) as a percentage of EU27 GNI.

Figure 12.1 shows the development of the size of the EU budget as a percentage of GNI since the beginning of the 1990s. While the 1993–1999 MFF had amounted to as much as 1.28% of GNI (including the European Development Fund), the volume of the two succeeding MFF decreased to 1.11 and 1.15% of GNI, respectively. The 2014–2020 MFF was reduced further to 1.03% of GNI for the EU28, which translates to 1.16% of GNI for the EU27 excluding the UK. Thus, the European Commission's recent proposal of a volume of 1.14% of GNI for the 2021–2027 MFF for the EU27 implies an increase compared with the 2014–2020 MFF for the EU28, but a stagnation if the UK is excluded.[12]

In absolute terms, the European Commission envisaged an increase in nominal expenditures (commitment appropriations) from €1083 billion to €1279 billion (i.e. an increase by 18%) (Table 12.5). To cover the additional financial resources needed to expand expenditures and to cover the Brexit gap, large traditional spending items were to be decreased (agricultural expenditures) or to be increased only moderately (cohesion funds), and new own resources were to be introduced.

The structural shifts within EU expenditures envisaged by the European Commission were rather moderate. According to the European Commission's proposal, the share of agricultural and of cohesion expenditures (regional and social funds) should decline to 29% of overall expenditures each. The share of the research framework programme Horizon would increase moderately from 7.3 to 7.6% of overall expenditures, while the share dedicated to cross-border infrastructure (Connecting Europe Facility) would stagnate at about 2%. The largest increases were foreseen for the areas of migration, asylum, border management, defence and external relations, which together would more than double their share in overall expenditures, from 7.7 to 15.5%.

The European Commission (2018e) also proposed several structural reforms for the EU system of own resources which were based on the recommendations derived by the HLGOR (2016). These reforms included a simplification of the system of own resources. Along with the elimination of the UK rebate, which will become obsolete with the Brexit, all other rebates for certain net contributing countries should be phased out. Moreover, the calculation method for the VAT-based own resource should be simplified.

In addition, a diversification of own resources was foreseen. Accordingly, new 'true' own resources should replace or complement, respectively, the EU's funding sources. The European Commission proposed to channel 20% of the revenues from auctioning emission trading certificates as well as the revenues from a share of 3% in a harmonized corporate tax base (CCCTB) and from a tax of €0.80 on non-recyclable plastic waste into the EU budget. These new own resources should raise a share of 12% of overall EU revenues in the future. The share of national contributions should thus be reduced from more than 80% to 71% by 2027.

These three new own resources indeed can be seen as 'natural-born' true own resources for the EU: the plastic tax owing to the cross-border nature of the environmental damage associated with plastic waste and the use of fossil

---

[12]   This is due to the fact that the UK's share in the EU GNI exceeds its net contribution to the EU budget because of the UK rebate.

Table 12.5 MFF 2014–2020 compared with MFF 2021–2027

	MFF 2014–2020				MFF 2021–2027		
	Million €	Percentage of total	Percentage of GNI		Million €	Percentage of total	Percentage of GNI
1a. Smart and Inclusive Growth	**142,13**	**13.1**	**0.13**	**1. Single Market, Innovation, Digital**	**187,37**	**14.6**	**0.16**
Horizon 2020	79,402	7.3	0.07	R & I	102,573	8.0	0.09
Connecting Europe Facility (CEF)	21,937	2.0	0.02	Horizon Europe	97,600	7.6	0.08
ERASMUS	14,775	1.4	0.01	European Strategic Investments	49,973	3.9	0.04
Other	26,016	2.4	0.02	Connecting Europe Facility (CEF)	24,480	1.9	0.02
				Single Market	6,391	0.5	0.01
1b. Economic, Social and Territorial Cohesion	**366,791**	**33.9**	**0.34**	**2. Cohesion and Values**	**442,412**	**34.6**	**0.39**
				Cohesion Funds	374,414	29.3	0.33
				Regional Development and Cohesion	273,24	21.4	0.24
				European Social Fund (ESF)	101,174	7.9	0.09
				ERASMUS	30,000	2.3	0.03
				EMU	25,113	2.0	0.02

Features and challenges of the EU budget

	MFF 2014–2020				MFF 2021–2027		
2. Sustainable Growth: Natural Resources	**420,034**	**38.8**	**0.39**	**3. Natural Resources and Environment**	**378,920**	**29.6**	**0.33**
Common Agriculture Policy (CAP)	408,312	37.7	0.38	Common Agriculture Policy (CAP)	365,006	28.5	0.32
European Agriculture Guarantee Fund (EAGF)	312,735	28.9	0.29	European Agriculture Guarantee Fund (EAGF)	286,195	22.4	0.25
European Agriculture Fund for Rural Development (EAFRD)	95,577	8.8	0.09	European Agriculture Fund for Rural Development (EAFRD)	78,811	6.2	0.07
Other	11,722	1.1	0.01	Other	13,914	1.1	0.01
3. Security and Citizenship	**17,725**	**1.6**	**0.02**	**4. Migration and Border Management**	**34,902**	**2.7**	**0.03**
Asylum, Migration and Integration Fund	3,137	0.3	0.00	Asylum and Migration Fund	10,415	0.8	0.01
Internal Security Fund	3,764	0.3	0.00	Border Management	21,331	1.7	0.02
Other	10,824	1.0	0.01	**5. Security and Defence**	**27,515**	**2.2**	**0.02**
				Security	4,806	0.4	0.00
				Defence	19,500	1.5	0.02
				Other	3,209	0.3	0.00

	MFF 2014–2020		
4. Global Europe	**66,262**	**6.1**	**0.06**
External Action	54,563	5.0	0.05
Humanitarian Aid	6,622	0.6	0.01
Neighbourhood, Development and International Cooperation Instruments	40,012	3.7	0.04
Other	7,929	0.7	0.01
Pre-accession Assistance	11,699	1.1	0.01
5. Administration	**69,584**	**6.4**	**0.07**
6. Compensations	**29**	**0.0**	**0.00**
TOTAL	**1,082,555**	**100.0**	**1.02**

	MFF 2021–2027		
6. Neighbourhood and the World	**123,002**	**9.6**	**0.11**
External Action	105,219	8.2	0.09
Humanitarian Aid	11,000	0.9	0.01
Neighbourhood, Development and International Cooperation Instruments	89,500	7.0	0.08
Other	4,719	0.4	0.00
Pre-accession Assistance	14,500	1.1	0.01
7. European Public Administration	**85,287**	**6.7**	**0.07**
TOTAL	**1,279,408**	**100.0**	**1.11**

Sources: European Commission, own calculations. European Neighbourhood Instrument (ENI), European Instrument for Democracy and Human Rights (EIDHR), Instrument for Stability (IfS), Partnership Instrument (PI), Development Cooperation Instrument (DCI), Civil Protection and European Emergency Response Centre (ERC), European Voluntary Humanitarian Aid Corps EU Aid Volunteers (EUAV).

fuels for plastic production; the other two options are directly connected with EU policies to cope with important European challenges. However, the contribution of these new own resources would be rather moderate in quantitative terms. The introduction of further tax-based own resources beyond the European Commission's proposals, along the lines presented in Section 3.2, could be expected to create considerable additional European added value.

12.8   CONCLUSIONS AND OUTLOOK

A comprehensive restructuring of the EU budget could be one key element to contribute to the targets of the Europe 2020 Strategy, to the Sustainable Development Goals, to the Paris Climate Agreement and to further central EU policies and strategies. It would also increase the European added value created by EU expenditure. Moreover, shifting EU expenditure towards European added value is also a key prerequisite for the implementation of tax-based own resources (HLGOR 2016).

How realistic is the implementation of such reform proposals in the political–economic context of the EU, and particularly in face of Brexit? As Begg (2017: 9) states, an important impact of Brexit will be the withdrawal of 'a powerful supporter of certain preferences for the EU's finances'. Accordingly, the UK's absence from the negotiations on the 2021–2027 MFF weakens the position of those Member States opposing a larger budget as well as demanding the cutting of common agriculture policy expenditures and a focus of cohesion funds on poorer Member States to create space for increased spending on competitiveness.

Brexit can be expected to promote future-oriented reforms of the EU budget directly via several channels. First, the UK is one of the most vehement opponents of tax coordination at the EU level. Therefore, its withdrawal from the EU should make the introduction of tax-based own resources (for example the financial transactions tax strictly rejected by the UK, or a share in a CCCTB, which is also not supported by the UK), but also other reforms in the area of taxation less controversial among the remaining EU Member States. Secondly, the UK is one of the fiercest proponents of the net position thinking, focusing mainly on the difference between payments into the EU budget and transfers received out of it instead of the European added value of EU expenditures. With the UK's withdrawal, the alliance of net contributor countries with a rather restrictive position regarding the level of the EU budget may be weakened (Brehon, 2017). Thirdly, the rebate for the UK will no longer be necessary, so that there is a good chance that the accompanying correction mechanisms (i.e. the various rebates for several net-contributing countries) can be abolished at last (HLGOR, 2016).

Indirect support may be provided by growing awareness at Member State level that the EU budget needs to deliver more added value for European citizens to prevent further acceleration of exit movements in other EU Member States. This might enhance the openness and willingness of Member States to agree to expenditure reforms towards European added value, and to accept reforms on the revenue side, in particular to consider certain tax-based own resources, and especially those that have some integrative power because they are appealing for many EU citizens (e.g. a financial transactions tax). Moreover, the Brexit gap, and the new tasks resulting from the challenges the EU has to cope with, draw renewed attention to the EU system of own resources and its obvious shortcomings, and may thus open up a new window of opportunity to its more fundamental reform.

On the other hand, Brexit and the financial gap might exacerbate the net position debate at least in the short run, which may lead to demands for cuts in the overall volume of the EU budget and/or new rebates for net contributors. Moreover, Brexit might delay discussions and decisions on reforms within the EU budget, depending on the progress in the negotiations about the 'divorce bill' and the future (financial) relationship between the UK and the EU.

Ultimately it will depend on whether EU Member States will be able to overcome the net position thinking currently blocking the route to an EU budget adequate in volume and size. This again requires the acknowledgement of the manifold benefits provided to all EU countries by their EU membership. Substituting a major share of national contributions by sustainability-oriented tax-based own resources may act as a catalyst to secure net-contributors' agreement to maintain or even increase the current spending level in exchange for a far-reaching reform of EU expenditure to enhance European added value. Therefore, one crucial success factor for a future-oriented reform of EU finances is to understand the need for package solutions. As stressed by Núñez Ferrer et al. (2016), these would include the expenditure as well as the revenue side of the EU budget. An obvious example is the concentration of cohesion funds on the Member States with lower per capita GDPs, which in the majority strongly object to any tax coordination as they regard the option of tax cuts or generally lower tax levels as one of the few instruments available to them to secure their competitiveness, in exchange for their agreement to the EU-wide introduction of tax-based own resources on a harmonized basis. Another package deal may include the introduction of carbon levies and specific support measures to further decarbonization for particularly strongly affected countries (Núñez Ferrer et al., 2016), possibly within agricultural or cohesion funds or expenditure on cross-border infrastructure. The absence of the UK, as a strong and financially powerful advocate of certain positions and 'no-gos' regarding size and structure of the post-2020 MFF, might increase the chances of reaching compromises based on such package deals that are necessary for far-reaching reforms of the EU budget.

REFERENCES

Auerswald, H., Konrad, K. A. and Thum, M. (2011), 'Adaptation, mitigation and risk-taking in climate policy'. CESifo Working Paper 3320.

Becker, S. O., Egger, P. H. and von Ehrlich, M. (2018), 'Effects of EU regional policy: 1989–2013', *Regional Science and Urban Economics*, 69, 143–152.

Begg, I. (2017), 'The EU's finances: can the economically desirable and the politically feasible be reconciled?' Mimeo.

Bertelsmann Stiftung (2017), 'How Europe can deliver'. Gütersloh, Bertelsmann Stiftung.

Bonfiglio, A., Esposti, R., Pagliacci, F., Sotte, F. and Camaioni, B. (2014), 'Regional perspectives and distributional effects of European regional policies'. WWW for Europe Working Paper 66.

Brehon, N. J. (2017), 'The budgetary impact of the Brexit on the European Union'. Foundation Robert Schuman Policy Paper 454.

Chomicz, E. (2017), 'EU budget Post Brexit. Confronting reality, exploring viable solutions'. European Policy Centre Discussion Paper, March.

Darvas, Z. and Wolff, G. (2018), 'Rethinking the European Union's post-Brexit budget priorities'. Bruegel Policy Brief 1/2018.

Dellinger, F. and Schratzenstaller, M. (2018), 'Sustainability-oriented future EU funding: a European nuclear power tax'. *International Journal of Energy Economics and Policy*, 8, 346–353.

European Commission (2011), 'The added value of the EU budget'. Commission Staff Working Paper SEC (2011) 867 final, Brussels.

European Commission (2017a), 'White Paper on the future of Europe – reflections and scenarios for the EU27 by 2025'. European Commission, Brussels.

European Commission (2017b), 'Reflection paper on the future of EU finances'. European Commission, Brussels.

European Commission (2017c), 'EU Budget Interactive'. Download data 2000–2016.

European Commission (2018a), 'A modern budget for a Union that protects, empowers and defends'. Communication from the Commission to the European Parliament, the European Council, the Council, the European Economic and Social Committee and the Committee of the Regions, COM(2018)321 final, Brussels.

European Commission (2018b), 'Proposal for a Council Regulation laying down the Multiannual Financial Framework for the Years 2021 to 2017', COM(2018)322 final, Brussels.

European Commission (2018c), 'Proposal for an interinstitutional agreement between the European Parliament, the Council and the Commission on Budgetary Discipline, on cooperation in budgetary matters and on sound financial management', COM(2018)323 final, Brussels.

European Commission (2018d), 'Proposal for a regulation of the European Parliament and of the Council on the Protection of the Union's Budget in Case of generalised deficiencies as regards the rule of law in the Member States', COM(2018)324 final, Brussels.

European Commission (2018e), 'Proposal for a Council decision on the system of own resources of the European Union', COM(2018)325 final, Brussels.

European Commission (2018f), 'Financing the EU budget: report on the operation of the own resources system', SWD(2018)172 final, Brussels.

Felbermayr, G., Gröschl, J. and Heiland, I. (2018), 'Undoing Europe in a new quantitative trade model', Ifo Working Paper 250/2018.

Gagliardi, L. and Percoco, M. (2017), 'The impact of European cohesion policy in urban and rural regions', *Regional Studies*, 51 (6), 857–868.

Haas, J. and Rubio, E. (2017a), 'Possible impact of Brexit on the EU budget and in particular. CAP Funding'. European Parliament, Brussels.

Haas, J. and Rubio, E. (2017b), 'Brexit and the EU Budget: threat or opportunity?' Jacques Delors Institute/Bertelsmann Stiftung Policy Paper 183.

Heinemann, F. (2016), 'Strategies for a European EU budget', in T. Büttner and M. Thöne (eds), *The Future of EU Finances.* Mohr Siebeck, Tübingen, pp. 95–112.

HLGOR (2016), 'Future financing of the EU'. High Level Group on Own Resources, Brussels.

Jones, B., Keen, M. and Strand, J. (2012), 'Fiscal implications of climate change'. World Bank Policy Research Working Paper WPS5956.

Keen, M., Parry, I. and Strand, J. (2012), 'Market-based instruments for international aviation and shipping as a source of climate finance'. World Bank Policy Research Working Paper WPS5950.

Körner, K. (2018), 'Post-Brexit EU budget – the next hot button issue'. Deutsche Bank EU Monitor, February.

Krenek, A. and Schratzenstaller, M. (2017), 'Sustainability-oriented tax-based own resources for the European Union: a European carbon-based flight ticket tax', *Empirica*, 44 (4), 665–686.

Krenek, A. and Schratzenstaller, M. (2018), 'A European net wealth tax'. WIFO Working Paper 561.

Krenek, A., Sommer, M. and Schratzenstaller, M. (2018), 'Sustainability- oriented future EU funding: a European border carbon adjustment'. FairTax Working Paper 15.

Negotiators of the European Union and the United Kingdom Government (2017), 'Joint report on progress during Phase 1 of negotiations under

Article 50 TEU on the United Kingdom's orderly withdrawal from the European Union', https://ec.europa.eu/commission/sites/beta-political/files/ joint_report.pdf (accessed 19 December 2018).

Nerudová, D., Solilová, V. and Dobranschi, M. (2016), 'Sustainability-oriented future EU funding: a C(C)CTB'. FairTax Working Paper 4.

Nerudová, D., Schratzenstaller, M. and Solilová, V. (2017), 'The financial transactions tax as tax-based own resource for the EU budget'. FairTax Policy Brief 2.

Nerudová, D., Dobranschi, M., Solilová, V. and Schratzenstaller, M. (2019), 'Sustainability-oriented future EU funding: a fuel tax surcharge'. FairTax Working Paper 21.

Núñez Ferrer, J. and Kaditi, E. (2007), 'The EU added value of agricultural expenditure – from market to multifunctionality – gathering criticism and success stories of the CAP'. Brussels.

Núñez Ferrer, J. and Katarivas, M. (2014), 'What are the effects of the EU budget? Driving force or drop in the ocean?' CEPS Special Report 86. Brussels.

Núñez Ferrer, J. and Rinaldi, D. (2016), 'The impact of Brexit on the EU budget: a non-catastrophic event'. CEPS Policy Brief 347.

Núñez Ferrer, J., Le Cacheux, J., Benedetto, G. and Saunier, M. (2016), 'Study on the potential and limitations of reforming the financing of the EU budget'. Study commissioned by the European Commission on behalf of the High Level Group on Own Resources. Brussels: European Commission.

Schratzenstaller, M. (2013), 'The EU own resources system – reform needs and options', *Intereconomics*, 48 (5), 303–313.

Schratzenstaller, M. (2017), 'The Next Multiannual Financial Framework (MFF). Its structure and the own resources'. In-depth analysis on behalf of the European Commission's Policy Department for Budgetary Affairs following the request of the Committee on Budgets of the European Parliament. Brussels: European Parliament.

Schratzenstaller, M., Krenek, A., Nerudová, D. and Dobranschi, M. (2016), 'EU taxes as genuine own resource to finance the EU Budget: pros, cons and sustainability-oriented criteria to evaluate potential tax candidates'. FairTax Working Paper 3.

Schratzenstaller, M., Krenek, A., Nerudová, D. and Dobranschi, M. (2017), 'EU taxes for the EU budget in the light of sustainability orientation – a survey', *Jahrbücher für Nationalökonomie und Statistik/Journal of Economics and Statistics*, 237 (3), 163–189.

The Institute for Government (2018), The EU Divorce Bill, https://www .instituteforgovernment.org.uk/printpdf/4686 (accessed 19 December 2018).

13. Conclusions

Ubaldo Villani-Lubelli and Luca Zamparini

This book has provided a multidisciplinary analysis of the EU budget encompassing historical, political, legal and economic perspectives. As it was highlighted in the Introduction, such a multidisciplinary approach has allowed to disentangle several topics for which single disciplines would not be able to provide a comprehensive evaluation. The contributions were carefully chosen in order to cover a wide spectrum of relevant themes characterizing the EU budget. Part 1 of the book (Historical and Political Profiles) has been identified given the consideration that there is a tight linkage between the evolution of the EU budget and the overall development of the European Union, especially in terms of integration among Member States. Part 2 (Legal and Economic Profiles) has been deemed necessary considering the ongoing debate on the need to reform the EU budget and of the trade-off between unity and flexibility. Moreover, legal and economic measures have a clear impact on the democratic legitimacy and on the political representation of the European Union. With respect to these issues, the adoption of a view that embraces a constitutional approach enables to really appreciate how the budgetary issues are one of the most remarkable factors to explain why many European citizens feel distant from the European Union (Chapter 4). On the other hand, policy-makers interested in enhancing the legitimation basis of the EU budget, also for international solidarity, may diffuse better information about the objectives and functioning of this redistribution mechanism (Chapter 5). Moreover, the division of the Multiannual Financial Framework (MFF) into two shorter five year cycles would align it with the European Parliament and European Commission political mandates, guaranteeing a higher degree of democratic legitimacy (Chapters 2 and 10).

An important issue that has emerged in several contributions to this book concerns the relations between the EU institutions. The European Union appears to be characterized by a peculiar legal background, with a constitutional nature, and by a complex set of institutions (Chapter 4). In this context, the EU budget is discussed and adopted in a negotiating process that involves a demo-cratic side – the European Parliament – and a technocratic body – the European Commission – both engaged to distribute costs and benefits among EU citizens

(Chapter 11). This is also due to the fact that the relationship between political representation and taxation has always existed and it is extremely relevant in the constitutional framework (Chapter 2). The right to have control of the budget has had a pivotal role in the definition of relations between government and Parliament in terms of decision and representation. It seems that the EU's institutional arrangement at the end of the second decade of the twenty-first century is marked by the weakening of the Commission and of the European Parliament influence (Chapter 7). The former has in fact lost relevance to a large extent in the European integration process, turning out mostly to be the administrative branch of the executive power represented by the European Council. The European Parliament, which has experienced a growth in its institutional legitimacy from Maastricht to the Lisbon Treaty, also with respect to budgetary policy, appears marginalized both in decision-making processes of key policy areas and in the Union's political sphere of influence. On the other hand, Chapter 3 has highlighted that, although the European Parliament is still not participating as an equal partner in the negotiation of the MFF, its increasing role has also favored the evolution of the EU budget towards a policy instrument. As regards the monitoring and control of the EU budget, these activities are structured around four EU institutions: the European Commission, the European Parliament, the Council and the European Court of Auditors (Chapter 9). The resulting framework is characterized by complexity and fragmentation, a tendency that accelerated with the implementation of the Lisbon Treaty, with the creation of many instruments and their corresponding monitoring and control arrangements. The *Better Regulation Agenda* aims at reducing burdens and inconsistencies. However, more efforts are necessary to improve the EU budget monitoring and control system.

The relationships between the EU institutions and single countries have also been highlighted by several contributions to the present book. Chapter 7 has provided a general analysis of the increasing involvement of national governments in the decision-making processes because of the weakening of supranational institutions. This has been achieved by means of formal institutionalized gatherings in the EU Council of Ministers and of informal meetings that normally take place among heads of States or ministers before or alongside official summits. Moreover, the adoption of a voting system based on unanimity or *consensus*, instead of fully or partial majoritarian systems, reduces the possibility of neutralizing national interests. The negotiation process is characterised by the net-payer/net-receiver logic as the main basic conflict line and by the necessity to coordinate national interests. The reconciliation of interests between France and Germany has often been a dynamic factor paving the way for compromise at the EU level up to the 2021–2027 MFF (Chapter 6). The unanimity rule, since the adoption of the 2007–2013 MFF, restricted the possibility of side payments and policy solutions for specific Member States

(Chapter 3). Chapter 8 has identified net payments logic, burden sharing and status quo bias as well as institutional struggles and power games as the main difficulties in reversing the trend toward fragmentation and differentiation in the Union's budgetary policy. On the other hand, these factors have also favored package deals that, given the increasing heterogeneity of preferences among Member States, have determined the concentration on programmes which generate an added value at the EU level. More generally, there has been a paradigm change in the perception of the EU budget, from a budget aimed at compensating Member States for their political compromises to a budget intended for solving EU-wide problems. The EU financial resources have thus been directed toward investments rather than mere expenses. The loss of the UK as an opponent to expenditures at a EU-wide level might further enhance the openness and willingness of Member States to agree to expenditure reforms (Chapter 12). On the revenue side, the UK's withdrawal from the EU should make the introduction of tax-based own resources, but also other reforms in the area of taxation, less controversial among the remaining EU Member States. It may also weaken the alliance of net contributor countries with a rather restrictive position regarding the level of the EU budget. Moreover, the Brexit gap and the new tasks resulting from the challenges the EU has to cope with have generated a renewed attention to the EU's system of own resources and its obvious shortcomings, originated by the concentration of national contributions to the EU budget (Chapter 3). Many tax instruments could potentially be mobilized to either replace or complement the current EU budget resources (see, i.e., the proposals of the High Level Group of Own Resources in 2016). With respect to the fiscal discipline in Member States, the Commission and the Council manage a system of strict controls, articulated in preventive measures (based on the concept of prudent budgetary policy) and in corrective control activities, which apply when the deficit of a Member State exceeds 3% of the GDP or is in violation of the debt rule (Chapter 11).

Another important issue that emerges from various contributions to this book is the relationship (trade-off) between unity and flexibility in the EU budget. Chapter 8 proposes a thorough discussion and confirms that a feasible combination of predictability and flexibility is difficult under the current circumstances and particularities of the European budgetary policy. For nearly five decades, starting with the first significant overhaul of the European budgetary policy with the introduction of the own resources system in 1970, the EU has searched for the right balance between the pragmatic political necessity of budgetary flexibility and the establishment of a single European budget. Even though a unified and universal budget should remain the norm of European budgetary policy, some exceptions should be allowed when specific political challenges or emergencies occur. A clear, although very limited, trend toward flexibility appears to have marked the evolution of MFFs (Chapter 3).

Since the mid-2000s, a larger emphasis has been put on regional policy and on research, as important factors of growth and competitiveness. Moreover, in the mid-2010s, two new headings explicitly referring to migration and to development and cooperation were inserted in the EU budget (Chapter 10). At a more general level, a higher reduction of rigidity of the MFF would, however, require the concession of greater political autonomy of the EU and the European Commission in interpreting the need for action and the scope of funding. In this respect, the monitoring and control activities may represent an important tool to find a balance between sound financial management and flexible implementation of the EU budget (Chapters 6 and 9).

A theme that has been considered by most of the authors contributing to the book is the need to reform the EU budget and the factors that limit path-breaking improvements. The EU represents a peculiar and unique institutional model, where its autonomy of decision and competence are derived from the will expressed by Member States (Chapter 2). In the context of the historical evolution of its budget, these factors have determined the difficulty of reforming it. More generally, they have also hampered the development and completion of the political project. Chapters 4 and 7 state that the Lisbon Treaty contributed to generate a legal framework where budgetary policy is constrained by a rigidity in spending and levying new taxes and by mechanisms that prevent those ceilings from being modified. In addition, the self-confidence of a given historical path for European integration has brought the Member States to create a budgetary system with few capabilities to make a real difference and to adapt to social transformations in Europe. Chapters 4 and 12 state that the current financing system has been attracting various criticisms over recent decades. These relate to its lack of transparency and complexity, but particularly to the fact that the EU system of own resources does not contribute to central EU strategies and policies. The introduction of sustainability-oriented tax-based own resources, partially substituting for Member States' national contributions, may strengthen the relevance of central EU policies (Chapter 10). Aiming to achieve this goal, the European Commission has proposed some reforms leading to a more efficient system of own resources. However, the focus on net contributions and *juste retour* dominates the policy and increases the reluctance of Member States to even consider any significant and ambitious option for reform (Chapter 8). It may be argued that the EU budget has developed into a path-dependent structure, somehow resilient to crisis situations (Chapter 6).

With respect to expenditures, it would be important that their largest share target policy areas in which Member States' uncoordinated actions would be insufficient owing to free riding, coordination problems and cross-border issues; or policy areas in which common European interests are at stake, such as trans-border infrastructures and decarbonization strategies (Chapter 12). In

addition, Chapter 3 emphasizes the increased conditionality in the re-distributing policies of the MFFs. Using the EU budget as a policy instrument can not
only mean budgetary spending according to non-obligatory guidelines and soft
governance, but also requires budget support to be tied more strictly to political
conditions. The EU's budgetary system and policy should also find a feasible
relationship and interaction between the necessary ability to react quickly to
new political challenges and the interest of the Member States in medium-term
stability and predictability of MFF resources and spending policies (Chapter
8). The flexibility guaranteed by new instruments to respond to emerging
challenges should not endanger the possibility of attaining sound financial
management and proper audit and control arrangements (Chapter 9).

Finally, there is an ongoing debate over the issue of whether the EU budget
should be increased, implying a higher level of international solidarity among
EU Member States. It remains to be seen, however, whether and how the size,
structure and degree of redistribution of the EU budget will be changed in the
future (Chapter 10). Public support for a larger EU budget currently is rather
low in many Member States. If policymakers would implement a reform that
increases the EU budget, then such a reform step would be made on a rather
weak legitimation basis (Chapter 5). Consequently, reforms at the structural
level for the 2021–2027 MFF are quite unlikely. This is because the structure
of the MFF has proven and still proves a certain degree of flexibility, which
means that it is capable of incorporating quite substantial changes while, at the
same time, providing actors (mainly at the national levels) with the amount
of security needed to commit themselves to a longer-term definition of their
burdens and benefits. However, changes will probably occur at the instrumental level where it is still possible to agree on new policy objectives or to
change certain rules for the distribution of funds (Chapter 6). The involved
actors, both at the national and at the EU level, prefer to agree on the lowest
common denominator in a familiar procedure rather than becoming entangled
in conflicts that an ambitious and significant initiative to modernize and
reform the European budget would imply – especially given that it would
contain the risk of the negotiations failing (Chapter 8). However, Brexit may
promote future-oriented reforms of the EU budget via several channels: more
tax coordination at the EU level, the weakening of the net position thinking,
and the abolition of the various rebates for several net-contributing Member
States (Chapter 12). Everything considered, it seems that the 2021–2027 MFF
will not lead to a revolutionary new budget. On the other hand, the negotiation
outcome may reinforce the paradigm change from a budget aimed at compensating Member States for their political compromises to a budget aimed at
solving EU-wide problems.

The conjoint perusal and analysis of the various contributions that constitute
the two parts of this book allow the series of relevant topics discussed above

to be underscored. Such issues are important not only in terms of theoretical examinations, but also as prospective inputs for rethinking and reforming the EU budget. This appears particularly relevant at the time of writing this book given the effects of the diverse crises that have marked the second decade of the twenty-first century in the European Union (sovereign debt, migration crisis, effects of Brexit among others). In this context, the necessity to provide the European Union with a more substantial and values-oriented budget will be the real historical challenge in the next decade, in order to put freedom, equality and rule of law at the political core of the European project. Such reforms will also strengthen the EU with respect to possible future social, economic, political, and humanitarian crises.

Index